In
Praise
of
Retreat

FINDING SANCTUARY
IN THE MODERN WORLD

In
Praise
of
Retreat

Kirsteen MacLeod

Published by ECW Press
665 Gerrard Street East
Toronto, Ontario, Canada M4M 1Y2
416-694-3348 / info@ecwpress.com

Editor for the Press: Susan Renouf
Cover design: Natalie Olsen

LIBRARY AND ARCHIVES CANADA CATALOGUING IN
PUBLICATION

Title: In praise of retreat : finding sanctuary in the
modern world / Kirsteen MacLeod.

Names: MacLeod, Kirsteen, author.

Identifiers: Canadiana (print) 20200384511 |
Canadiana (ebook) 2020038483X

ISBN 978-1-77041-473-0 (SOFTCOVER)
ISBN 978-1-77305-654-8 (EPUB)
ISBN 978-1-77305-655-5 (PDF)
ISBN 978-1-77305-656-2 (KINDLE)

Subjects: LCSH: Solitude. | LCSH: Solitude—
Psychological aspects. | LCSH: Spiritual retreats.

Classification: LCC BJ1499.S65 M33 2021 | DDC
155.9/2—dc23

The publication of *In Praise of Retreat* has been generously supported by the Canada Council for the Arts and is funded
in part by the Government of Canada. *Nous remercions le Conseil des arts du Canada de son soutien. Ce livre est financé en
partie par le gouvernement du Canada.* We acknowledge the support of the Ontario Arts Council (OAC), an agency of the
Government of Ontario, which last year funded 1,965 individual artists and 1,152 organizations in 197 communities across
Ontario for a total of $51.9 million. We also acknowledge the support of the Government of Ontario through the Ontario
Book Publishing Tax Credit, and through Ontario Creates for the marketing of this book.

PRINTED AND BOUND IN CANADA

PRINTING: MARQUIS   5   4   3   2   1

MIX
Paper from
responsible sources
FSC® C103567

For Marco

I will arise and go now, and go to Innisfree,
And a small cabin build there, of clay and wattles made;
Nine bean-rows will I have there, a hive for the honey-bee,
And live alone in the bee-loud glade.

—WILLIAM BUTLER YEATS

Contents

Mapping
the
Ground

OF SACRED GROVES, INNER MOUNTAINS

AND THE ART OF RETREAT

An Introduction

If you let yourself be blown to and fro,
you lose touch with your root.

—Lao Tzu, *Tao Te Ching*, transl. by Stephen Mitchell

I'm sitting on the old footbridge that leads to my cabin in the woods. Beaver Creek passes silently below. Ducks fly overhead. Ferns, cardinal flowers and moss grow amid grey rocks at the water's edge. Spiders wander over my notebooks, which are spread out on the bridge's rough planks, pages held open by stones.

This is the place that inspired this book. By the creek and in the forest, I discovered a rich inner dimension I didn't know existed. Far from my city life and work-obsessed routines, I began to see what gives my life meaning. I recognized the value of protecting a divine spark, though I'm not religious, and of amplifying the extraordinary—nature, spirit, art, creative thinking—in impoverished times. A retreat means removing yourself from society, to a quiet place where moments are strung like pearls, and after long days apart spent in inspiring surroundings, you return home refreshed and with a new sense of what you want to do with your life.

In the fraught modern era, you'd think our timeless human desire to retreat would feel more urgent than ever. Yet taking a step back has become an act of 21st-century rebellion when disengaging, even briefly, is seen by many as self-indulgent, unproductive and anti-social. But to retreat is as basic a human need as being with others. To withdraw from the everyday is about making breathing space for what illuminates a life.

For millennia, people have retreated from human concerns as a corrective, spiritual and otherwise. This is a universal impulse, evident in all times, in all cultures. Throughout history, opinion has swung between two poles on the question of how to find fulfillment in life—in solitude, or in society? In the sixth century BC, when early philosophies for a good life dawned in China, Confucius said the key was to meet one's social obligations. Lao-Tzu said the key was to avoid them—though his teachings show that he cared deeply for fellow humans, and for the natural world.

Lao-Tzu left few traces, and even his name is uncertain; likely translations include "the Old Master" or "the Old Boy." He fled corrupt court life, legend has it, through the western mountain passes of China, disguised as a farmer and riding a water buffalo, or a blue ox, or a black ox, depending on the source. The sage was supposedly recognized by a border guard and asked to share his wisdom before he departed. Lao-Tzu dictated the *Tao Te Ching* and then disappeared, likely to become a hermit. *The Book of the Way*, as it's known in English, imparts its lucid counsel about living a self-directed life and has inspired kindred spirits ever since, including the "Sage of Concord," Henry David Thoreau.

In the 21st century, when we over-venerate the active and the social, I find myself in deep sympathy with the Taoist philosophers of antiquity, who viewed the universe as a flux of paradoxical opposites. Early terms they used to describe this were "the firm" and "the yielding"—later referred to as yang and yin. Visually, this indivisible unity is represented by a circle, half light and half dark, each containing a dot of the other shade. The idea is that energies are in interchange, universal energies from which everything emerges, and their dynamic balance brings cosmic harmony.

Contrary to Western dualism these opposites are not at war but hold equal importance, permeate one another, and create a whole. The world of being "arises out of their change and interplay," explains Richard Wilhelm, who translated the *I Ching*, or *Book of Changes*, into German in 1924, thus opening up the spiritual heritage of China to the West. The *I Ching* is the common source for both Taoist and Confucian philosophy and was first published in English in 1950.

Westerners may consider such concepts esoteric or mystifying, but they are common in the East. And common sense, I believe. It seems logical that we need action and engagement, yang energy, and also the complementary yin, which is solitary, reflective and receptive. This does not mean passive, as it's often misinterpreted in the West. Wei wu wei, or "effortless effort," describes yin's power, observable in the action of a river on rock. To quote the *Tao Te Ching*, written between 300 and 600 BC: "Nothing in the world / is as soft and yielding as water. / Yet for dissolving the hard and inflexible, / nothing can surpass it."

Similarly, to retreat is about widening our perspective, about the pursuit of the whole, developing yin attributes rather than rejecting them. In a historical time when solitude and silence are conflated with boredom, and no one wants to be seen as a weird "loner," retreat has become a countercultural notion. I admit to being irritable about this. I believe independent people like solitude, and retreating is healthy for everyone at particular times of life, for particular reasons. A retreat is different from a holiday: it's a temporary, voluntary withdrawal from everyday life for a purpose—for personal, social, environmental, spiritual, artistic or even professional reasons. It's about deep engagement and, often, dissidence.

Granted, not everyone wants to flee permanently through the Han-Ku Pass as Lao-Tzu did, or has the means to do so, including me. That's why over the past 20-plus years I became a serial retreater, creating islands of space and time, a week here, a month there, to answer a faint call, barely heard above the din of the everyday: "There must be something more—where can I find it?" One good retreat led to another, and slowly, my life transformed.

Retreat is an adventure, and it involves uncertainty. Whether we go to the quiet woods to rest or make art, walk a pilgrim path or sit in silent meditation, we're in some way seeking a new way to be. We're creating space for change.

I'm not dismissing ordinary, active, social life and its routines: that's how we keep the lights on, the dog fed and the world turning. No one needs reminding of the value of the everyday, or of relationships and work. But I believe we have mistaken this half of reality for the whole. As modern times sweep away the extraordinary, the transcendent and our attention, retreat offers a way to reclaim what's being lost. Like many people, I don't want to be blown about by the wind, always in company. I have other priorities, which is where retreat comes in.

I have often wondered why I am so interested in retreat and its yin companions, solitude and silence. This book is my chance to consider the question, for myself and everyone else who wants to inhabit a slower, quieter, more thoughtful world than the 21st century usually offers. Drawing on my own experiences, and the wisdom of hermits, monks, pilgrims, naturalists, writers and artists, solitary thinkers and other independent spirits, living and dead, I will explore the art of retreat and how it can reconnect us to our essence—and why this is a matter of urgency for personal and planetary health in modern times.

Here, beside the creek in the forest, it's time to concentrate my thoughts and write down what I've discovered. I'll begin with the story of my retreat to Beaver Creek, where this journey began . . .

Green
Cathedral

The cabin is a mile down a winding logging road, deep in the green forest. There's no running water, unless you count the creek, and no electricity. It's far from everyone and everything.

The bumpy road in is overgrown with weeds and wildflowers, and ends at Beaver Creek. A rough footbridge spans the water, planks nailed between two tree trunks that were pulled into place by a neighbour's horse. We fill our arms with supplies from the truck and walk over: drinking water, wine, cooler, bags of food, bedding and towels, maybe a saxophone, the stories of Chekhov—"the hockey player" my husband, Marco, deadpans—or fat yoga and philosophy tomes we don't have time for in the city.

Stepping onto the bridge's weathered boards, I feel something lift and wash away in the rush of water and wind in trees. It's the sensation of a gorgeous absence, as when a pain that had been constant suddenly vanishes or when a noise unheard for always being heard disappears. All the cells of my body relax. Below, the creek pours on without beginning or end. At the far shore I step between the tall poplar and the woodpecker-riddled cedars and onto the land.

Up ahead the cabin, shaped like a tiny barn with cedar-plank siding and a blue steel roof, rests amid tall trees. On the front porch, I peer into the mud-and-moss nest in the eaves while two adult phoebes peep in alarm from a nearby maple sapling. Four upturned beaks. This means we'll be using the back door again this spring, until the babies fly. I pull out my keychain, a blue globe, and open up the front door. Of all the places on this planet, this is where I feel most at peace.

A retreat in the woods is the last thing I expected to have, or even desire. For 20 years I lived in Toronto. I loved cities. I had zero interest in wilderness. I thought it anti-social to spend time alone and would never have considered leaving the smoggy, edgy metropolis for a place where biting insects likely outnumbered people. No culture, no clubs, no cappuccino—I got uneasy at the very idea of being "miles from a lemon," just like Reverend Sydney Smith, an English writer who once remarked of his new country parish, "My living in Yorkshire was so out of the way that it was actually 12 miles from a lemon."

Then one summer, quite suddenly, I got fed up. I'd been working on contract for the provincial government, wondering how my journalism career as the next Oriana Fallaci had come to this. My boss was in a constant state of panic about legislation we were working on and she paced, spritzing peppermint essence into the air. My friend and I, two lapsed magazine writers with no clue about how laws are made, lived in perpetual fear of getting fired. Each evening we'd ride the streetcar home together, limp from tension and amazed to still be employed. The money was stellar, but the days were consumed by absurd dramas and counterfeit crises.

About the same time, home became inhospitable. Marco and I were renting a three-bedroom brick semi with a small yard near St. Clair and Oakwood. Mighty Q107 rock blared nonstop in the yard next door. Out back, our neighbours kept their tiny city lots pristine by sticking all their junk out of sight behind their sheds— the view from our rear door. They hacked down trees, which they considered a messy nuisance that blocked sun from their tomatoes. Then a dead body was found in the trunk of a car that had been parked outside our house for a week. Much later, Marco told me he never corrected the rumour that we were brother and sister; thus the hostile stares whenever we walked down the street holding hands.

Worst of all, many bored kids lived nearby. They called to me, "K, what are you doing?" I longed to read in peace, so Marco constructed me a hideout in the back corner by our shed. He used the springs of a bed frame and let green beans grow all over it, an aesthetic not appreciated by our neighbours. They went more for garden gnomes and had a back-gate sign that said "Garden of Earthly Delights"—I guarantee they weren't familiar with the painting.

In my leafy retreat there was just enough space for a chair. It was so pleasant in the dark green shade. Before long, the kids discovered me and their calls became ever more plaintive. One day, exasperated, I stood in the yard with my arms spread wide and shouted to the skies, "All I want is me squared of peace!"

I'm inside the cabin, gazing out and up into the green cathedral. Boughs of balsam, maple, white pine, birch and cedar fill the windows. The phoebe chicks cheep in their porch nest. I hear the rush of wind in the trees, the nearby whir of hummingbird wings, a woodpecker's knock. Green chiaroscuro light dapples the forest floor down the short slope to the creek. At the water's edge, two white birches and a tall cedar, the trunks enmeshed, arc up, leaning on one another. At intervals ducks, beavers and muskrats coast silently by.

The cabin's main floor is 12 by 24 feet, with two rooms up steep wooden stairs for sleeping. In this space is a tiny washroom, a kitchen with our luxuries—a full-sized propane stove and pine cabinets—a retro grey table and chair set from the '50s, and a tall bookshelf loaded with nature books, childhood classics such as *Black Beauty* and *The Black Stallion*, plus volumes of fiction and poetry. A daybed piled with pillows sits beside the Atlanta Homesteader woodstove. Everything one needs in life, all within sight.

At night, we pull down random books and read to one another by candlelight. This excerpt—from *The Lonely Forest Dweller* by Prince Tissa Kumara, the youngest brother of King

Ashoka, who spread Buddhism through his vast realms in 250 BC—resonates with us across time: "If nobody is to be found,/ In front of one or behind one,/That is exceedingly pleasant/For the lonely forest dweller."

We repeat the next stanza, laughing and substituting deer or moose: "Pleasing, and joyful to sages,/Haunted by rutting elephants,/Seeking my goal alone, quickly/Will I go to the wild forest."

This morning it's raining. Drops ping on the metal roof, tree-tops rustle in the wind and the fire makes burning sounds—not crackling, but the roar of combustion. A log shifts in the wood-stove and Marco's hard rubber boots tap outside on the deck. I finish my coffee, pull on rainwear and step out the sliding door to the small deck that looks down toward the creek.

My favourite walk loops around the edge of our 47 acres, skirting the central "Unknown Regions"—swampy, dense bush where branches poke and bruise and shadowy animals glide by in the half-light. Up the path in the field, wildflowers have taken over from hay. This was once part of the Old MacKay Farm. There's now a clearing where the pioneers' house had been. The barn's old stone foundation and apple trees still stand. Fresh water still bubbles from an artesian spring in the woods nearby.

At the end of the field is Moose Point, marked by a patch of scrubby cedars and a pile of fieldstones. Black bears fling the heavy rocks around, looking for insects. I find the overgrown path in the bush and then teeter over the top of the beaver dams. Pushing aside cruel raspberry canes with my beaver-whittled walking stick, I wend past the fiddlehead patch and veer slowly right, clapping, watching for bear scat and continuing on the path's curve until the hardwood forest.

Here, under the tall maples and cherry trees, there's a hush. My thoughts become quiet. I pass the rocky hummock, the highest point on the property, and soon hear the gurgle of water. From the creek I wander downstream, past the wide pond where wild rice grows, and along the deeryard path, moss inlaid with white quartz underfoot. At the end, the path emerges back beside the footbridge and the cabin. The land's intricacies, traced into memory by years of my footfalls here.

Free of everyday concerns I follow the rhythms of the body: eat, walk, swim, walk, sleep. I do yoga on the bridge and the red squirrel scolds, his claws scrabbling toward me along the branch that serves as a railing. He loses his nerve at the last moment and makes an angry about-face. How can I tell him I won't hurt him? More and more, I want to protect the peace here. We don't allow hunting, so this is a safe haven for fish, deer, elk, moose, mink, grouse, ducks.

In the solitude and safety of this place I feel relief from life's rushing and chafing. "We are driven to distraction by the pursuit of the fragmentary," writes Bengali writer Rabindranath Tagore in his essay, *The Religion of the Poet*. Never more true than in our technological age, which for all its benefits exacts a steep cost. We have constant connectivity; yet our gadgets untether us from reality in deeply disturbing ways.

Shortly after my "me squared of peace" plea, Marco and I started to tag along with friends on their house-hunting expeditions up north, dreaming that perhaps we could afford a summer place even though a city house was out of reach. We met Merv, a stocky man in his fifties with a boyish face and a deep laugh, who became our real estate agent and rural decoder. He introduced us to black-flies, bug jackets and properties around Bancroft. By late fall we had resolved to buy a mouse-infested cottage near Maynooth that teetered beside a raging torrent and had only a rickety bridge for access. Some other impractical souls beat us to it. We were sad and resolved to keep looking in spring. To our surprise in February, Merv rang. "Guess what, kids—I have something to show you." The property had more going for it than the other place, he promised. "And I'd be your neighbour."

That week we met him in Bancroft on a cold, sunny day. Merv told us his plan: we'd hike in the back way over a neighbour's property—the man had made paths while logging with his horse—and then cut across a frozen beaver pond. Merv wound duct tape around the tops of our boots to keep out the deep drifts, and we began the long slog in. An hour later, out of breath and shivering, we paused on the crest of a hill. We spotted the cabin below: a charming blue steel roof amid snowy pines. Hastening our steps we slid-bounded down the slope.

Inside the little cabin Merv fired up the ancient woodstove and invited us to sit on the godawful orange sofa, where snow from our boots melted onto an old braid rug. He lounged in the matching orange grandfather chair and told us the details. The beavers would build at the low point in the access road "once in a while." Our right-of-way ran over a logging company's land. "They're the kind of neighbours you want—they'll come to cut a few trees every 12 years or so." The right-of-way was shared by a neighbouring property—the access road ran right through the creek and past the cabin's front door. But this wasn't a problem: the owner lived in Alberta, Merv explained, and the only person we'd see was Doug, a friend of "Alberta's" who kept an eye on the place and who had permission to hunt next door.

Once we'd warmed up, Marco and I went back out to stand on the little bridge over the creek, which led to the logging road, the fair-weather way in. Blue sky above, sun sparkling on snowy boughs and the frozen creek, still flowing fast in the centre. "I wonder what's under all this," I said, waving my hand at deep snowdrifts. We shrugged. Whatever it was, a graveyard for rusting Chevys perhaps, we both knew it was for us.

The deal for our "nature-lovers' paradise," as the real estate listing had read, was done by April, shortly after my fortieth birthday. I was working on another government contract and life on Bay Street was a speedy grind, driven by "the sky is falling!" panic—about volunteerism awards. I stayed marginally sane by sneaking out with a friend to do yoga at Trinity Church at lunch, writing poems with titles like "Bored Brain," and reciting Theodore Roethke's "Dolor," about the tedium of office life, with its "misery of manilla folders and mucilage."

Now new vistas were opening up. We had a retreat in the woods, far from noise, speed and stultifying routines. The snow had finally melted, the logging road was passable and the cabin beckoned. We rode through the mud on Merv's ATV and he walked us around the property, pointing out landmarks: the secret spring, the foundations of an old house and barn, the corner post in the beaver pond, cherry trees in the forest. Merv knew and loved every corner, as he'd grown up here. There were no rusting hulks—just trees, water and sky, the vast wilderness at our backs.

Today it's sunny, and the weathered boards of the dock warm my bare feet. I look into the sun-lit water at cedar reflections. Fallen trees—so many lose their footing and topple into the creek—appear as wavy lines, while the live trees are green rectangles that ripple when the wind touches the surface. The creek widens and deepens here in front of the cabin, before turning the corner and flowing down over a waterfall.

Curious black bass come and hover. I step into the cool water, down three natural steps in the rock until I'm submerged. When the sun's up I can see right to the bottom as I swim: brown-gold water, companionable fish following me—Are you food?—and the stem of a water lily growing up from the muck. I never feel so clean.

The creek is the liquid heart of this retreat. I can think of no greater gift than clean water and spend hours swimming in its everlasting rush and clarity. All that's negative, depleting, gets washed away. The cold shock of water on my warm body, the joy of being immersed in the new element, the beaver's-eye view of water, the grey shore festive with green ferns and water irises or cardinal flowers, woody cedars rising from the banks, white and yellow birches that guide the eye up to the sky. I encounter other creatures of the creek made light by the waters—a beaver, a curious watersnake, a bass protecting her nest—all of us persuaded by the currents, baptized here.

I've always loved water best, its constant flow and movement. The way it reflects the truth of change both within us and around us. On it goes, running downhill, powerful, yet taking the path of least resistance. Limerick Lake to Beaver Creek to Crowe Lake to Lake Ontario to the St. Lawrence to the sea to the sky to the earth, perfect cycles of fall and flow.

At first, kneeling by the creek, I'd cup my palms and try to drink the sparkling water quickly, before it escaped. Now I experience the cascading water as a deep, unending source that always finds its way.

In the early days, all I wanted was me squared of peace. I didn't quite know what to do with 47 acres. Sometimes I felt compelled to tidy up the messy sticks in the woods. Or I hid indoors, persecuted by deer flies, thinking, "This is not what I signed up for." I couldn't have told you the name of a wildflower or the differences between evergreen tree species. One evening, having a drink by the dock after our four-hour drive from Toronto, Marco and I were startled when, after half an hour, what our blind eyes had mistaken for a rock started to swim away—a giant snapping turtle.

I liked the natural world vaguely, but it was more what was absent than what was present that appealed to me. Asked to explain this to my urban friends, I'd quote Dorothy Parker's poem, "Sanctuary":

"My land is bare of chattering folk;/The clouds are low along the ridges,/And sweet's the air with curly smoke/From all my burning bridges."

Even just for weekends it felt wonderful to escape the accumulated scandals, failures and baggage of 20 years of living in Toronto. Led away by the cabin, after two years of being stuck in traffic with all the other cranky Torontonians going home on Sunday nights, we moved to Kingston—two and half hours closer to Beaver Creek. In "The Country North of Belleville," poet Al Purdy calls the cabin's region "the land of our defeat," where settlers worked the thin veneer of earth on top of the ancient rock. Up in our field, the farmers had grown hay and taken it out by horse wagon to Sutton Road, following an old track. Snake fences and cairns of fieldstones in the woods remain, testament to their backbreaking labour.

As our nature enthusiasm grew, it became evident that few people in our circle shared it. My dad surprised us by liking the place—it's good to have a "bolt hole" to run to when the apocalypse comes, he said. My friend's druggie brother was excited to hear we had a remote property with an open field and a good water supply. He sidled up at a funeral and asked, "Would you like an opportunity to augment your income?" My sister Kath and Talisker, her dog, were the only ones who loved the cabin as much as we did.

Most everyone else visited once and never returned. They were, as I was at first, annoyed by bugs, the outhouse, the small indoor space, the lack of running water, electricity and cell signal. How could they not be won over by the solitude, open space, natural beauty, trees, wildflowers and the ever-flowing creek? Clinging to familiar comforts separates us from reality, like the seasons changing and the rhythms of the natural world, leaving us in a fake fantasy world of our own creation, I'd opine to their eyeball rolls.

At first I was sad that the place was too "rustic" for everyone. Soon, however, I appreciated the peace, first as a guilty pleasure, and then as a luxury I revelled in. Gradually my desire for peace became a deepening hunger for solitude. Before long I rarely invited anyone up to the cabin by the creek.

Occasionally someone would arrive unexpectedly. One afternoon I looked up from my book to see an elderly woman clinging to the bridge, legs kicking. "Grab my canoe!" she shouted. I jumped into the water and caught it, noticing a rod and reel and many large, dead frogs. Maggie from St. Ola was 82, she told us as she climbed back in her canoe, and liked to make fires on islands in the stream and do some fishing. As well, a local man injured in a chainsaw accident, who often left his carvings on people's porches and window ledges, would suddenly walk past and wave.

As Merv had predicted, we seldom saw anyone except Alberta's friend Doug, who was a pest but kept a good eye on the place. His presence only became unrelenting in September as hunting season approached. Walking in the field one day, I saw him leaving apples out for the deer on the neighbouring property so they'd make easy prey when he returned with his shotgun. One November, we met Doug and his friends on the road. Six men with guns, all of them likely doused in deer pee so the animals couldn't smell them. They asked if they could hunt at our place. We told them emphatically no.

Hunters, especially bear hunters, make me edgy. When I'm in the woods, I don't fear black bears or wolves, only hunters. One day, we walked up our logging road toward the main road, specu-lating about where Doug had found the "IGA bag full of morels" he always bragged about. Two big sweaty hounds, tongues practi-cally dragging on the ground with thirst, came bounding up to us through our open gate.

We poured water into an upturned shovel for them to drink and noticed a phone number on their collars. Minutes later, a white Toyota Tacoma came barrelling in past the gates and started to roar up our road. We stepped out from the trees and it stopped. The driver was clean cut, and beside him was a hairy guy with a long beard wearing dungarees.

"This your place?" asked the clean-cut man. We nodded. "Have you all seen our other five dawwwggs?" he drawled, opening the tailgate, allowing the two hounds to jump up into the kennel custom-built onto the back of the truck. Tennessee plates.

Apparently more of their dogs were running free in the bush. How did the dogs get away? we asked. "Pappy's been coming up to Coe Hill for 30 years to hunt bears," the clean-cut one replied. We looked puzzled. "We let the dawgs loose, they tree 'em, and then we shoot 'em," he explained.

"Not the little ones though," Dungarees added, noting my look of horror.

"We'll call the number if we see them," I said.

Reluctantly, muttering "Pappy's gonna whup us sure," they turned around and roared off.

My heart beat erratically. Why can't people respect this place and leave the wild animals alone? I thought about the few undis-turbed places left on Earth, of plants and creatures at risk, of the links to human exploitation. Even here: footprints, ATV tracks in the meadow, litter—chip bags, plastic bottles, tin cans, cigarette butts, spent shotgun shell casings. Plastic washed downstream. The menacing black military airplane that flew along the creek.

People, always making incursions. The nature of a sanctuary: it can be violated.

Tea-hued water passes under my feet. I glimpse it through the gaps between the bridge's planks and see two little fish looking up. Cardinal flowers flash red amid the green fern-ribs, and wild peppermint grows on the grey rocks. Above the tall silver birch, protected from beavers with a wire skirt, the sky is wide. The sentry trees, two cedars, are pecked with holes, so their resin drips onto the bridge.

Disturbances at the cabin feel magnified, yet vanish quickly, like a stone thrown into water. The quiet swallows them. They are overcome by the creek's fluent voice, jays squawking, the great blue heron's silent shadow passing overhead, the flitting of woodpeckers, warblers, chickadees in the branches.

On the bridge I do what I'd have considered an inconceivable waste of time in my old life: sit and stare. When I first arrive, the trees are a welcoming green expanse, and the bird calls, a chorus. Soon, shades appear, variegated trees, and birdsong becomes the phoebes' nervous *cheep, cheep*, the barred owl calling *who cooks for you*, the mad cackle of the pileated woodpecker. The longer I stay, the subtler my perceptions become. Undisturbed, I can go inward, return to myself, and notice the world around me.

I write on the bridge, and my pen is stilled when a dragonfly lands on the page to rest. It seems to say, "Look at me. No, really look." Four black-lace wings, gilded red bubble eyes and body. Then a spider crawls across the white page of my book. My knee is a landing place for powder-blue dragonflies and metallic blue-green ones—perhaps they've grown from the nymphs that practise flying, dancing up and down high in the air at dusk.

I have often felt out of place, jangled, unable to truly relax into the moments. Peace is rare and fleeting, soon to be broken. I always identified with birds, the way they can't rest, their twitching motions, fear of cruel claws. But here, where I feel safe, I'm learning to be present. Experiencing the beauty of the dragonfly, or a blue-spotted black salamander asleep under a plank, or the bright stars twinkling above, makes me, in that moment, conscious of being part of it, not apart. In the quiet forest, I can begin to see the patterns of reality. To retreat is to stop, gain clarity and make space for change.

Inspired by our experiences in taking a step back to the cabin, Marco and I make plans to attend a month-long yoga retreat in India, to fully immerse ourselves in study and practice. I've been reading about India's ancient forest dwellers. They preached that the perfect relation with this world is the relation of union. As Tagore writes, the forest hermitage in classical Indian literature is "the place where the chasm between man and the rest of creation has been bridged." I read these words, seated on the bridge with my back against a tall cedar tree, and heave a satisfied sigh. Observing the complex unfolding in these woods, I've experienced the truth of relatedness, so different from the duality of everyday life. Not long ago, I'd felt that humans were somehow separate.

We can learn so much from our bodies, and from the book of nature. Some think to retreat to the woods is to stick our heads in the sand in a time of ecological crisis. I attended a reading where a poet spoke dismissively of the poet Mary Oliver. "She lives in a national park," this poet said, meaning, "She's out of touch with reality." But don't we first need to recognize what we need to preserve? "I like to think of myself as a praise poet," Oliver said in a rare magazine interview. Others write well of the coming devastation, she added. "Yes, I try to praise. If I have any lasting worth it will be because I have tried to make people remember what the Earth is meant to look like."

In this forest, I become quiet, observe. Then I move back into the world, transformed by my new respect for insects, plants, animals, seeing the interdependence of the natural world and all creatures on this planet. "Attention is the beginning of devotion," Oliver writes in *Blue Iris*. Ecology of the spirit leads to ecology in the physical world.

It's nearly autumn and the crisp air feels urgent, vital. Beside Beaver Creek, rose-breasted grosbeaks flit in the cedars as thrushes flute the sun to sleep. The creek gurgles and the dog begins to snore on the rug as we sink into the rapture: another quiet night deep in the forest.

It was a warm February evening on the spice coast of Malabar when I first realized our forest retreat had inhabited me in unexpected ways. Marco and I had finished our yoga studies and were dining at a guest house, set in a lush coconut grove on a bluff by the sea. We sat with a couple from London, UK—he was in tax law, she was a tourism executive—and a dancer and a sociology professor from Paris. Urban professionals with city concerns, like me in my Toronto days.

We swapped stories. I found myself talking not about our yoga retreat adventures, such as the rampaging temple elephant that nearly trampled Marco and then picked up its trainer and threw him against a tree (the mahoud lived but was taken to hospital with serious injuries), or the passionate embrace we received from Amma, India's most famous female guru. No, I talked about the cabin.

The others seemed receptive so I evoked some scenes. "In spring, trilliums carpet the forest in white or deep purple; yellow and purple violets peep out from under the dead leaves; and we forage for edible plants coveted by chefs, such as fiddleheads and morels." The French people nodded in approval.

"And all the creatures have come back: young deer feed in the fields; migrating warblers and white-throated sparrows sing; woodpeckers chatter; and garter snakes hold orgies on the warm rocks. By the way," I asked, "did you know that garter snakes have two penises?"

They exchanged incredulous looks and laughed openly as I continued to regale them with stories about our cabin in the woods, and how its influence had slowly transformed our lives, even acting as the catalyst that led us to India. They looked puzzled. "A retreat is about creating space for what's meaningful to you, but you don't have time for in everyday life," I explained. The sun sank into the liquid gold of the Arabian Sea, and as we clinked glasses, I was aglow in a warm vision of Beaver Creek— how it flows, falls, loses itself.

That spring, my friend Wendy—a "naked yoga" teacher from New York whom I met during my first yoga teacher training retreat in Bahamas—visited us at the cabin. As we got out of the truck, frightening clouds of mosquitoes descended. She gamely pulled on a bug jacket that zipped over her head, and then lit a cigarette. "These things have a design flaw," she noted, puffing through the mesh.

That night by candlelight over dinner I held forth about how landscape and divinity are closely linked in India. She listened awhile and then said, "You've turned into a nature freak." We laughed at the "life is a comedy" aspects of my tale: I was yet another of India's disillusioned spiritual seekers, one who went on a yoga retreat 5,000 miles away only to find peace at a small cabin two hours from home.

Despite shady gurus and other lively disappointments, India was fascinating and provided new ideas about sacred topography and the forest. In Vedic tradition, life is divided into stages. When your hair is grey, you have wrinkles and grandchildren, and your family and worldly duties are completed, you may enter what's called the "forest dweller" phase. This is when a couple may go to the forest to become hermits, to live simply but not grimly (i.e., sex is allowed once a month), and have a spiritual life.

While the hedonism quotient at the cabin wildly exceeds Vedic guidelines, the parallel seemed obvious: I came to the cabin when I was forty, and in this place, began to explore the natural concerns that arise at middle age and changed my trajectory. I moved to a smaller city, became a yoga teacher and focused on literary writing, work long deferred.

A forest hermitage dominates Kalidasa's famous play, *Shakuntala*. The spirit of the forest retreat he describes as "sharanyam sarva bhutanam" (where all creatures find their protection of love). I read these words while swinging in my hammock by the water and had to put the book down. An epiphany: at this retreat, a missing inner dimension had been restored. I was refreshed and now spilling over with my "protection of love."

Literally the next day everything changed. First we found out that our absent neighbour, Alberta, had given his property to his son. Inexplicably, Alberta's old friend Doug suddenly became like a burr we couldn't unstick. Nearly every time we visited that season, there he was: examining the bridge and talking about building a bigger one, making elaborate plans to improve the road, scoping out places he might park a caravan.

One dark night, the mystery of his constant presence was solved. It was 10:30 p.m. and we were nearly asleep. A blaring car horn shattered the quiet. We ran outside to find Doug standing on the far side of the bridge. First, he launched into a rambling tale about how he'd taken in a relative who'd suffered brain damage in a logging accident. Always a sucker for a colourful story, I said, "Uh huh," at the appropriate moments. Then he got to the point:

he had permission from Alberta's son to log the few remaining trees. In exchange, Doug was to build him a road to the waterfront and clear a building site.

The next morning, a Saturday, Doug was planning to bring heavy logging equipment over the stream—at 6 a.m. Marco and I looked at one another. We shared the right-of-way with the neighbouring property and Doug had permission, so there wasn't much we could do. We'd always known that the right-of-way passed over the bridge or through the creek, a stone's throw from where we swim, from the cabin's front door. We shrugged, asked Doug to avoid early mornings and weekends in future, and told ourselves it was temporary.

Doug, who is a terrible listener, besieged us for months: at all hours, he was chainsawing, machines and tree torsos trundled in and out, and the new road—which snaked all over the property next door where Doug cut trees, versus taking a direct route that made sense—looked like a giant had come and uprooted everything. A few stumps were uncomfortably close to our property line. Doug met every protest at how inconsiderate he was being with an excuse. He was like an old fire horse, his blood up, crazy to snuff the trees. When I talked to Alberta's son about it he seemed unconcerned, said he would likely sell the place instead of building there.

Walking in the field one day, I spotted Doug dozing in the cab of his truck. As usual, he'd tossed his candy wrappers out the window. He was diabetic and brought his treats here to savour far from his wife. I was furious with his littering. But I always softened. He loved this place, he was old and had a serious heart problem, and he likely did not have many seasons left. Temporary, I told myself.

I kept walking along the loop trail, confused. How could this be? Just as I'd felt grateful and at one with everything, chainsaws appeared in the sacred grove? As I walked through the hardwood forest and to the creek, my mind turned over something I'd never quite been able to grasp: the Buddhist concept of attachment, and how it leads to suffering. With the cabin I'd always wondered, "How can we not be attached to what feeds us?" Now I was getting some insight. Everything changes.

In consolation, and to mark our ten-year anniversary at Beaver Creek, I resolved to write about our beloved cabin in the woods. I packed up all my notes and naturalist journals, ready to begin. We arrived to find a real estate sign nailed to our front gate: "70 acres, waterfront, right-of-way, call for details." A huge arrow pointed down the logging road toward the cabin. Tracks from an ATV went around the gate, flattening the tall flowers and grass. I saw tire imprints in the muddy spots all the way in, and just past the cabin, a red marker tied to a tree, well within our boundaries.

Strangers—and soon, neighbours—in this space. ATVs in the temple. "The retreat story is taking a new direction," I wrote in my journal in consternation. We had known that change was in the air. Doug had died a few weeks before of a heart attack. Also, Alberta's son had mentioned he might sell the property—which we couldn't afford to buy anyway. But we were still shocked.

A droning sound approached and then the real estate agent and his clients rolled through the creek on their ATVs. I reasoned with myself, "Really, is it so hard to coexist? Maybe all will be well and the new people will be nice, even new friends." Or they could be noisy hunters.

Peace was suspended. I constantly thought I heard engines. Sometimes I really did, and ATVs or pickups would appear and drive through the creek. Feeling sick, frozen in my hammock, I hoped they'd get out quickly. We had passive aggressive exchanges with the real estate agents—two young guys with preppie haircuts. "Hope you brought your bug jackets," we'd say, happy when the deer flies were truly awful. They'd reply, "We know what to expect up here." Or "Is this your only showing this weekend?" we'd ask, and they'd counter, "Are you here every weekend?"

We sent the dog to bark at them, were happy when they arrived as Marco was looking his most eccentric, hair long and wild, wearing pink shorts and sharpening his axe. When the people left looking harried, we felt triumphant. It was an invasion of our privacy, our peace, but we knew we couldn't win.

New people arrived on ATVs. Marco spoke to them: three guys from "Camp 40." Doug no longer held hunting rights on the logging company land we cross over to get to our place, and now these hunters were leasing it. The one who said he's "the captain" told us we'd never see them, except maybe for two weeks in November during deer season.

Before long the real estate sign came down, and the new neighbours—two couples with many grown kids, extended family members, friends and dogs—introduced themselves. They were social, shared our feeling that this place was paradise. I struggled to be civil despite how obviously sweet they were. I recognized that they needed to get to their place somehow and couldn't just walk over the bridge as we did. I recognized their right to be here and truly wanted them to enjoy the place. And I loathed their presence.

Marco was gracious, while I hid and felt besieged whenever they cut their engines outside and a booming voice called, "Howdy, neighbours!" Or when they zoomed through the creek in the morning to get bacon, disturbing my swimming. One night, after they dropped by to say hello unexpectedly—ten of them and three dogs—I wept. Next, the logging company came to cut the trees. I avoided Beaver Creek all that fall. I had to regroup. The world had arrived.

I'm at the cabin, sitting by the creek and leaning back against my favourite cedar. A woodpecker raps on the tall white birch and a grouse gains altitude, wings beating. A duck quacks upstream in the pond. I watch the ever-changing flow of the current. I dangle my fingers, create a temporary wave of resistance.

Where is the stream taking me? On. After years of peace here, it seems I've taken it in, found a sanctuary of the heart. The cabin, the creek, the woods: the outer reflection of my unconscious desire all those years ago in Toronto to retreat and find a new way to live. Turns out it was I who was the call.

Now, the whole "ATVs in the temple" storyline seems like a cosmic joke. Ten years of nearly perfect peace; I resolve to write about retreating to a small cabin and within months, we have scores of neighbours, hunters appear to lease the right-of-way land, and the logging company cuts down the trees across the creek. Much else has happened in the decade since. Before, these events would have made me feel the peace and stability were being snatched back, another of life's cynical tricks. But I've changed. I've been filled. Maybe events are hinting at a new call—for community?— that's arising now.

The cabin has gone from being something I thought I didn't need or want to a guilty pleasure, to a luxury I drank in greedily, to a deep need met, to an emotional geography, a quiet place I carry within.

As ever, when Marco and I arrive at Beaver Creek we make plans to build me a writing hideout down the deeryard path beside the pond and discuss renovations and solar panels that would make the cabin liveable if we wanted to spend more time here. Then, the neighbours drive in and out to pick up relatives, milk or more beer, and we wave and talk about perhaps finding a new place, somewhere more private.

In a way, it doesn't matter whether we stay or go. After so long in this place, our strides are long, our hearts light. We feel blessed on the Earth and open to the flow. Whatever happens, just last night, I saw the stars go from white light to variations of blue and red, and in the quiet, I returned to myself as to some longed-for source. In the green cathedral, wind still ripples the water, and most of all, the creek's steady pouring . . .

The Art
of Retreat

Now and again it is necessary to seclude yourself among
deep mountains and hidden valleys to restore
your link to the source of life.

—Morihei Ueshiba, founder of aikido

M ountain caves, sacred groves, purifying deserts, holy wells and waterfalls—wild places are where humans first went to contact divine forces. Later we constructed new sanctums: hermitages, monasteries, pilgrim paths, forest cabins and other quiet havens for creativity, deep thinking and introspection. These spaces are the tangible reflection of our timeless human desire to retreat.

Finding seclusion today among deep mountains, or anywhere else, has become a feat of ingenuity. Even longstanding cartoon tropes are getting a modern twist: the *New Yorker* recently depicted a bearded monk meditating on a mountaintop, while on the next peak, a second monk grinned beside a billboard: "Coming Soon: Enlightenment and Pizza by the Slice." In times when a monk can't find a quiet mountain and daily life makes the hellscapes of Hieronymous Bosch feel eerily familiar, what of our corresponding inner spaces, our psycho-geographies?

Space for retreat, or lack thereof, has consequences: for personal and spiritual fulfillment, for our connection to nature, for culture and creativity and for clear thought. Paradoxically, at a moment when taking a strategic step back would be of particular benefit, we've forgotten how retreating fits into our busy, lopsided lives.

Retreat as an idea is rarely discussed except in terms of its result: perhaps wisdom or art, a new scientific theory, clarity or healing. In part the reason is that inner transformations are devilishly hard to articulate. Retreat is also challenging to isolate as a topic, because it crosses great shifts of time and space, diverse spiritual and secular practices, and it overlaps with related subjects such as silence, solitude and sanctuary. It's like a great river that flows down the mountains and spreads widely and unpredictably across the plains. This book is an adventure, an attempt to follow the tributaries without getting lost, exploring yet keeping the focus on the fluid phenomenon that is retreat.

While retreat itself is undocumented in scientific literature, solitude, one of its common elements, has been widely studied. Once considered a virtue, solitude is "more devalued than it has been in a long time," says Matthew Bowker, a psychoanalytic political theorist at Medaille College in Buffalo, New York, whose work on the collective beliefs that shape our social and political landscapes includes research into being alone. Departing from old ways, we moderns rarely see the need to withdraw for a time and pay attention to what's holy to us—however secular that may be. "Holy" is not to say religious—the words "healthy" and "whole" derive from the same root, signifying wider meanings.

As I begin this exploration of our human retreats, I feel like someone who has made an amazing discovery that no one is interested in. Perhaps it's as Albert Einstein once said, "I live in that solitude which is painful in youth, but delicious in the years of maturity." When we're young it's a torment and we don't see why it's important, when we're middle-aged we're too busy, and when we're older, we may realize the rich benefits and wish we had started earlier. Is retreat passé, or is it part of our humanity? I'm longing to get below the surface discourse to what I see as the seriousness of retreat; people think it's a holiday when in my experience, it's about what we value most deeply.

Historically in the West, retreat was religious, for divine and scholarly purposes, practised by hermits, monks, nuns and pilgrims since the third century AD. By the industrial age that began around 1760, under the influence of the Romantics and the Transcendentalists, nature and culture gained on scripture, and our revisionist retreats—focused on creation rather than Creation—drew us to the forests, national parks and modern arts temples for making culture, as well as to museums and galleries for appreciating it. Since the 1950s, millions seeking a personal experience of the divine without pews and pulpits have also embraced yoga and meditation—two spiritual traditions that value retreats and have radically changed the way modern people take a step back. Our retreats link to what we consider sacred, to what transports us beyond our small selves, our ordinary sense of being in the world, to where the transcendent dwells.

The shift in our Western ways of retreat, away from religion and toward spirit, nature and culture, was on my mind when one night, I had a vivid dream. In it, I go to a cathedral with the manuscript for this book, planning to lay out the chapters in an office just off the main church. I stride up the wide stone steps, worn by many feet, and open the heavy wooden door. In the spacious interior my eyes sweep over an expanse of empty wooden pews, up to the vaulted ceilings and rest on exquisite light that floods in through the stained-glass windows.

I continue to walk but find my way blocked by a golden chair. Thwarted, I decide to leave, but find I can't get out: first I exit into a courtyard enclosed by a black wrought-iron fence, and then into a sunken courtyard with walls too high to climb. Uneasy now, I walk more quickly and the setting transforms—into a windowless shopping mall of shining marble that goes on and on and on.

What stays with me now is the image of the church's illuminated, empty space. And the strangeness that I couldn't find my way out—is our religion perhaps not wholly deleted? The dream had a wistful feeling that brings to mind Chen Chen's poem "I'm not a religious person but": the speaker meets a rookie angel, and then God, and they play a game of backgammon. When he asks about the afterlife, the angel and God leave and never return. He misses them, "Like creatures I made up or found in a book, then got to know a bit."

To my conscious self, the dream's literal-minded, empty-cathedral-straight-to-the-mall aspect seems simplistic. People are less religious today, but studies show we're not less spiritual—we're simply finding new ways to seek meaning. And though religion continues to decline many people still believe in God, which may or may not be an omnipotent man with a beard. Some believers identify as "spiritual but not religious" (SBNR), the fastest growing faith group in the West, which includes many millennials. No one actually knows how many Canadians self-identify as SBNR, writes Anne Bokma in *Broadview*. Statistics Canada won't ask about religion on a census until 2021, but about a quarter of Canadians, nearly eight million, said in 2011 that they had no religious affiliation, up by 50 percent in the decade since 2001.

While in previous centuries it was unimaginable not to believe in God, today organized religion has become one possibility among many. In the near past, when most Western people went to church or synagogue or its equivalent, the weekly service was a short retreat—a sacred space was held for us. We knew how to enter and rest in it, guided by rituals we found meaningful. By studying sacred texts that expressed our faith we knew how to contemplate greater forces and our own souls. But now tradition—along with "holy days" away from work, school and everyday life, outside of ordinary time—has largely vanished. In our more secular world, retreats can recreate what organized religion offered, but without the trappings or the traditional beliefs. People have always needed to step away from their ordinary lives, so the question becomes, How do we find this space for what's extraordinary ourselves? We've lost the method, it seems, but not the need.

One characteristic of our SBNR times is we pick and choose what works from different traditions—even in Christian retreat centres today, it's not unusual to find reiki, tai chi, yoga or meditation on offer, and many former seminaries have been repurposed into wellness hotels and ashrams for spiritual retreats. There is criticism of this trend from many quarters as being self-indulgent, flaky spiritual materialism. But where some see spiritual shoppers, I see pioneers. If spirituality is, as I believe, simply the desire to think deeply, seek meaning and acknowledge life beyond the mundane without involving a deity, perhaps a more compelling issue is: How do we recreate sacred space outside organized religion?

Architects are grappling with a version of this question. "I have not experienced the miracle of faith, but I have known the miracle of ineffable space," said Le Corbusier, whose famous Notre-Dame du Haut in Ronchamp, France, completed in 1955, marked a watershed moment in the history of modern religious architecture. The Catholic church had asked for a pure space without extravagant detail and ornate religious figures. The sculptural building he created heralded many qualities of contemporary sacred spaces: ethereal, meditative, with reverence for natural materials and adaptable for worship and community needs.

Like our retreats, church buildings are becoming more spiritual and less religious, yet they still offer experiences of timelessness, awe, silence, solitude, devotion, a place where humans can step closer to a higher power. These sanctuaries of light, peace and beauty—and often, empty soaring space—correspond to our own inner cathedrals.

The word precedes the world, so our vocabulary needs reinvention if we are to discuss retreat today. Many secular people get a rash using the religious words, yet we have few others to describe our attempts to touch Le Corbusier's "ineffable" realm. Retreat is the most serviceable word I've found to name modern-day sacred space. What can we say instead of sacred, divine, God? Poetry is where language goes to renew itself. It excels at the unsayable, what's beyond what we have words for, at dwelling in that liminal space between the everyday and the transcendent. This is the space retreat also occupies as we reach for something intangible, greater than ourselves.

For ideas I look to Marie Howe, the former poet laureate of New York and author of *Magdalene* and other works that attempt to bring the sacred back into the modern world. Howe, noting that Shakespeare invented hundreds of words, says we need a new, non-religious vocabulary. What is god? she asks. "It doesn't mean anything anymore, how can we even approach the power that is animating the universe, and all the universes that might be? We must choose another word, find another way of describing it that honours the vast unspeakable energy of it whatever it is . . ."

Retreat offers one time-tested and capacious way to link us to spirit, the Muses, the natural world, and "whatever it is." This helps us in changeable times, when it's hard to maintain a sense of personal responsibility and connection to what's most important to us—another of religion's useful functions that's being swept aside.

Against the backdrop of today's world, the art of retreat seems more relevant than ever. What's unprecedented at this moment, I believe, and many agree, is the unhealthy way the hard-wiring of our brains is being exploited by contemporary forces— notably, technology and commerce. We've become dangerously distracted, a word that comes from the Latin dis (apart) and trahere (drag), signifying the effect on our thoughts. Silicon Valley insiders admit that social media companies deliberately make their products addictive, "like taking behavioural cocaine and just sprinkling it all over your interface, and that's the thing that keeps you like coming back and back and back," as former Mozilla and Jawbone employee Aza Raskin, a leading technology engineer, told the BBC. As a result, it's becoming easier than ever to confuse a busy life with a rich life, to swap fleeting interactions for true connection and to squander our downtime on screen time. There it is, the apple with the bite out of it, the fall of humanity every time we turn on our computers. Retreat can be an important way to push back, an act of dissidence that has social and cultural importance.

It's hard to convey to someone who hasn't experienced it how different, how spacious and embodied, life felt before we were always turned on. Having lived roughly half of my life analogue and half digital, I can tell you there's been a rapid decline in both the ability to find quiet space and the value we accord it. The transformation has been swift and decisive, and dates from when we got our first cellphones, intensified by the arrival of social media. Expectations about solitude and inner space, and the place of interiority in our lives, have undergone a sea change. Collective amnesia about paying attention has swept over us with incredible speed.

The new age arrived for me one afternoon in the 1980s when I heard a loud voice on my way home, near Barton Avenue in Toronto. I glanced up to see a well-dressed man walking a large black dog. Was he addressing Rex? The man held something about the size of a brick in his hand, which was in fact a phone. I remember the scene clearly, my first taste of an experience that's commonplace now that connectivity has become our default: being held captive to one side of a conversation.

The ongoing invasion of my cognitive space that dates from this moment on feels like an infringement on my freedom. It leaves me with a new mood of anxiety, a destabilizing sense of permeability, like my windows are stuck open and the wind is blowing in and disturbing my peace—or often, extracting it. Rings, pings, yet another data breach warning or phishing attempt, or emails about spray-on hair regrowth products and nail fungus remover, vexatious dinner conversations punctuated by cellphone calls, texts and searches for forgotten facts, or my incredulity as people walk babies past my house in carriages, engrossed by another new face we're always looking into—our screens.

Not long ago, knowledge seemed both pleasure and power, before a mind-numbing flood of information made clear thinking elusive. This flood makes my—our—limited attention a valuable commodity, one many are aggressively monetizing, prompting calls for us to "Join the Attention Resistance." For me, solutions like apps that block social media—on smartphones specifically designed to be addictive—or short digital detoxes aren't nearly enough to restore my cognitive quiet. I have to close my windows, return to myself, and from time to time retreat physically to allow my headspace to clear of sensory pollution.

Headspace: what I once thought was an inviolable sanctuary.

Neurologist Oliver Sacks wrote in his essay "The Machine Stops" that our gadgets have "now immersed us in a virtual reality far denser, more absorbing, and even more dehumanizing" than ever. Clutching a device every minute means we have "given up, to a great extent, the amenities and achievements of civilization: solitude and leisure, the sanction to be oneself, truly absorbed, whether in contemplating a work of art, a scientific theory, a sunset, or the face of one's beloved."

This sounds antique, even to me, though I agree wholeheartedly. Sacks, as a scientist, feared what "being caught in a flutter of ephemeral, ever-changing sensations" is doing to people without a memory of "how things were before, no immunity to the seductions of digital life. What we are seeing—and bringing on ourselves—resembles a neurological catastrophe on a gigantic scale." He wrote these words while facing his own imminent death, from cancer, in 2015. With his dire warning, he also dared to hope we'd get a grip, for the health of humankind and the planet.

Yet our new conditioning makes it acceptable that our solitude is swept away, and our data harvested, as we gorge on Likes like rats in an experiment gulping down reward pellets of food. Privacy is no longer a "social norm," said Facebook CEO Mark Zuckerberg.

We seem heedless to the disturbing machinations of corporations that exploit how we are hardwired to connect. That many computer executives bring up their children technology-free, and founded organizations to educate about its dark side, should be a warning. In China, there's now a state-organized system of social credits, which rewards and punishes routine behaviours, giving "good" people perks, such as discounts or the ability to jump medical queues, and banning "bad" people from buying so much as an airplane ticket. Add to the forces of conformity that our lives are more and more virtual: in ways never experienced in human history, we're losing touch with the material world, with experience and embodied life, with what's *real*.

As I said earlier, I do recognize that a busy, social life can also be rich, full of enlightenment. Nothing can replace the magic and meaning of friendship and familial love, and we are, after all, social animals. But my subject is the ignored yin side of our experience, without which life is incomplete. Unlike other animals, we seek meaning. It's as though we're choosing to live in half of our houses, just when the urgency of preserving a sacred precinct for whatever we love is high, and new technology is penetrating every corner of our lives.

We rarely stop to consider the implications of giving up control—of our time, and our attention. Addicted to gadgets and one another, our inner lives wither, work blurs into free time, creativity and new ideas are crowded out, and privacy disappears—we're the most tracked and surveilled people in history now that we all have a computer in our pockets. Google Earth easily invaded my sanctuary: anyone can go online and see the bridge and the blue roof of my cabin. Your wi-fi router could spy on you, watching you breathe and monitoring your heartbeat. Worst of all, we're bombarded with information and confused, unable to discern who is telling us what, and why.

Given today's world, to retreat may seem a counterintuitive response. People tend to dismiss retreat as a way of escaping engagement. But why should social action and taking a step back be mutually exclusive? In fact, they are complementary. Activists, social workers and engaged others know the importance of not burning out, and all of us benefit from a measured response rather than a reaction—which only serves to make us *feel* we're doing something. Reactiveness, in my view, is a more common form of avoidance than retreating. It's often painful to be in reality, to stay present. In poet Karen Solie's *The Caiplie Caves*, a seventh-century Scottish hermit considers a question still relevant today, whether to live a contemplative life or an active life. Solie writes, "To make our own the righteous anger / that keeps some people alive / feels like doing something / so grief and fear don't stir / under their blanket, don't open their eyes." On retreat, we're challenged to look squarely at our reactiveness and our vulnerability, charged with making sure life doesn't escape us, and with taking a longer view. In doing so we're likely to encounter the sublime, the night-marish and everything in between—in a word, totality.

Retreat is far from the only remedy, or the only way to push back against the life-diminishing aspects of our age, and to make space for and amplify what has meaning. But in this moment— when mystery, beauty, truth, sanity, independent thought and even unmediated experiences are viewed as unimportant in a secular, speedy, capitalistic and technology-obsessed world—its role, its meaning and place in our lives is a pressing question.

Our brains will adapt to changes, but are we adapting in ways that are good for us, for other people, and the planet? Along with sacred space—and not unrelated, I believe—much that's precious is disappearing: ice is melting, species are dying, silence is being swallowed by noise and even dark skies are becoming a thing of the past. Unparalleled in human history are the conditions of environmental peril, the desecration of the sanctuary, for lack of non-religious words. These are high-stakes times, yet we're more distracted, can't discern the difference between what's new and what's important and fall prey to misuse of technology and unreliable information in our post-truth age.

What's irreplaceable is vanishing. Once it's gone, will we ever remember we needed it, or loved it? Will we be gone too?

Under these conditions retreat can be seen as both a space to cultivate vital peace and perspective, and as a radical act of refusal. Poet Mary Oliver, known for her lucid wisdom—when not being disparaged for her "accessible" work, that is—reminded us of one of the greatest gifts of retreating. "To pay attention," she wrote, "this is our endless and proper work."

For centuries, the retreat, which has its roots in Buddhist, Chinese, Hindu and Western philosophies, has offered a way to cultivate an inner life and wisdom. Tension has always existed between the social and the solitary, action versus contemplation. And while the value of developing inner calm in a world in crisis might seem evident, it now requires an effort of conscious will to step out of the fast-moving stream.

It also requires time, and a place to go. Parents of young children, caregivers, or those who can't afford time away from work can't easily retreat, but that doesn't mean it is for only the privileged few. (Many places, such as yoga ashrams and arts residencies, recognizing retreat's importance, offer work-study programs, bursaries and scholarships.) Once our survival needs are met, according to psychologist Abraham Maslow's hierarchy of needs, other innate needs—for love, belonging and meaning—begin to motivate our actions. We become "self-actualizing" individuals, who experience "peak experiences" of the kind often found on retreat, characterized by wonder, beauty, awe and the feeling of being connected to the cosmos. These in turn give rise to a sense of purpose and greater happiness.

The desire to retreat is constant throughout recorded history in all places and religions. Always for nonconformists, it is, as ever, today being embraced by those who want to reclaim freedom to just be, spend time outdoors in nature, make art, think deeply, tend their spiritual life, heal—and often, marshal energies for future action.

The link between the history of retreat and seeking wisdom is clear: early exemplars include Buddha meditating under the Bodhi tree alone, Jesus fasting in the Sinai desert wilderness for 40 days and 40 nights being tempted by the devil, and Muhammad, who withdrew periodically to his mountain cave retreat near Mecca for Ramadan. All these retreats from the everyday world brought revelations. China's hermits took to the mountains, India's ancient rishis retired from society, the Christian desert fathers and mothers lived in remote, solitary caves and intrepid Celtic monks of antiquity in the British Isles withdrew to remote and wild places. Countless other religious figures, ancient and contemporary—as well as artists, thinkers, scientists, adventurers and anonymous solitary spirits over the centuries who we know nothing about—have taken a step back, recognizing that retreat leads to transformation.

Since time immemorial, people have consulted the man on the mountain, or the wise woman healer—because we think they have wisdom to offer us, perspective gained from their vantage point on the margin. Retreat, we believe, is a tested approach for gaining insight in seclusion, which can then be shared with society.

Retreat. I wish there were another word, free of the baggage of Western prejudice about passivity and weakness. Nothing could be further from the truth. Retreat is an inner adventure, a foray into the unknown. Loosening our habitual patterns leads to change: we retreat to advance, returning with new ideas and deliberate actions that enhance collective life. It's just the opposite of turning a blind eye.

What exactly do I mean by retreat? Basically, it's a voluntary, temporary step back from everyday life, either alone (a remote cabin), or in a community of like-minded people (a yoga retreat), with a purpose. But it's more nuanced than that.

The *Oxford English Dictionary* defines "retreat" as "a quiet or secluded place in which one can rest and relax." The word originates from the Latin retrahere, to "draw back, withdraw, call back," and the old French retret. Retreat as "a step backward" is first recorded circa 1300, as "a military signal for retiring from action or exercise" in the late 14th century, as a "place of seclusion" from the early 15th century on, and as a "period of retirement for religious self-examination" from 1756. Retreat as an "establishment for mentally ill persons"—another word for an asylum—appears in 1797. Also related is the word sanctuary, which derives from the Old French sanctuaire, from Latin sanctuarium, from sanctus, or "holy." Retreat has a double meaning: it is a place and also an act of independence, linked to rest, seclusion and self-examination.

The Greek word temenos better captures the expanded idea of what I mean by retreat: it's a sacred precinct set apart from common uses and life. Temenos is a sanctuary, or holy grove, or enclosure dedicated to a deity. For Swiss psychiatrist Carl Jung, it was a sacred space and container for your own inner work, a safe place for soul-making—in his case, Bollingen Tower, where he spent several months each year and said he felt "in the midst of my true life" and "most deeply myself." By establishing a protected temenos, we can meet ourselves and, Jung writes, "isolation, so uncanny before, is now endowed with meaning and purpose, and thus robbed of its terrors." The fruits of inner work in this extraordinary space are meant to be shared with the world.

The Chinese idea of retreat as a strategic step back is also valuable, and runs counter to Western ideas—we tend to think of retreat as running away. The Chinese sense is described in the *I Ching*: in its conception of reality, chance is immensely important, while the causality of Western science is barely noticed. "Just as causality described the sequence of events, so synchronicity to the Chinese mind deals with the coincidence of events," wrote Jung in his introduction to this ancient book.

Intrigued, I decided to consult the I Ching Online about the best approach to this book and tossed the virtual coins six times. Each toss defines one line of a hexagram, built from the bottom up. In an example of synchronicity, out of 64 possible hexagrams, the answer I received was 33, Retreat, which relates to a balance of natural forces, the yin and the yang of existence: "Mountain under heaven: the image of retreat. Thus the superior man keeps the inferior man at a distance, not angrily but with reserve. Unwavering will to remain persevering and not submit."

Retreat, then, is not a forced flight of the weak, but a tactical withdrawal of the strong. "The power of the dark is ascending," the text continues. "The light retreats to security, so that the dark cannot encroach upon it. This retreat is a matter not of man's will but of natural law. Therefore in this case withdrawal is proper; it is the correct way to behave in order not to exhaust one's forces."

Retreat as a remedy in dark times is an ancient idea, which entails drawing back at the right time and in the right way, not trying to force anything, but "persevering in small matters," maintaining solidarity and resistance until conditions change. Retreat lets us cultivate what sustains us, focus on what we love, guard our flames of humanity and marshal our forces with "unwavering will" to never submit—the essence of its dissident power. More than just moving away from chaos, to retreat expresses our human desire to connect to something larger: the spiritual, the natural world or transcendence through arts and culture, and often, an interweaving of all these.

I discovered the potential of retreat inadvertently, and over time. When I was in my twenties, I holed up in a tiny cabin in the jungle in Costa Rica for two weeks. I'd gone from being a keen journalism school graduate to a bored fashion magazine freelancer in just over a year and wanted a quiet time out for life strategizing. I chose the Cabañas Escondidas purely for the name, flew to San José, and caught a packed Easter-holiday bus over the Mountain of Death and down a dirt road along the Pacific coast. Descending in a cloud of dust in front of a locked gate, I sat on my suitcase smoking as I watched the red sun sink into the sea. Eventually my host pulled up in her truck in the pitch dark and said portentously, "I'll take you to the other side." We drove across the road and up the mountain in the warm darkness.

I had no company at my lofty cabana, except for the hummingbird that woke me each morning with a whir of wings as it investigated my stick of incense and searched the upturned broom for bugs. Red crabs climbed up from the shore, rustling in the dry leaves. My perch was wild and inspiring, with a clear view of the sea below. I worked into the tropical nights on my first fiction-writing project, wrote my earliest poems. I considered how to jump the journalism tracks to do more of this once I got home.

I still have a photo of that cabana on the shelf in my study, framed like a credential. It reminds me of a dreamspace I entered, alone and free to imagine. Retreat is not an orderly progression, where you meet the curriculum and get your PhD. Its benefits are deep and hard to measure, and often things don't go as planned. I thought I was at Cabañas Escondidas to consider my next move in journalism, but that wasn't quite it. From that time on I valued solitude—though it took me decades to really protect it—and my notebook morphed: interviews in the front, and new creative experiments in the back.

When I got home from my cabana my fashionista magazine colleagues were mostly interested in my tan, how it improved my look, and my weight loss plan (eating mangoes from the trees and little else). But they were also curious about the solo nature of my trip. Weren't you afraid? they asked. I certainly had moments: like when I heard a rustling and my flashlight beam picked out a rearing snake that slithered back into the dark jungle behind my cabin.

I didn't know it then, but I'd planted the seed of a life-changing discovery: time away from everyday life, alone or with like-minded others, yields insights, clarity, inspiration and agency.

"The being one creates of oneself" is what Alice Koller calls this in *The Stations of Solitude*, her book about the stopping places where we make choices about the life we want and the person we want to be. "In this, Sartre is surely right: persons are not born but made. The choice lies inescapably within ourselves: we may let it wither away, or we may take it and run."

Koller, who has a doctorate of philosophy from Harvard University, is author of *An Unknown Woman*, a surprise bestseller in the '60s that was based on her three months on an island in Nantucket, with her dog for company. Philosophers since Kant have distinguished two aspects of freedom, she writes, "Not duplicitous because of its two faces but rather whole like the moon, all of whose sides we can at last see. Free: not only having no restraints but also being self-governing according to laws of your own choosing."

Being alone well is something Koller describes as "luxuriously immersed in doings of your own choice, aware of the fullness of your own presence rather than of the absence of others."

Solitude is an achievement, she adds. "It is your distinctive way of embodying the purposes you have chosen for your life, deciding on these rather than others after deliberately observing and reflecting on your own doing and inclinings, then committing yourself to them for precisely these reasons."

What has inspired people, ancient and modern, to retreat? Conveniently, the three most illuminating sources I found to answer this question approached it from multiple perspectives: a philosopher, a Christian solitude seeker and writer, and a psychologist. I was fascinated to see how much their findings about solitude, a common element of a retreat, overlapped.

At its most basic, stepping back can be a simple break. "Escaping to such a solitary place—often called a retreat—provides respite, relief, a time for healing of wounds," writes Philip Koch in *Solitude: A Philosophical Encounter*. But, he warns, it's not just a way to restore ourselves so we may return to the frenetic lifestyles and social contact that many think is the real meaning of human existence. Koch, having read through 25 centuries of literary reflections on solitude—Lao-Tzu to Sappho, Petrarch, Teresa of Ávila, Montaigne, Percy Shelley, Thoreau and Proust—attributes to it five main virtues. These are tributaries that flow through one another, and illustrate what retreat offers beyond restoration of the spirit. These virtues, which apply equally to retreat, are freedom, attunement to self, attunement to nature, reflective perspective and creativity.

In *How to Be Alone*, author Sara Maitland, a self-described "Anglo-Catholic, socialist feminist," observes that over the centuries, people who retreated gave surprisingly consistent reports of its rewards. She describes the joys of solitude as consciousness of the self, attunement to nature, creativity, freedom, and in place of Koch's "reflective perspective," she puts "relationship with the transcendent (the numinous, the divine, the spiritual)."

For psychologist Anthony Storr, imagination, individuality, healing, the search for coherence and the desire and pursuit of the whole are the main reasons for retreat. "Removing oneself voluntarily from one's habitual environment promotes self-understanding and contact with those inner depths of being which elude one in the hurly burly of day-to-day life," he writes in *Solitude: A Return to the Self.* The value of time alone increases for people later in life, he adds, and the capacity to be alone is especially vital when changes of mental attitude are required, such as bereavement, divorce or other calamities.

Retreating from the crowd has always been the way of outliers. Hermits, monks, pilgrims, meditators and spiritual seekers aren't the only ones who withdrew into silence and solitude; traditionally, artists, composers, writers, philosophers and creative thinkers of all kinds have also been vocal proponents of time alone, which is why they're overrepresented in all explorations of the art of retreat. That's not to say retreat and inspiration are limited to these exemplars—in my mind, they serve as stand-ins for anyone who can benefit from taking a purposeful step back.

"We must reserve a little back-shop, all our own, entirely free, wherein to establish our true liberty and principal retreat and solitude," advised 16th-century essayist Michel de Montaigne. "In solitude alone can be known true freedom." Cultivating a well-stocked mind, he believed, is also a protection, because all troubles can be endured if you have rich inner resources. (On the frequent occasions when people tell me they'd be bored on retreat I admit I wonder snarkily about their well-stocked minds.)

Goethe echoes this idea: "One can be instructed in society, one is inspired only in solitude." This was true for him personally: "Nothing will change the fact that I cannot produce the least thing without absolute solitude." Mozart too: "When I am . . . completely myself, entirely alone, and of good cheer . . . it is on such occasions that ideas flow best and most abundantly." "The happiest of all lives is a busy solitude," said Voltaire. Thoreau called solitude "medicine to the soul."

Retreat can also be a powerful feminist statement. "A woman must have money and a room of her own if she is to write fiction," famously wrote Virginia Woolf. "*I* care for myself. The more solitary, the more friendless, the more unsustained I am, the more I will respect myself," declares Charlotte Brontë's Jane Eyre. Emily Carr painted her most powerful works in British Columbia's coastal forests while retreating in an old caravan. Aviator and author Anne Lindbergh left family and career obligations for a beachside cottage, where she penned the classic *Gift from the Sea*, concluding, "Every person, especially every woman, should be alone sometime during the year, some part of each week, and each day." May Sarton, in her *Journal of a Solitude*, wrote: "I am here alone for the first time in weeks, to take up my 'real' life again at last. That is what is strange—that friends, even passionate love, are not my real life unless there is time alone in which to explore and to discover what is happening or has happened." Anne LaBastille wrote of her retreat in the Adirondacks her *Woodswoman* memoirs: "the cabin is the wellspring, the source, the hub of my existence. It gives me tranquility, a closeness of nature and wildlife, good health and fitness, a sense of security, the opportunity for resourcefulness, reflection and creative thinking. . . ."

Running parallel to the long history of enthusiastic retreaters is the other track: objectors who view it with fear, loathing or ambivalence. Settling into silence, solitude—alone or communal, for a weekend or a month—and its new routines can be strange, even scary at first. Resistance arises: we get bored, fear missing out or not having others to reinforce our sense of self, feel upset about wasting time and not being productive, a sin in our capitalist, Puritan-influenced reality, and ultimately, quiet and emptiness make us anxious, being not unrelated to death—the only thing many people fear more than being alone.

Humans are so contradictory: in our society we value independence, yet we are either terrified of being by ourselves or we don't value solitude or retreat. No wonder people today find themselves alone and panic—it's unfamiliar. When was the last time you spent 24 hours alone voluntarily? Solitude makes us uncomfortable so we don't retreat, and because we never retreat, we lack the skill.

French philosopher Blaise Pascal famously wrote in the 15th century, "All of men's miseries derive from not being able to sit quiet in a room alone." This was prescient: noting that few studies had been done on "simply letting people go off and think," researcher Timothy Wilson of the University of Virginia tested 700-plus people in 11 experiments in 2014. His findings? Most subjects would rather inflict a mild electric shock on themselves than be alone with their thoughts for six to fifteen minutes. How Pascal would cringe to see our agitation when the Internet is down or there's no cell signal, and marvel to know that one-third of young people surveyed said that marooned on a desert island, they would rather go without sex than their smartphone. People's fear of boredom, other studies demonstrated, is on par with their fear of cancer.

Discoveries like these make me want to institute conscription, so people are required to retreat periodically and develop interiority, which steadies and enriches. Of course I'd think that: for me, the need to withdraw feels as strong as the need to be social. Over the years I've often felt guilty about declining an invitation because I wanted to rest, or read, or simply take a bath. It's akin to admitting you're a crank. Privately though, I'd wonder how in the scheme of things time spent alone is somehow vastly inferior to drinking downtown with friends, which is social. I'd wonder, Am I weird, or just independent? Is it really always better to be with others than by oneself? What about a healthy need to be alone, to be self-reliant or to make space for individual differences?

Meanings get blurry whenever we begin to talk about solitude and silence—common elements of retreat, which are known to promote clarity, inspiration and conversations with the self, the Muses or God. "The state of being or living alone; solitariness," is how the *Canadian Oxford English Dictionary* defines solitude. Yet even early hermits, the most solitary and ascetic of retreaters, were not fully alone. They had supporters to bring food, took time out from cave life to teach and even had visitors—think of the many depictions of white-bearded friends St. Anthony and St. Paul the Hermit, accompanied by the raven who brought a loaf of bread to their cave each day. Nearer in time there's that icon of solitude, the poet William Wordsworth, who "wandered lonely as a cloud"—accompanied by his sister, Dorothy, with whom he saw the "golden daffodils."

Muddying the waters more we use often use solitude interchangeably with related words such as loneliness, isolation, privacy, and alienation, when they're not the same thing. Loneliness is solitude with issues. In Koch's *Solitude: A Philosophical Encounter*, he examines the unique characteristics of solitude, which he refers to as voluntary time apart, and tries to define it. "A solitude is a stretch of experience disengaged from other people in perception, thought, emotion and action," he writes. Koch's emphasis on disengagement from others, as opposed to complete isolation, takes in the truth that people can be alone together. Later Koch adjusts "disengagement" to the idea of "indirect engagement." In this way he recognizes a paradoxical truth that applies equally to a retreat: even when we're alone, we're always in relationship.

Definitions of silence are similarly slippery. "The absence of sound or noise," says the *Canadian Oxford English Dictionary*, and "abstinence from, or renunciation of speech, especially as a religious vow or payment of respect to a deceased person or group." So an absence of sound or speech. Yet to me, and many others, silence is the absence of human-made sounds, like voices, or engines from airplanes flying over my cabin, but not natural sounds, like wind in pines. Silence is always defined in negative terms, of what it is not—when in my experience, there's rich inner space, something in the void.

To complicate matters further, "There's no such thing as silence," says composer and Zen meditator John Cage, who enacted this in his conceptual work "4'33'''": a pianist sat down and made no sound for four and a half minutes. "You could hear the wind stirring outside during the first movement," Cage says, recalling the 1952 premiere. "During the second, raindrops began pattering the roof, and during the third people themselves made all kinds of interesting sounds as they talked or walked out." Even in the deep silence of an anechoic chamber, we hear the sounds of our own breathing and digestion and heartbeat. And what about silence as the lack of a response?

Conflicting definitions aside, human beings tend to distrust loners, a term usually reserved for serial killers, and stigma is a given for anyone seeking interludes of solitude and silence—or especially, a life of it. I come from a long line of Scottish contrarians, which means I'm insulated from the sting of judgment about my episodic retreats, but society does seem to hold that no one normal, especially a woman, is alone on purpose. Spinster is an insult, though in medieval times it meant someone, usually a woman, who was self-supporting from spinning well. Maybe prejudices will change given that living alone has actually become the Western norm, the biggest demographic shift since the Baby

Boom. In Canada for the first time in our history, a phenomenon mirrored in Europe and the United States, more people live in one-person households than in any other arrangement.

"Wherever there is affluence, and a welfare state, people use their resources to get places of their own," says sociologist Eric Klinenberg, author of *Going Solo: The Extraordinary Rise and Surprising Appeal of Living Alone*. This trend is not negative, he says, nor is it the cause of the terrible epidemic of loneliness in the West, a modern malady with complex causes. "We need to make a distinction between living alone and being alone, or being isolated, or feeling lonely. These are all different things. In fact, people who live alone tend to spend more time socializing with friends and neighbors than people who are married. So one thing I learned is that living alone is not an entirely solitary experience. It's generally a quite social one."

And yet the ignominy of going solo remains: Carmen Callil, 73, a British publisher who is founder of the feminist Virago Press, told the *Guardian* about her experiences, "Living alone means freedom, never being bored, going to bed at eight if I feel like it." But, she adds, there are great tediums. "Men—Auberon Waugh and Lord Longford spring to mind—have occasionally insisted to my face that I was lesbian. I felt this to be an insult to women who are lesbians as well as to myself. I hate getting invitations addressed to 'Carmen Callil & Friend' and am often tempted to bring my dog." In the same article, TV presenter Alex Zane, 33, said that living alone balances his busy social and professional life: "It's not about selfishness, just knowing what you like and doing what you want without having to take another person into account." Then he added apologetically, anticipating criticism, "I know how selfish this sounds."

Equating being alone with being selfish is a common objection to solitude, and to retreat. But if time alone is simply a counterpoint to everyday time spent with others, as I suspect, why the judgments? For one thing, it's that confusion of loneliness, isolation and alienation, which are painful states, with chosen aloneness, which is glorious. "The cure for loneliness is solitude," observes poet Marianne Moore with incision.

Are there, perhaps, prerequisites for solitude to be beneficial? Yes, says Kenneth Rubin, a developmental psychologist at the University of Maryland. His study found it must be voluntary, people have to be able to regulate their emotions and join a social group when desired, and they must have existing positive relationships. "Aloneness implies a conscious choice by the individual for quiet solitude, and doesn't carry with it the negative emotional conditions associated with loneliness," Rubin notes.

Ancient fears about being alone, however, run deep. People feel time alone is unnatural because humans evolved as social animals. Evolutionary theory, social anthropology and archeology confirm that we're a social species that survived by cooperating. So being banished from the hunter-gatherer group on the savannah in equatorial Africa meant death: no more group hunting, opportunities for reproduction or security from predators. As the medieval French proverb clarifies, "Homme seul est viande aux loups!" ("A man alone is meat for wolves!")

Fear of being ostracized may go back to our tribal origins, but philosophy and theology have often reinforced the idea in our imaginations that solitude—and by extension, retreat—is bad. In the ancient Greek world, execution was the only punishment worse than exile. Think of Prometheus chained to the side of a remote mountain for stealing fire and giving it to mortals: having an eagle eat his liver every day only for it to regrow would have been considered the secondary punishment. Solitaries were occasionally praised but mostly frowned upon. Aristotle said in the fourth century BC that the highest good is contemplation.

But he also maintained, "The man who is isolated, who is unable to share in the benefits of political association, or has no need to share because he is already self-sufficient, is no part of the polis, and therefore must be either a beast or a god."

Biblical sources exert a strong influence. In the creation story in the Old Testament, God makes the world and each time says it is good—until the sixth day, with Adam: "And the Lord God said, It is not good that the man should be alone: I will make him an help meet for him." So he creates Eve. "Woe to him that is alone! For, if he falleth, there is none to raise him up."

But what if it's the case that just as we have an instinct to herd together, we have a drive to seek time apart? Is retreat just for outliers, or can everyone benefit? Psychologists pose a similar question: Do humans need solitude as much as sociability? While studies have led to different conclusions, there's agreement that solitude has benefits, and that variables, such as personality traits and stage of life, affect how much a person needs to be alone. Also relevant to ideas around retreat, psychologists emphasize that in the past, too much focus has been placed on relationships. Yes, love and friendship make life worthwhile, but they are not the only source of happiness. Solitude, which is about the relationship with oneself, is the other side of the coin. Many modern scientists say solitude is as basic a human need as being social, but that we give it short shrift.

In Koch's *Solitude*, a delightfully thoughtful book, he maintains that both solitude and engagement are essential for becoming a fully developed human. I was surprised to find a reproduction of the yin/yang diagram in a chapter titled "Images of Solitude," which he used to portray "the proper places of solitude and encounter in a human life." Solitude also improves relationships, he writes, because even when alone, we often focus on others. "In many ways the virtues of solitude find their completion in encounter."

Similarly, clinical psychologist Ester Schaler Buchholz writes in *The Call of Solitude: Alonetime in a World of Attachment*, "Aloneness is a biological and psychological essential and just as important as the heavily documented need for attachment." This, she says, has obscured the need for solitude for our development in both children and adults. If we're unable to be alone or don't make room for it in our lives, she adds, we hamper our "ability to find a sense of inner ease, at best, or at worst, end up dependent on others or drugs in unhealthy ways." Buchholz, like Koch, believes solitude strengthens our attachments, and that everyone needs time alone, not just the select few—though in different amounts. "Regardless of the dosage, solitude is a deep, soothing, and persistent call in life."

Modern psychoanalysts have long focused solely on relationships as a sign of emotional maturity, while ignoring the ability to be alone. "The burden of value with which we are at present loading interpersonal relationships is too heavy for those fragile craft to carry," writes psychiatrist Storr in *Solitude: A Return to the Self*. Many of history's greatest thinkers and artists spent most of their time on work and not on relationships, he says, which is just as meaningful. He examined the lives of artists to see what he could learn for all of us, and notes that "a retreat from the crowds has always been necessary for the formulation of brave new ideas." The need for solitude is important for society, he adds, not just because it improves our relationships with others, but so we can be at peace with ourselves. And it's not just for artists and the gifted—all people need to realize that love and friendship are not the only source of happiness.

We have been very slow to embrace these ideas. The first to identify the ability to be alone as a vital sign of maturity in emotional development was Donald Woods Winnicott, an English pediatrician who became a psychoanalyst, in his 1958 classic paper, "The Capacity to Be Alone." He called for investigation into the positive aspects of solitude—versus the fear or wish to be alone, which was already well documented. An infant's quiet time with all needs satisfied in the presence of the mother, or mother surrogate, Winnicott suggested, is the origin of the ability to be alone comfortably in adulthood. Without this the experience of positive silence can't develop, which leads in later life to a false self that complies with wishes of others, versus acting on authentic feelings or instinctive needs.

Some development of the capacity to be alone, Storr echoes, "is necessary if the brain is to function at its best, and for humans to fulfill their highest potential. Human beings easily become alienated from their own deepest needs and feelings. Learning, thinking, innovation, and maintaining contact with one's own inner world are all facilitated by solitude."

A retreat is always both a step away from something—a noisy world, perhaps—and a step toward something—a simple rest, or time to focus on what's of passionate importance to us, like the hermits of old who retreated to the desert to become "wholly aflame." I don't think it is a coincidence that I began to retreat at more regular intervals when digital technologies arrived and the world sped up. Or that I retreated in greater earnest—alone, with my partner and as part of a group—when I turned 40, the life stage at which it begins to hold greater appeal. Midlife is when we typically realize we have not been marching to our own drum. The long span of life after the reproductive years has significance. "It is then that the impersonal comes to assume a greater importance for the average person, although seeds of such interests may have been present from the earliest years," Storr says.

In my case these seeds were present, though I wasn't aware of it. Counter-culture millennials, it seems to me, discovered the benefits of solitude and retreat early in life. With a reputation for being hyperconnected, many also know the value of unplugging, even prompting talk of "the rise of millennial hermits." As well, youthful "rubber tramps," who live in vans and cars, and cloud-connected millennial "hobos" are leaving society behind for a time. Swedish environmental activist Greta Thunberg, 16, surprised me with her reply when asked by a reporter what she would miss about being on the water, having sailed from England to New York for a climate summit. "To not have contact with anyone, and to just literally sit for hours and stare at the ocean, not doing anything," she said. "To be in this wilderness, the ocean, and see the beauty of it."

Myself, I stepped back at times in my twenties and thirties, mostly to consider career dissatisfaction. I tried meditation retreats too, which made some impression, though my life remained chaotic. In my forties I went on nature and yoga retreats and got calmer, and in my fifties, I widened my repertoire to include artistic retreats, sometimes in religious places that welcomed outsiders. Like many people, for years my work was not my vocation. Retreats helped me to keep my inner flames alive, and gradually provided needed oxygen for the shift toward a more spacious and passionate life.

Given the evidence that we can all benefit, I began to wonder about an optimal dosage. What influences how much is right for each of us? "The events of early childhood, inherited gifts and capacities, temperamental differences, and a host of other factors may influence where individuals turn predominantly toward others or toward solitude to find the meaning of their lives," according to Storr.

Temperament is a well-studied aspect of personality that influences our need for time apart. The idea that psychological types, introverts and extraverts, shape our individual needs for solitude is well accepted by psychologists. Recent research shows that the types relate to one's sensitivity to stimulation. Extraverts are motivated from the outside and directed by external, objective factors and relationships. Introverts, on the contrary, are motivated from within and directed by inner, subjective factors. For extraverts, psychic energy flows outwards toward the world, while for introverts, energy is withdrawn from the world. Jung believed these tendencies coexist in us, and when either is exaggerated, it leads to neurosis. "Extreme extraversion led to the individual losing his own identity in the press of people and events," Storr explains. "Extreme introversion threatened the subjectively preoccupied individual with loss of contact with external reality."

It's fascinating how our societal preferences swing. Especially in the 1950s and 1960s it was deemed more desirable to be an introvert, notes Merve Emre, the author of *The Personality Brokers: The Strange History of Myers-Briggs and the Birth of Personality Testing*, who taught English at McGill University in Montreal. "There was something very suspicious about the extravert," Emre writes. "The extravert is the people-pleaser, the social man, the superficial one. And the introvert is the serious, creative intellectual who commands respect because he or she will not change herself to meet the demands of others."

This flipped in the 1970s, Emre believes, and since then we've lived in the age of the extravert "with a strong bias towards a person who is incredibly flexible with their personality and who can change themselves to meet the demands of any given situation. In some ways it is because that's what is utterly necessary to succeed in today's economy, right? You have to be a kind of constantly flexible labourer." Notably, not all cultures have an extravert ideal: one study compared eight- and ten-year-olds in Shanghai and Southern Ontario and found that shy and sensitive children are shunned by their peers in Canada, but are sought-after playmates in China.

Today, with modern scientists saying we all benefit from time alone to dip our toes into our imaginary Ganges or withdraw for a mountain interlude, retreat has much to offer modern people—religious, spiritual and secular. Even Superman had the Fortress of Solitude, where he went to take a break from saving the planet. The fortress's existence was secret from all but his closest allies, such as Lois Lane and Batman. Originally, his refuge was depicted as being built into a mountain on the edge of Metropolis. It was also styled as a castle in a wasteland, and located in the Arctic, though it appeared in other wild places—Antarctica, the Andes, the Amazon rainforest. The Fortress of Solitude was the only place Superman could truly be himself: only there could he openly display statues of his parents holding kryptonite.

In one way we all experience retreat every day. Nature insists we enter the solitude and silence of sleep for a third of our lives. Though we know more about it than ever, no one can say with certainty why we sleep, except that it has to do with restoration. It's the yin element of life, without which we're wakeful, exhausted, impoverished—which hints at the role of retreat in our modern lives. "Were there no darkness to restore the soul," writes Czech philosopher Erazim Kohák, "humans would quickly burn out their finite store of dreams."

So how in the 21st century can we take a temporary step back? Where do we find the seclusion of deep mountains and hidden valleys—geographies both inner and outer?

The
Old
Ways

OF HERMIT CAVES, MONASTERIES AND PILGRIM PATHS

A Hut of
One's Own

To live as a hermit is to be untrammelled by the things of the world;
it is like drawing a length of bamboo out from a dense thicket.

—Kyobutsu, 13th-century hijiri (Japanese wandering monk)

I'm looking out the window of my rented hermitage in Scotland's northwest Highlands, a place apart. Open sky, the round-shouldered mountain and the shining loch appear in painterly swathes of blue and brown. Sheep and lambs dot the dun spring fields, and in the hermitage's small garden, high winds are blasting the daffodils.

The Scottish Gaelic word cuilidh means a retreat, or a quiet place that affords privacy. The way of the hermit is solitary—or more accurately, on the solitary end of the spectrum. Hermits are less alone than we usually imagine: even the most ascetic in desert caves had social interactions, and communities of hermits have long been the norm. Myself, I plan to experience full days of hermit time in this small stone cottage, sharing meals and evenings with Marco, my like-minded companion, with whom I have often retreated over our long marriage.

Of all the "old ways" of retreat, being a hermit is the most rarefied, more rigorous than the monk's or pilgrim's way. Far from being an escape for the weak as we tend to stigmatize it, this most solitary path has always been a training ground for the strong. Hermits were the original outsiders, living in edgelands and on the fringes of social acceptability. The earliest Western hermits were religious, seeking God, and braving the hostile desert to wage spiritual warfare with the devil. In modern times, we often use the word "hermit" to describe anyone living a life apart from society, or spending interludes of time away. These dauntless rebels, regardless of motivation, are at ease with being alone.

As I gaze out at the old mountain, I get an inkling about why the Celtic hermits, the early Christians they emulated and hermits from the East were all drawn to caves—our most primordial shelters, they are made of solid rock, which surely steadies the mind. I hope my quiet stone hermitage will do the same. The previous winter I'd doubted that being a hermit of any description, even for a time, was possible in the modern day.

Christian settings don't allow for amateur hermits—to be an official hermit takes years of probation and advanced training; you have to prove your mettle in the monastery first. This was a huge relief. Not being a person of religious faith, nature, art and yoga retreats are more my style. And yet exploring the earliest Western ways of retreat appealed strongly. I'm interested in the metaphysical and consciousness, and feel we're influenced far more than we realize by our religious past.

Of all the old ways, hermit life fascinates me most. Many people have a negative impression of the solitary retreat, preferring communal ways, but I feel a strong affinity for these singular figures. I was curious to learn why hermits retreat—and why and how I might too. My search for a place to become a self-directed hermit brought a fascinating array of nonconformists to light. In the mountains of Europe, sociable professionals still practise the hermit's vocation. "Are you an idealistic, religious person who enjoys meeting people?" read a job ad placed by the small Swiss city of Solothurn in 2014. The town's hermitage, built into the rock face of a gorge, has been occupied for 600 years, and the successful applicant was a German ex-policeman with a bushy beard who studied meditation and theology. He took up residence in 2016, beating out 22 hopefuls. His duties? Caring for the chapels, taking part in baptisms and weddings, and counselling a steady stream of day-tripping tourists. For this he gets about $24,000 per year, plus paid vacation and a rent-free mountain cottage.

A 350-year-old hermitage in Austria advertised for a replacement in 2017 after its hermit, former priest and psychotherapist Thomas Fieglmueller, returned to Vienna after just one season. "Life in the hermit's cell is spartan, but the nature is very beautiful.

I met lots of nice people and had good conversations," he told the *Salzburger Nachrichten* of his hermit experience. "But there was also criticism from apparently arch-conservative Catholics because I didn't have a cowl or a beard . . . Maybe I was the wrong person."

The last thing I expected to find was a throwback to ancient times, a stylite living atop a pillar—not to be confused with a tree-dwelling dendrite. Twenty-five years ago Eastern Orthodox Father Maxime Qavtaradze climbed up the 40-metre Katshki pillar in a remote part of the Caucasus. Asked why he chose to live an isolated hermit's life, he said: "I need the silence. It is up here in the silence that you can feel God's presence." For the first two years on his eagle's nest that overlooks the mountainous region, he had only the bones of the last stylite, thought to have died 600 years ago, for company, and slept in an old fridge to keep warm.

Now there's a small church on top of the limestone monolith and a tiny stone cottage with one shade tree. Up there Father Maxime prays, reads and prepares to meet God. Predictably, he isn't completely alone: a religious community has gathered at the foot of his pillar, and he has a phone to speak to the monks below. Father Maxime is a former crane operator and unafraid of heights, and he can still do the 20-minute climb up and down the rickety iron ladder. But once he can't, he plans to pray atop the pillar and die there, adding his bones to his predecessor's now buried in a crypt under the church.

Seeking something a little less radical for myself, I came across two hermits with a peculiar role: they act as spokespeople for hermits. Karen Karper Fredette, who led a solitary life for six years in a tumbledown cabin in the West Virginian woods before she met and married hermit Paul Fredette, defines a hermit as someone who "chooses to live in solitude for spiritual reasons." The couple publish a quarterly hermit newsletter, *Raven's Bread:*

Food for Those in Solitude, which has more than 1,000 subscribers, about half urban and half country hermits. *Raven's Bread* is named for the bird that fed the prophet Elijah during his desert retreat, and aims to give "nourishment to seekers of solitude and to assure them they are not alone in their search for quiet in a noisy, busy world."

While expressions of the hermit lifestyle vary, the reasons people choose this life "classically involve silence, solitude, simplicity of life, and prayer," the couple explain. "A necessary degree of interaction with others allows a religious solitary to earn a living and maintain a simple lifestyle in the modern world," they add. Their book *Consider the Ravens: On Contemporary Hermit Life* examines "a vocation as old as spirituality itself." The couple also mentor people seeking a solitary life and offer a secluded mountain retreat, Raven's Rest in Western North Carolina, for people to try out hermit life.

I wanted to inhabit an ancient hermit landscape, so my search continued. I discovered many secular hermits improvising on ancient traditions, mainly bearded white guys who value solitude and self-sufficiency. Writers and photographers curious to know what solitary life is like had rooted them out on all continents and a few islands. We don't tend to take secular hermits as seriously as the religious ones—they aren't institutionalized, so perhaps they're easier to dismiss as cranks? But many were far from being dilettantes.

Take Pete, "one of New Zealand's last hermits," who lives in the bush near the rocky Kaikoura coast in a small hut and survives off the land and his garden. He had been in Asia for years and couldn't adjust once he returned to New Zealand. He lived in a Cistercian monastery for a year, and then "kind of wandered, living in old churches and under bridges and stuff." Tiring of his itinerant ways he retreated to a cave right beside the sea and to a surfers' hut, where the authorities told him to move on. Then a kindly sheep farmer gave him a piece of land to live on. "This has been home for the past 30 years. I've always loved solitude," Pete says.

Asked what it's like to be a hermit, Pete proves his secular solitary wisdom credentials, in my opinion: "A lot of people ask me if I get lonely. But loneliness is just a feeling. It's no big deal. For a lot of people, it's as if loneliness is some sort of fearful creature, but it's not. One time when someone asked me that, I had this image of temples in Thailand. At the entrance there'll be creatures that look incredibly demonic and fearful, but they're just the guardians of the temple. And I think loneliness is a bit like that—one of the guardians that has to be encountered and then, gradually, it turns into a friend—an extraordinary friend. It doesn't have to be escaped from."

A good hermitage is hard to find, I soon realized. Now, watching the lambs outside frolic in the fields, I feel grateful to have stumbled across the leaseholder of this stone retreat. Sara Maitland is a well-known author and an unlikely hermit. She grew up in a loquacious upper-class Scottish family, danced with Prince Charles once at a debutante ball, and in 1970 was introduced to feminism by her close friend Bill Clinton, also a student in Oxford, who "invited her to accompany him to a lecture by Germaine Greer, whom he had heard had great legs." Maitland's debut novel, *Daughter of Jerusalem,* won the UK's Somerset Maugham Award and established her as a leading feminist thinker, and since then, she's written about 30 books. Maitland, variously, married an Anglican vicar, had two children, got divorced, became a Catholic, wrote a screenplay with Stanley Kubrick and became a hermit when she fell in love— with silence.

Her fascinating *A Book of Silence* explores a subject that's inherently difficult to write about. A wonderful storyteller who by her own admission loves to talk, she chronicles personal experiments into silence and solitude, and those of many historical figures. Among her quests, the intrepid Maitland retreats to an isolated Scottish cottage on Skye and spends 40 days and 40 nights alone—"It seemed possible but substantial, as well as ironic," she writes—to understand silence better. Vile weather, deep fear, ecstatic bliss and auditory hallucinations are among her experiences. Ultimately, after experiencing its "good" and "bad" varieties, she falls for silence. "It was interesting, demanding, exciting, good fun and deeply joyful. It has informed my choices for my life ever since."

There are few female hermits as guides, and Maitland intrigues me. Reading about her enviable experiences is what first got me thinking about retreat as an adventure, with as many peaks and valleys as any mountain expedition—except you go inward. If you announce you're going to sail a boat around the world for two years, Maitland observes with exasperation, people get excited, whereas if you say you're going to stay home and talk to no one for two years, it makes people think you've lost your mind. "We declare that personal freedom and autonomy is both a right and good, but we think anyone who exercises that freedom autonomously is 'sad, mad or bad.' Or all three at once," Maitland notes. If you're not in a relationship, you're considered sad: tragically lonely and deficient, possibly with mental health issues, or sociopathic—mad. If you say you actually *like* being alone, that solitude is your ideal of happiness, you're bad: selfish, or reprehensible.

Social unacceptability be damned, Maitland has lived a self-styled hermit's life of isolation and self-denial in a shepherd's cottage in southern Scotland for the past 20-plus years, in a place she calls the "Huge Nothing," amid miles of wild and empty space. Her chosen terrain of silence, the moors where she grew up, has "high hills with enormous views, rough waterfalls and tiny lochs, roofless castles and abandoned farmsteads." She doesn't, however, live in complete isolation—she sees the postman most days, has a phone; the Internet and a car; and goes to Mass and shopping on Sundays. "What I want to do is live in as much silence as is possible at this moment in our history," she explains.

Why has she chosen a hermit's life, so out of step with the times? "Silence makes me happy," Maitland says simply. Long periods alone in silence yield rewards, she thinks, for religious and secular explorers alike. "Silence is a place in which I can find ecstasy. I only get it in silence and most people I know only get it in silence. It is just a fabulous feeling. You know, you're walking along and quite suddenly you just say, 'Yes!' It's an extraordinarily intense response. Totally joyful."

In *A Book of Silence* Maitland diagnoses the need for silence and how we may not know we need it. A surprise bestseller in 2009, the book generated widespread media attention. Maitland began to receive many letters from people asking how to experience silence and solitude. The cottage is her answer. Not surprisingly holiday rentals catering to hermits are scarce, so she offers this place to people who want to experience a measure of the hermit's life. For the past decade she, and a previous leaseholder, have made it available to rent or borrow, depending on means.

The cottage is that rare place where an aspiring modern-day hermit can withdraw without the framework provided by a religious or other community. It has everything that's required: it's simple yet comfortable, accessible yet isolated, peaceful, with dramatic scenery and many wild creatures—pine martens, deer, wildcats, ospreys and eagles—to inspire awe. So far, Maitland told me, the main hermits have been Buddhist and Christian meditators, and writers—people self-emptying, and filling the creative well.

Maitland has inspired many others to explore the joys of hermit life, even temporarily. Like most hermits she is drawn to deserts, moors and other wild places. The wise old person who lives in the wilderness or on the outskirts of town, outside convention, is a universal archetype. Present in all ages and cultures, archetypes are charged with a sense of the sacred, unconscious reality shared by humans, our ancient psychic structures. Through history we have been called to consult the wise sage on the mountaintop, or the crone or grandmother in the woods—or to seek wisdom by being in solitude or living alone for a time ourselves. The wise one personifies our higher self, whose knowledge transcends the mind and comes from experience.

In modern times one common place we see the archetypes is the Rider-Waite tarot deck, published originally in 1909. The card for the hermit shows a cowled man with a lantern, suggesting Diogenes the Cynic, who famously shone a light in broad daylight searching for an honest man. Diogenes, who lived as a beggar and often slept in a wine barrel, does not represent isolation or idleness, but the active cultivation of introspection, wisdom and spiritual maturity. While people often scorn hermits as eccentrics, or consider them misanthropic, there's a part of many people that fantasizes about their positive aspect. Whenever I mention hermits, certain friends get starry-eyed, say things like, "Oooh, a little mountain hut . . . with maybe just a little bonsai to water." To be alone for a time, or to live alone, free, self-sufficient in a simple, wild place—this has enduring appeal.

The hermit impulse has roots in Eastern and Western philosophies: from Lao-Tzu's rejection of the social ideal of Confucius, to Japan's wandering monks, to the ancient sadhus of India and bhikkhus of Tibet, to the Greek pre-hermits such as Diogenes, to the Christian desert hermits—considered the first true Western hermits, who retreated to caves in the third century and valued asceticism as a path to knowledge and a meaningful life.

As for me, I've come to this rugged place of moors and mountains to taste the experience of being a hermit, to use the time to study the history of hermits and what modern people can learn from these outsiders. The Highlands is a suitable locale for such an inquiry, with eremitic traditions recorded since the fifth century. Not only is the land here rich in the artifacts of the hermit traditions of northern Scotland, but it's also a place I'm connected to. I was born in Glasgow, came to Toronto when I was three, and my ancestors are from the Highlands and the Inner Hebrides. People who inhabit a landscape are also created by it. Perhaps I'll also learn something of my own wild, solitude-loving, transplanted self?

The Rough Bounds, or Na Garbh Chriochan in Scottish Gaelic, describes the mountainous coastal lands where I am, which have attracted solitaries for centuries. The hermitage is on the Ardnamurchan Peninsula, which juts into the sea, the most westerly point of Britain. Jagged sea lochs run mainly east to west, making travel by water obligatory except in places where a single-track road snakes along the shorelines.

Daunted by the prospect of driving in this rugged place, Marco and I hired a local driver to pick us up from the train station in Fort William. Ewen navigated his van for an hour and half down winding roads in the rain, the scenery a dramatic blur of mountains and lochs. Finally we slowed for a hairpin turn and rolled down a steep, narrow road past a farm. Ewen said Bonnie Prince Charlie once slept there when he was a fugitive, hidden by loyal supporters after the battle of Culloden in 1746, which ended his hopes of claiming the thrones of Scotland and England. We passed a jetty, opened a gate and headed down a muddy track that wound through tall Scots pines beside the long, narrow loch.

I felt disconcerted when Ewen said he was familiar with my Scottish family, from a small community on the Isle of Skye. Likely he knew more than I did, because my father never spoke of them, to me anyway. Like many here, Ewen has family in Canada, where he'd visited many times. In the merchant navy for years, he now stayed home, playing the bagpipes and driving for a living.

"Why have you come here?" he asked, emphasizing the final word.

"To be hermits," I replied.

"Och, well," Ewen said with his lilting laugh. "The most exciting thing that's liable to happen to you here is a funeral on the Green Isle." Since ancient times, he explained, burials have taken place on a tiny island in the nearby loch, the most recent just two weeks before. "The old coffin route comes over the hill," Ewen said, pointing left, "and then mourners take the dead across from the jetty," he added, pointing right, "to bury them."

"I'd hate to miss that," I said, meaning it. My immediate family shares a peculiar enthusiasm for cemeteries, and my backyard borders one back home in Kingston.

"Don't worry," Ewen said. "You'd hear the bagpipes."

We pulled up to the muddy entrance of the property, marked by a riot of rhododendrons. The small stone hermitage sat on a small square of land cut out from the farmer's fields, beside a collapsing byre, and with a few fruit trees and a small garden. We fished the old mortise key from its hiding place and opened the door. Ewen helped us in with our bags, and with a wave and a grin, he left. A note from the previous hermits, another couple, greeted us. "There are mice and bats in the ceiling, the fire's ready to go, and we hope you enjoy the chocolate biscuits—our favourites."

On our first night as hermits we saw a spill of stars in the dark, black sky. This morning we're already on familiar terms with the cranky stove and fridge, the touchy CO alarm, the saggy, comfy couch and the spirited little Morso woodstove with squirrel designs on its iron sides, which heats the house. Luxury of luxuries, the woodstove also heats water for a bath.

Each day here I plan to read, to walk and to sink into the silence. I am the fixed hermit, the cottage my cave. Marco is the wandering hermit-monk: he's already out in the hills this morning taking photos. Historically, hermits and wandering monks were the more solitary renegades, in contrast to regulated monks or nuns and their regulated hermit brothers or sisters, who lived the other model of contemplative life, in communal monasteries.

I go outside, stand in the weak morning sun and breathe a sigh of relief. I've been longing to shed the activities of ordinary life awhile, to explore hermit life. I've spent enough time in quiet places to know that silences differ, and I'm curious about the qualities of this one. Ben Resipol still has snow on top, and the old mountain, the most westerly of the big Highland peaks, commands the windswept hills below. Its ancient rock is the physical manifestation of this silence, which has grandeur, spaciousness and solidity. It brings to mind the words of Orkney Island poet George Mackay Brown: "Stone is an enduring material."

Landscapes have long been of vital importance for solitaries in both Eastern and Western traditions. Hermits and wandering monks are especially drawn to wilderness—mountains, forests and extreme places. Like the first Christian hermits who heard the call of the desert, they are summoned to live on the uninhabited edges. The Rough Bounds is among the emptiest parts of Scotland, though it once had a sizeable rural population. During the Highland Clearances from the 1780s to 1880s, half a million Gaelic-speaking Highlanders were violently driven and burned out of their homes— to make way for sheep. The quiet here is tinged with melancholy, the residue, perhaps, of a cultural collapse. I know that wild and not wild land is a false distinction: early hunters and farmers, as well as modern miners and crofters, all worked here. But those seeking the wild are still drawn to edgelands, as much idea as physical place.

About a thousand years ago, the landscape from the Middle Eastern deserts to the furthest corners of the known world, Ireland and Scotland, was full of hermits in cells and caves—and later, in hermitages within convents and monasteries, apart from the other nuns and monks. Ancient Christian saints on the edge of darkness, of civilization, settled this particular wild place. Thousands of Irish monks and hermits, an influx of devout pilgrims called peregrine, arrived between 500 and 1000 AD. They sailed their fragile boats across treacherous seas, leaving the familiar behind forever for wild terrain that reflected their inner asceticism.

These adventurers founded the Celtic Christian culture of retreat. Matching the austerities of the earliest desert hermits they emulated, they waged spiritual warfare in the harshest conditions, studying scripture and communing with God. The holy wanderers travelled on foot once they arrived in Scotland, believing that the spiritual journey of life requires putting oneself in God's hands without knowing where it will lead.

Citizens of heaven passing through life like strangers, they carved hermit cells for prayer into rock cliffs facing the fierce Atlantic storms, built beehive stone huts for shelter, erected monasteries made of stone, driftwood and peat for worship on windswept islands. They built tombs and dug cemeteries for their dead, raised Celtic crosses on headlands and braved the wild mountains and forests. To this day several place names in the Rough Bounds begin with "Kil," meaning "cell," which indicates that a hermit or missionary once lived there—Kilchoan in Knoydart and on Ardnamurchan, Kilcumin in Morar and Kilmory in Arisaig.

I take in the sweep of space around me: moor, water, forest, mountain, sky. To the Celtic Christians, and the Druids before them, all creation was sacred. The given world—this was their sanctum sanctorum.

Excited to begin my hermit meditations in this auspicious place, I go back inside and find that the solar panel isn't functioning. This means I have one battery charge of about eight hours for my computer, unless I can fix the invertor or find a new power source. Pens and notebooks it is. I begin to write longhand and fight a regular impulse to check the Internet: for email, for the weather and, for some reason, to find out whether there's a laundromat nearby. Every thought I have, I react to, seeking an answer instead of concentrating on the task at hand. I had no idea I was afflicted with this irritating habit. A phrase from a Douglas Coupland show I'd seen at the Art Gallery of Ontario pops into my mind: "I miss my pre-Internet brain."

My mind compulsively spins on, uneasy about being cut off from data. When I finally realize that despite no cell signal there's a landline and more important, that retro accompaniment, a phone book full of numbers I could call, I'm strangely elated. With no wireless or cellphone, and no electricity either, this hermitage is going to be the ideal setting to explore whether being a self-imposed hermit is possible in the modern world.

Along with the early Celtic hermits, and me, I was surprised to learn that the scouts for a reality show called *Eden* had also selected this stark, boggy landscape for an experiment in leaving society behind. Months later I read a dark, often-hilarious article in the *New Yorker* and discovered that filming for *Eden* had wrapped up just down the loch the week before I arrived. "A group of 23 skilled strangers would live in the wilderness, isolated from the world, for a year. . . . The cast members would build their own shelters and hunt and grow their own food while a small embedded crew and a rig of remote cameras observed every moment of the embryonic society."

Two doctors, a paramedic, a vet, a carpenter, a shepherd, a gardening expert, a gamekeeper, a chef and a Canadian life coach were chosen out of the 2,000 who applied. No utopia, it was a cautionary tale about a dark side of stepping away from society: the community quickly descended into infighting, bullying, breakdowns and hunger—cast members were supposedly spotted at the dentist in town getting their teeth treated after eating chicken grit. Worse perhaps than the biting midges, terrible gales, brutal cold and other dreadful conditions they'd have endured, the producers had left the cast in the wilds even after the show had been taken off the air. (Many, traumatized, had already escaped by then.) Later, new episodes aired, rebranded as *Eden: Paradise Lost*, prompting the media to pronounce it "the reality show that no one watched."

As for my own hermit experiment, it feels surprisingly good to write by hand at the square oak table, sun falling on my pages. After a few hours I stop to wolf down cheese and bread and then pull random volumes off the hermitage's tantalizing bookshelves. I flop on the sofa with a luxurious pile and read interrupted only by the need to throw the shrieking—and, I hope, malfunctioning— CO detector outside.

First I untangle hermit terminology, or more correctly, eremetic terminology, which is tricky. In the early Christian era, the words hermit, monk and anchorite, all from the Greek, were used interchangeably. Hermit derives from eremia—desert; monk from monos—alone; and anchorite from anachorein—to withdraw. Early traditions were diverse, and travel was a key feature of monastic life, so it's hard to separate the hermits from the monks, who were sometimes also pilgrims. By the Middle Ages, meanings and models for contemplative life had changed and the words had come to specify distinct vocations. For the most part, hermit came to mean the independent solitary, itinerant or otherwise, and monk came to mean someone living in a settled, regulated community. The meaning of anchorite changed too, and became associated with a particular kind of solitary—usually a woman, bricked into a small cell called an anchorhold on the side of a church for life, "closyd in an hows of ston."

In our day we add to the confusion of terms by using the words hermit and recluse interchangeably. I'm in agreement with anonymous hermit-blogger "Meng-hu, resident of the Hermitary," who has gathered a wealth of hermit lore and resources: "Strictly speaking, with a few technical exceptions, a recluse has a psychological fear of people, whereas the hermit does not." The so-called North Pond hermit of Maine, he continues, is "a classic recluse who dared not encounter people, though his fear of them was because he stole from them, and is certainly not a hermit."

To the list of non-hermits I'd add haters, and the unsound of mind—Unabombers, misanthropes, the mentally ill or dangerously obsessed. Controversial figures like Christopher McCandless, a young man who starved to death in an abandoned bus while living "in retreat" in Alaska, a tragedy made famous by the book and film *Into the Wild*, are not hermits by my definition. Nor are the hikikomori of Japan: an estimated half a million social recluses, mainly men, stay home and refuse to interact with others, often for years. One hypothesis is that conformity may promote mental health issues, and it's more acceptable in Japan to withdraw than act out.

Ornamental hermits, who lived in grottos and ruins on country estates in Britain in the 1800s, don't count either. These faux hermits appeared as part of a craze among the Georgian gentry that resulted from a fashion for "pleasing melancholy." They were paid £600, enough that they never had to work again, provided they engage with guests and not cut their hair or wash for six years. The living symbol of rural retreat, they survive in our garden gnomes.

Serious retreaters, such as religious hermits and hermit-meditators exploring deeper realities, tend to train for solitude, the way an athlete trains for a triathlon. Building stability and strength are self-protective prerequisites because extreme solitude and silence are challenging, even destabilizing. The idea is to prepare and gain wisdom—not to deny the world or go unprepared, risking psychological wildfires. Hermits are known to experience altered states of consciousness. Accidie, "spiritual or mental sloth, apathy," as the *Oxford English Dictionary* defines it, is one danger, also called "the noonday demon" and known to afflict monks and hermits. Accidie was one of the eight deadly thoughts before the seven deadly sins were developed in the sixth century, and means "not-caring" in Greek. For ancient ascetics it was a specific, afflictive spiritual condition akin to depression. There may also be wild ecstasies, spiritual visions, hearing voices, elation, self-transcendence and feelings of union with the divine—as experienced by mystics such as Persian poets Hafiz and Rumi, and centuries of Christian mystics such as Saint Teresa of Ávila and Julian of Norwich, an anchorite who wrote the first work in English that was certainly authored by a woman, *Revelations of Divine Love*. Secular retreaters also report altered states of time and other unusual perceptions.

While the Greeks are considered their ideological precursors, the early Christian desert fathers and mothers are the first true Western hermits. Radicals who lived for years in silence in remote caves in the wilds of Egypt, Syria, Palestine and Arabia, often considered a dangerous cult, they were not simply leaving society, they were actively moving toward God. Wrestling with their demons—with no map, as there were no written rules—they prized a life of contemplation consecrated to God more than they did applying their religious experiences to human relationships. The hermit's ascetic spiritual life was traditionally regarded as the purest form of religious life in Christianity.

I admire the desert hermits' discipline, their determination and courage—it's like they were preparing for the spiritual Olympics. And I admire their unlikely founding of a long tradition that continues to support modern-day solitude-seekers. We still draw from their ideas and their infrastructures—hermitages, monasteries, convents, abbeys, pilgrim paths. But the more I learned, the more mystified I became about one aspect of desert hermit life. Mortifications. Why? Why wear animal skin shirts in the scorching sun? Why the scourging and bloody self-flagellation? Why extinguish lust with pain? Why drink muddy water and eat hard bread, why fast to kill appetites, why near-starvation? Why pillars, why harsh deserts and barren wastelands—why the desertum of the Celts, bricked into freezing caves that faced the wild Atlantic storms?

I suppose that like us, they were people grappling with eternal quandaries and questions of meaning—only they believed that the world, the flesh and the devil were the three sources of temptation. Fasting and flagellation were thought to quench desires, while prayer and psalms drove away evil thoughts. Wearing hair shirts was just part of what free hermits, monks and anchorites did to fight for salvation, Earth their purgatory. It wasn't mere penance, but a practical solution to cleanse sin. By mortifying the flesh and praying, the desert hermits, people believed, were transformed and could act as intercessors with God.

Perhaps a hermit's most important mission was to fight demons, those invisible agents of darkness. Demons lurked especially in old temples and on remote hillsides, and to sin was to be overcome by their power. St. Anthony, the first desert ascetic, gave a pithy explanation of what hermits do all day: "Let your heart be silent, then

God will speak." St. Anthony fought a demon or two. His trials are one of the most repeated subjects in Western literature and art. He moved to a mountain cave and resisted a series of temptations by the devil and demons who mocked him, assaulted him physically and tortured him with horrible or seductive visions: monks bringing bread when he was fasting, wild beasts, sexy dancing girls. To puncture his lustful desires he'd throw himself into the thorn bushes outside his cave. The hermit's fame grew as he withstood these assaults, and his ideals spread far and wide from Egypt.

The Christians of Europe under Rome's influence embraced living in communal monasteries. But in Scotland and Ireland the Celtic hermits and monks, whose territories hadn't ever been conquered by the Romans, drew inspiration directly from the desert fathers. (As for the Druidic tradition they were supplanting, little is known about these oak-venerating ancient priests, renowned for wisdom. They had an oral tradition, leaving no written record, and little archeological evidence exists. The Christians were known to bless the holy wells and other sites of Druidic worship thus claiming them for the new faith.)

The Celtic Christians, in their desertum of the coastal wilderness, matched Byzantine extremes of asceticism. They "deliberately sought out the most wild and deserted places—the isolation of lonely bogs and forests, the bare crags and islands off the Atlantic coast—where they could find the solitude that they believed would lead them to God," writes William Dalrymple in From the Holy Mountain. "The proudest boast of Celtic monasticism was that, in the words of the seventh-century Antiphonary of the Irish monastery of Bangor: 'This house full of delight / Is built on the rock / And indeed the true vine / Transplanted out of Egypt.'"

The fringe-dwelling Celtic holy men found further inspiration for their ascetic feats in books, notably Life of St. Anthony of Egypt by Athanasius of Alexandria. It was likely the most-read volume in Europe after the Bible, and the model for early Irish and Northumbrian gospel books. These amazing books were "portals of prayer," writes Michelle Brown, curator of illuminated manuscripts at the British Library, and the "act of copying and transmitting the Gospels was to glimpse the divine." Just as St. Cuthbert, a monk, bishop and hermit, one of the revered saints of early Christianity, struggled with his demons on the Farne Islands on behalf of all humanity, she adds, so the monks who produced the gospel books "performed a sustained feat of spiritual and physical endurance as part of the mission of bringing the word of God to the furthest outposts of the known world and enshrining it there within the new temple of the word and embodiment of Christ—the Book."

Unlike the desert fathers, who eschewed anything they saw as a distraction, the Celtic monks and hermits loved learning, poetry and art, as evidenced by their elaborate carvings, Celtic crosses and manuscripts, such as the exquisite Book of Kells. Created on the holy island of Iona, the book was saved, though many monks were slaughtered and their work destroyed during Viking attacks in 806 AD.

In spirit, the Celtic Christians remind me of Asia's wandering hermit-monks—independent, art-loving wilderness itinerants. The ancient Japanese hijiri gained power through austerities in the mountains. Seeking the world beyond, they believed, must entail a journey. By medieval times, the plain robe and bare feet of Japan's wandering monks reflected commitment to a life of poverty, and the staff to a roving existence without a fixed dwelling. Similarly, the wandering monks of China abandoned worldly ambitions and joined the ranks of fugitives and outsiders, living in the mountains, practising shan shui painting, which translates literally as "mountain-water-picture," and poetry as vehicles for philosophy. The earliest hermits of China left the settled world for secular and philosophical reasons, rather than religious ones, and though disillusioned with life in society and its constraints, they often kept ties with friends.

I love the passion and rigour of the Celtic hermits, who travelled from Ireland to remote places in northern Scotland and the islands, and of the early desert hermits they emulated. But I don't understand their body-hating asceticism, the harsh idea that humans are programmed for sin. This much I do know: we're all solitary wanderers in the wilderness.

By mid-afternoon what's wandering is my mind—to the maps on the shelf beside me, and the world outside. I pick up a booklet, *Exploring Sunart, Ardnamurchan, Moidart and Morar*, which tells me that much of the early history of this area stems from the arrival from Ireland in the sixth century AD of St. Finnan, "who established a holy cille on tiny Eilean Uaine, the beautiful Green Isle. The sanctity of this was such that for centuries it rivaled even that of Columba's Iona as a place of pilgrimage and internment."

I can't believe my luck—a holy hermit's cell just down at the loch?

We are not that far from windswept Iona, the island where St. Columba, the earliest hermit saint, chose to settle for his desertum, uninhabited even by the rugged Scots and Picts when he arrived in 532. Columba seems capricious to me: he banished women and cows from the island insisting that "where there is a cow there is a woman, and where there is a woman there is mischief." The builders of his abbey had to leave their wives and daughters on the nearby Eilean nam Ban (Woman's Island). He also banished frogs and snakes, though how he accomplished that is not documented.

Today Christian ecumenical retreats are offered there, and the Findhorn Foundation—a famous eco-village, holistic education centre and spiritual community in northeastern Scotland, which incidentally has a Canadian co-founder—owns an Iona retreat house where participants join with community members for worship, meals and education, social activities and chores.

I'm loath to winkle myself out of the shell of this hermitage to visit Iona, and resolve instead to seek out St. Finnan down at the loch. I pull on my boots and walk in silence down the muddy sheep's path to the water. Scotland's landscape is embedded with ancient sacred places: hermits' caves, stone huts, holy wells and shrines. Ontario too is encrypted with ancient places sacred to Indigenous peoples. Always in-between, I feel I can't fully read either landscape. I've always had a sense of inner homelessness. Being here is making me question a long-held, unconscious conviction: that it's always better to go than to stay, like the Irish monks in their resolute self-exile. But is this really true?

The light waxes and wanes with the passing clouds, blue sky one moment and then sudden gloom, as though a dark wing is passing overhead. The freshwater loch was sealed off from the ocean by a passing glacier eons ago. Along the shore, pebbled beaches backed by wind-sculpted oaks and holly trees are linked by meandering sheep paths. A large bird with a white tail flies above—a sea eagle? When the wind intermittently dies down, the silence feels active, not an absence but a presence. The old rocks of Resipol emanate solidity, and there's that unique, elemental clarity I only feel in northern places near the sea.

Just ahead the old grey stones of the rock jetty to Green Isle, known also as St. Finnan's—the burial place Ewen had told us about—lead into the blue water. St. Finnan died in 575 AD but his ruined chapel survives, built on the site of his devotional cell. The island is a few hundred yards across, and from this angle, I can see a tall, slender Celtic cross that tilts skyward. Finnan had been a disciple of St. Columba, who, with his travelling monks of Iona, visited this place. I'd found a 1950 book on the hermitage bookshelf, *Moidart and Morar*, by local author Wendy Wood. She writes of Columba's miracle: he told the people, "Cast your net again in the river, and immediately you will find a large fish which the Lord has prepared for you." Wood, who often got the unpleasant job of gutting, wonders whether God *really* prepared the fish, and then adds, "They drew up salmon of wonderful size."

Her wry humour is in evidence in describing a visit to the island's medieval chapel on the saint's day, March 18: "It is still something of a penance to visit the ruins of this church because of the nettles, and not having a stick, I was very properly stung." The Green Isle cemetery was Catholic until the Reformation, when Protestants began being buried on the south end, likely over top of the Catholic dead. Given their reverence for nature this may have once been a sacred site for the Druids—though their stone circles were most often placed beside a stream, in the shadow of sacred oaks, or in high places, such as the summit of a hill, where cairns (large stones) still mark their places of worship.

To dispel the cold I begin to flap my arms and walk quickly on, wondering how I can get over to the Green Isle. Marco is up ahead, stretched on his belly on the stones taking photos, vivid in his red raincoat. When my boot gets sucked off in a peat bog, I cling to a woody gorse branch on one leg until he notices and silently retrieves it. We walk the sheep paths and find spring's emissaries—one yellow violet, one white violet and three ferns. Darkness is gathering as we return to the hermitage, light candles and fire up the Morso. After a simple supper of beans, rice and kale, I boil water and fill the hot water bottle, defence against the heavy, damp blankets. I shiver to think of St. Finnan and his cold stone cell on the island as I tuck the bottles into their hand-knitted covers and into the bed.

I've always had hermit sympathies—which I considered a quirk of temperament, or a streak of romanticism. I've never been a loner, exactly, but I have always liked ample solitude amid my social routines. Now I've begun to wonder, Is it bred in the bone? Do my roots in this place explain the default attraction to solitude-seekers, rebels, edgelands, outskirts, wild people and places? I adore the margins. And suspect that outliers know something the rest of us don't. I have the utmost respect for resolute, valiant people who assert their independence and seek new wisdom and new ways.

I climb into bed and lie wide awake, listening to the fierce wind howl in the chimney. Many today think that being a hermit, even temporarily, smacks of the utopian. From where I stand, the way we live now, our assumption that we can continue to consume the world without disastrous results, is the capitalist impracticable fantasy, the unrealistic path that will never lead to happiness. Ancient hermits, though extreme, valued self-sacrifice over self-interest, renunciation over consumption, independence over conformity. Do these early explorers have something to teach us? Or have we become insensible to their wisdom, to the call of the desert, the wilds?

Each day spent at the hermitage is a version of the last. Mornings, Marco heads off to take photos and search for an abandoned village Ewen had mentioned, which involves skirting bogs, tramping up and down hillsides, fighting his way through dense forest and rhododendron thickets, taking "shortcuts" and, inevitably, getting lost. Later we read about two experienced hillwalkers in Ireland who were trapped in an impenetrable rhodo-forest and were finally freed after a dangerous, five-hour rescue mission.

For my part, I read, write, sit and often just stare out the window. And wonder how the hermits managed to cross the dangerous seas to here, while I still can't figure out how to get over to Green Isle. I'm enjoying being alone and all that happens. And things do happen. In the deepening quiet, my senses are getting sharper, for one thing. I've started to notice the subtle, complex beauty of the soundscape. Days with sun, sweet brown birds and yellow birds sing outside at the feeder. When it's overcast, there's just the wind, and the *meehh* of the sheep. In the rare lulls, no sound at all, pure possibility. Evenings we walk by the loch to flutelike nightingale songs. Inside the hermitage at night the fire soughs like a sigh of relief, and when the wind picks up, there's ghostly moaning in the chimney. Only the shrieks of the CO detector bring me back into regular time, which has begun to lose its linear, forward-motion feeling.

I feel part of, though apart from, the world. My companions? The steadying expanse of Ben Resipol, the narrow loch, sheep moving on the yellowy but greening tableau of fields, and the farmer, who bounces up the lane in his tractor or quad at 9:30 a.m. on his hay delivery or moves livestock to one pasture or another, busy with spring calving. And Marco. For me, being a hermit is less about being completely alone than about being able to follow my internal rhythms unimpeded, which solitary days provide. Chosen solitude is about agency, self-reliance and gaining clarity. When the churning mind-waters settle, I can begin to dip into the wellspring of my life. If I stay quiet long enough I begin to forget myself.

My daily hermit readings lead to unexpected places. I begin to realize that most of what we think about them is wrong. There's this popular idea, for instance, that hermits withdraw from people because they hate them. On the contrary, for solitary religious hermits, others are the whole point. As an intercessor to God, a hermit's purpose is to pray for the salvation of humanity. Thomas Merton, the 20th century's most famous author-monk, a Trappist and peace activist, writes: "The hermit's whole life is a life of silent adoration. His very solitude keeps him ever in the presence of God . . . His whole day, in the silence of his cell, or his garden looking out upon the forest, is a prolonged communion." This is the power of the hermit's way: we can focus fully on whatever we want to commune with.

As for the durable misconception that hermits are always alone, Merton struggled to reconcile his celebrity and his longing for a life of silence and contemplation as a hermit. By the time he'd been at Gethsemane in Kentucky for a decade he'd grown impatient with conventional monastic life. Desperate to escape the monastery's togetherness, he even considered "exclaustration," revoking his vows, so he could be a hermit. Allowed only three-day private retreats, he spent time reading, writing and meditating in a forest woodshed "hermitage," named in honour of St. Anne. Eventually, Merton was allowed to move to Mount Olivet, a combination of hermitage and retreat centre, where he was briefly a hermit. He then decided to travel and died in Thailand, likely electrocuted by a faulty fan.

Just as St. Anthony depended on friends to bring him food when he locked himself away, here at this hermitage I am supported by a web of others who supply propane, wood and necessities. Typically hermits have also connected to society through work: the desert hermits wove rush baskets to trade for bread, while modern-day hermits often earn daily bread online, by teaching, for example, or offering calligraphy services.

Hermits cultivate solitude, yet people seek them out. As a rule, hermits are actively prevented from privacy. When St. Anthony retreated to the desert to dedicate his life to prayer, he had to move numerous times to get away from people seeking his advice. The struggle to protect solitude has been the common lot of hermits ever since. I find it a wonderful irony that even hermits have had to make a conscious effort of will to get away, even temporarily, from society. For modern-day hermits, the media are typically the ones in hot pursuit, as a proxy for curious readers.

Even today, in these parts, a hermit isn't hard to find—though I later discover that Canadians are better at their vocation, and thus more difficult to track down. Our most famous hermit is not even a hermit but a recluse, and like many others who moved to the backwoods to avoid combat, he's American born. Willard Kitchener MacDonald, the "Hermit of Gully Lake," who died in 2004, lived in the forests of northern Nova Scotia for 60 years, ever since he jumped a troop train during the Second World War.

In the *Scotsman* I came across an article about "Hermits who have called Scotland Home," that featured those "who have shunned it all and whose stories of survival, endurance and solitude linger on." Note the admiring tone—in North America, this would more likely read, "Meet some weirdo recluses." I read hungrily, fascinated by their beliefs and why they chose the hermit's life. Their responses remind me of Federico Fellini's reply when asked why he made films. "You might as well ask a hen why she lays eggs," he said—it is just what he did.

Three of the article's five solitaries, unsurprisingly, are from northern Scotland. Though these hermits are sociable enough to talk to the media, the urge to live a life apart is clearly still with us. Jake Williams has lived alone in the nearby Cairngorm Mountains since the 1980s. Tired of the rat race, the former teacher moved to a ramshackle hut in the middle of the forest. "It's perfectly conventional to me—nothing startling at all. As far as I'm concerned I'm just a normal homeowner. It's everyone else's lives that are strange," he says. James McRory Smith, the "Highland Hermit," who lived for 30 years in a remote bothy (a rough hut) in northwest Scotland, died in 1999 at 73 and said he'd walked probably "thousands of miles" to collect his messages and pension from the nearest post office. And media darling Tom Leppard, "the Leopard man of Skye," who had spots tattooed over 99 percent of his body, lived as a hermit in a lochside bothy for more than two decades. "I'm never lonely," said the former soldier, whose derelict croft had an earthen floor, no windows or electricity, metal sheet roofing and a bed made from polystyrene board. Leppard paddled his kayak across the fast-flowing waters to collect supplies and his pension for years, and died at 80 in 2016—a matter for personal regret, as I'd hoped to meet him.

Sara Maitland is usually the only woman in articles like this, or Emma Orbach appears—strangely, she's another Oxford graduate turned hermit. Orbach lives in the Welsh wilderness in a mud and horse-dung roundhouse she's constructed, without electricity or running water. She grows her own food and keeps chickens and goats, and plays her Celtic harp at night. "This is how I want to live. This lifestyle makes me feel really happy and at peace and this is my ideal home," she says. The *Scotsman* journalist writes of Maitland that she "shuns television and social media in favour of sewing and praying for several hours a day. She likes to say as little as possible and at one point did not speak a word every Tuesday and Thursday. She described mobile phones as 'a major break-through for the powers of hell' although she does have a landline for essential communication."

One afternoon I walk in the woods above the house, keeping my eyes open for another solitary: the ferocious Scottish wildcat, which prowls on the fringes of woodland and moorlands, making its home in boulders, tree roots, disused dens and open moorland. Only 100 are left in the wild. I wander until the wind picks up suddenly, and I'm propelled back downhill as though pushed by a strong hand. Inside the hermitage it's warm, and we make a dinner of chickpeas and rice and kale, followed by the biscuits left by the previous hermits. I take a glorious bath, and we drink whiskey on the couch by candlelight, listening to the forlorn sound of wind in the chimney. Earlier, Marco had found the abandoned village. A waterfall was gushing between the walls of old dwellings subsiding back into the stony ground. I tell him about the threatened wildcats.

When we encounter a wild place, it's also an encounter with the wild inside, with untamed forces. So what happens when the wild is pushed into extinction? Do we lose touch with our selves, and all that lies beyond our safe, secure lives? How will the world be if edge-dwellers, both human and animal, disappear?

Our last morning is silent, without wind or even birdsong. The sheep are lined up at the feeder as usual, woolly backsides providing scale in the vast landscape. The winter-beaten grass is greener each day, and the loch, mountains and sky are composed into new layers by weather. My only regret is that I never made it to the Green Isle to visit St. Finnan's hermit cell. The farmer, too busy with the spring calves to take us across, apologized and offered us his boat. As two landlubbers unaccustomed to driving speedboats in wild winds, we decided against it.

I sit at the oak table, turn on the computer and give it a reflexive click, as I've done every day, and then remember about lack of electricity and turn it off again. I can't get used to not checking email, my biggest compulsion, though my resistance to being offline is gone. Away from society's thicket and its techno-gadgets, in the open spaces of the trackless moor, I feel uncluttered. My concentration is better. In the fullness of the silence I can think. The early religious hermits chose solitude to get closer to God. Perhaps for modern, secular people, God, or gods, can serve as a metaphor for the mystery of existence? For all that puts us in touch with the deepest part of ourselves, and our human need to belong to something larger? For the wilderness that calls us, which is the call of the desert?

Merton describes the freedom and peace of a wilderness existence as "a return to the desert that is also a recovery of (inner) paradise. This is the secret of monastic renunciation of the world. Not a denunciation, not a denigration, not a precipitous flight, a resentful withdrawal, but a liberation, a kind of permanent 'vacation' in the original sense of 'emptying.'" Similarly, being a hermit, even temporarily, is about freedom.

Wondering about the experiences of the modern hermits who have stayed here before me, alone or with another, I spend the hour before we depart reading the hermitage's guest book. I open it at random and smile to read a previous resident's entry, about a hermit seated in his hut, not wanting for anything, while streams meander and red flowers bloom red on their own.

Many write that their time of silence sharpened their senses: honeysuckle smells sweeter, bat shit more horrible, food more delicious. One man rhapsodizes about breakfast, joking that he's no ascetic. Others say time feels fluid; that escaping Brexit and politics temporarily is a balm; how the simplicity and ability to "just be" is deeply refreshing. Others worry—about being selfish for taking time alone, or about feeling lonely or nervous about being out of touch, or they're scared of wild animals, bats and ghosts. Other hermits express gratitude for the chance to explore solitude in this safe space, building on solo camping trips, borrowed cottages and crofts, and other previous tastes of being alone. One hardy hermit stayed a whole winter, saying he welcomed the privations and joys and left feeling energized.

The hermit diaries are interspersed with photographs: the cottage with its roof missing, and later replaced, in all seasons.

To my delight there are images of the Green Isle: mist lifting, mossy rocks and gravestones on a sunny spring day, blue flowers in the green grass and the tilted Celtic cross, a stone altar, a carved wall-crucifix and an old bronze bell. And what I'd most wanted to see: the old stone chapel, and below it, St. Finnan's ancient stone cell. I feel a thrill to imagine these passionate hermits, responding with body and soul to the urgent questions of their times.

For me, this hermit retreat has been a chance to work at the oak table undisturbed and plunder the shelf of books and its bounty of hermits, monastics, silence, solitude, zen, wild places and local history. Held in this conducive, private place, I effortlessly worked five hours a day, exercised for two and sat quietly for one. Usually, when I also teach yoga, write paid assignments, buy groceries, do taxes, fix the holes in my sock and so on and on, my attention is scattered and I'm fatigued by the day's end. This is one of the most marked differences between the everyday world and going on a retreat: "A hermit is one who renounces the world of fragments that he may enjoy the world wholly and without interruption," writes Kahlil Gibran. For the ancients this meant a focus on God; for many of us it means whatever is meaningful that we choose to devote time and attention to. Like hermits, the fierce attention of our wild and most exacting selves.

My imagination has loved the gaps, the open spaces, how the empty landscape evokes free thinking and dreaming. I had begun to see things differently, my mind a clean slate for insights, new thoughts, ideas, creative connections, which naturally arise in silence. The peaks of Ben Resipol evoke solidity and the heft of earth, providing a steady, immovable silence in which to think and feel deeply. My purposes are a far cry from the Christian hermit's religious goal of getting closer to God. But I'm getting closer to something. I feel I'm restoring to its rightful place what's being lost—darkness, silence, wildness—and all that corresponds within me.

It's odd to find that I feel more connected, not less, during my hermit-lude. To the mountain, to the farmer, to the hermit benefactors who make this space available, to the other hermits who shared parallel experiences like the shrieking CO alarm, nightingale songs—Marco says one lives in the byre. And to the Morso, its heat and light dispelling the cold and darkness. I feel connected to the ancient hermits, fellow travellers who came to the northwest, like St. Finnan. The wild winds that blew through me brought new thoughts and perspectives, my imagination and spirit free to roam in the gaps and open spaces. I've learned something of my own rough bounds: I feel kinship with the hermit-monks, who thought life was a journey, one of trust, of voluntary inner homelessness.

Even in the modern world, I've discovered, it's not as hard as we may think to trade a cellphone for a hermit's cell, of sorts—though it's the least accessible of the old, religious-rooted ways for contemporary people. But the very existence of this hermitage, and the sheer number of modern hermits, tell me people are enduringly fascinated by this life. Many are choosing to live on the edge, even briefly, themselves, to become the single length of bamboo drawn from the dense thicket.

As with retreat in general we don't always value the hermit's gifts, in part because we mistake silence and solitude for a lack, for emptiness. As poet Adrienne Rich writes so beautifully, silence is more like a plan, a presence, a "blueprint to a life"—not to be confused "with any kind of absence."

Monasticism
for Moderns

*There are hundreds of ways to
kneel and kiss the ground.*

—Rumi; transl. by Coleman Barks

My cell is white and austere. It has thick walls of stone and a high ceiling supported by rough wood beams, and silvery light waves filter in through the irregular old windowpanes. I kick off my shoes, unfold the bright, handmade quilt and lie on top of the single bed. Unlike on the highway—I've just driven for six hours from Kingston—it's tranquil here. I feel safely enclosed, like I'm inside a honeycomb.

This is reassuring. I'd been nervous about exploring what monastic places have to offer moderns, having experienced an acute attack of cloisterphobia six months before. I'd been at a Christian religious centre for the first time, for a writing retreat. My uneasiness began right away, after one of the lovely, welcoming sisters showed me to my room, named for Agnes. I read a booklet about the saint's history. St. Agnes was either hanged or burned to death at the age of 12, it said, for "being bold with a pagan king" —she had refused to marry his son or renounce her faith. That night I slept poorly, a rare thing for me. I tossed and awakened in my cot from a terrible nightmare: I'd been pinned on the cross, but upside down.

As the retreat got underway, participants began to read their work, with many "dear Lords" and passages about obedience to a father and a son. The room felt suddenly unbearably hot and stuffy. Despite my efforts to think of God as a universal field of potential, or Being itself rather than a being, my oppression-o-meter steadily rose. When it was finally time to go, I ran down the path as fast as I could to catch the bus, propelled by a mysterious religious recoil reaction. Thankfully I don't sense that anything of the sort will befall me in this place, for nearly 400 years the convent of the Augustinian Sisters of the Mercy of Jesus, set in the heart of Old Quebec City.

As I sink deeper into my sinfully comfy bed I imagine generations of ghostly nuns, habits rustling as they walk the wide hallways, issuing forth from identical cells for work and prayer. The few nuns who remain now still follow the *Rule of St. Augustine*, a guide for living in religious community written in the year 400. As well as poverty, chastity and obedience, their vows include service to the poor and the sick. After long days of saving bodies and souls, the sisters would have returned from the hospital to white rooms like this one. Removed their shoes. Knelt to pray. Hung their veils on round-topped hooks, designed to prevent wrinkles. Fallen into an exhausted sleep.

I think of the bravery of the convent's three founding sisters, only in their twenties when they left France in 1639, sent to the new colony by King Louis XIII to alleviate spiritual and physical suffering. Among the earliest female missionaries, these young nuns belonged to an order that had been nursing in the seaport of Dieppe, Normandy, since about the year 1200. The perilous sea crossing took three months. "The travellers slipped past enemy British ships and pirate ships, went through severe storms, grazed an iceberg 'as big as a city' and survived infectious diseases," writes Canada's History Society about their voyage. The sisters arrived on the shore of the St. Lawrence River below the fort in September, and clambered up through the woods to get a first view of the hospital site up on the cliff. "Great was their disappointment after they reached it through a pathless tangle of stumps, dry branches, and brush. Only the foundation had been laid and not a drop of water was to be found on this high promontory," an article in the journal of the Canadian Catholic Historical Association notes.

The sisters faced many hardships. They'd only just set up a temporary ward in an unfinished house when a terrible smallpox epidemic broke out among the Algonquins and Montagnais, and the nuns rapidly used up medical supplies meant to last two years. Shortages of food and water, exhaustion and overwork, threats from Iroquois and British raiders and long, cold, cruel winters were among the trials of their new lives.

The hardy nuns prevailed and founded Hôtel-Dieu de Québec, a grey stone complex I passed on my way here, and the first hospital in North America north of Mexico. Over time more nuns arrived to help care for sick and wounded European settlers, as well as the Indigenous people, who taught them their languages and the properties of local healing plants. For centuries the nuns worked as pharmacists, growing herbs in the Hôtel-Dieu garden, and as nurses and administrators. Eventually they established and ran 11 other Quebec monastery-hospitals, all of which were integrated into the province's public health care system in 1962. To this day, doors lead directly from the old convent's chapel into the adjoining Hôtel-Dieu de Quebec, now a 15-storey teaching hospital and a national historic site.

The convent's walled cloister, cemetery and garden are enclosed once more within Quebec's old walled city. While the nuns' legacy is visible for all to see, what's disappearing is the Augustinian sisters themselves. From their heyday, when 200 lived at the convent, just 12 remain. Like ancient religious orders worldwide, the sisters, faced with an aging community and few new recruits in the 1980s, had urgent decisions to make.

The radical change they decided on altered their lives, perhaps as deeply as when they left the cloister in 1965, no longer confined to the convent and hospital. This time the nuns were embarking on a $40 million makeover of their precious heritage building, transforming it into a 65-room secular wellness hotel. Le Monastère des Augustines opened its doors in 2015, with new architecture to symbolize the sisters' reinvention for the modern age: a glass and exposed steel beam addition meets the old 17th-century stone structure, preserving its façade. This modern section houses a light-filled reception area and serves as a hub for various wings of the old convent, both religious and secular.

The beautiful, light-filled space was dubbed the "Cool Cloister" by *National Geographic Traveler* in 2016, when Le Monastère was featured as a top locale internationally for "a mental and physical reboot." There are no in-room TVs or telephones here, though the hotel does have wi-fi. The front desk will babysit your cellphone, slipping it into a wool case made by the staff's knitting club.

For centuries, the sisters' days have alternated between contemplation and action. This is reflected in the hotel's activities—yoga, meditation, chi kung, offered morning, noon and late afternoon. Wellness classes take place in a studio in the cellar vaults, where British cannonballs, found by the nuns while gardening, are displayed. In another nod to the nuns' contemplative ways, Le Monastère has communal spaces for quiet reflection and a healthy food restaurant where breakfast is eaten in silence. Beyond the cloister's gate is Rue des Remparts, with a view over the river, and cobblestoned streets that lead to the nearby shops and restaurants of Rue Saint-Paul.

Visitors to this urban retreat are encouraged to engage with the healing values and history of the nuns, but in a secular way. My room on the third floor is part of the "monastic package" nun's cells that have been "reimagined" for modern-day visitors, with shared washrooms down an old hallway lined with religious paintings. My head brushes the lintel above the crooked wooden door of my room each time I go in or out. It's a reminder that people were smaller in times past—and of how we inhabit the same spaces through the ages. We relate to one another in ways we rarely think about, human beings struggling to lead meaningful lives.

A feeling of protected silence permeates the convent—created by centuries of prayer? Contemporary rooms are up a crooked wooden staircase from 1757, and an original ascetic room has been preserved for visitors to see, that of a Sister Brigitte: a simple bed, dresser, a place to kneel and pray, the special veil hook, a water pitcher and bowl, a candle.

On the first floor is the museum, which traces the order's history and how it intertwines with the history of health care in Quebec. Where the front doors to the old convent once stood there is a spinning shelf marked "Tour." Families once placed sugar pies or presents inside for their cloistered relatives, and then rotated it for no-contact delivery inside the convent. Besides family gifts, the nuns also received many surprises, including abandoned babies with notes pinned to their diapers—1,375 of them during tough times between 1801 and 1845. The museum features an array of medical paraphernalia, including a full apothecary with mortars and pestles, ceramic jars for creams and ointments and an impressive-looking tin and linen mask for use with chloroform anesthesia that was designed by the nuns in 1848.

A 12-piece nun's habit and a white "bride of Christ" dress give me the willies. I learn that in the 17th century if a young French girl dreamed of becoming a nurse, she had to become a nun first. Who knows how many independent spirits became nuns, a career as their main motivation? Old photographs depict the nuns skating outside the convent, young and numerous. A poignant film plays on repeat, giving testament to the sisters' diminishing numbers, image by image, over the years. Like an old-fashioned TV screen that's gone off the air, at the end the images fade to "snow."

Believers and nonbelievers alike are retreating in droves to places like Le Monastère to escape the information-barraged, material-istic modern world for peaceful sanctuaries where silence, beauty, history and a sense of the sacred are preserved. Is it progress when a convent transforms into a hotel and museum? How much can—and should—religious organizations change for the modern age? The Augustine sisters considered these questions carefully. They see their wellness hotel as a modern way of continuing their mission, delicate given the backdrop of Quebec's Quiet Revolution and scandals rocking the church. Hospitality, health and the healing of body, mind and spirit have always been part of the nuns' vocation. Hôtel-Dieu literally means "hotel of God," where everyone is treated as though they were Christ. Secular expressions of this strike a chord with modern people, who are drawn to holistic health, to spirituality, and who crave freedom from distractions.

"It was the nuns' own initiative to start the hotel," says Isabelle Duchesneau, Le Monastère's executive director, who guided the transformation from convent to secular hotel run by a nonprofit. Earnings from paying guests, workshops, corporate retreats, massage treatments, the gift shop and the restaurant support the nuns' healing and heritage missions. The nuns know first-hand that for those in healing professions, taking time out is vital so they may continue their work without burning out. That's why Le Monastère gives reduced rates to caregivers, whether professionals or family, who find respite to pray or reflect or simply wander in the garden. Hotel earnings also support the museum and archive centre. An entire floor was added above the sisters' residence—they now live in an adjoining wing off the hotel— to house a conservation facility for the collections of all the Augustinian monasteries in Quebec, with 40,000 artifacts—proof that the thrifty nuns never threw anything out.

I enjoy seeing the sisters, who rub shoulders with guests in the garden, gift shop, elevator and museum. I'd come here thinking "out with the old and in with the new." The church is rightly vilified for countless abuses of spiritual authority, but now I see that doesn't mean these nuns aren't admirable. In fact, in many ways they are women for our times: ambitious, capable, innovative, in service to others. I confess to a great respect for nurses—my mother is a retired nurse, which I think is a heroic and unsung profession.

I ask whether the sisters are surprised by the success of their monastic retreat. "They're very touched by how people respond," Duchesneau says. "They agreed this would be a nonreligious place. Religion was always an answer in the past centuries, but now the churches are empty and people are looking for meaning. Modern society needs this kind of place, where people are free to live their own spirituality the way they wish."

As well as the peaceful infrastructure, the nuns have centuries of expertise in balancing their spiritual and social mission. They have much to share about how to retreat *and* keep our day jobs. Sister Sarah MacDonald joined the Augustinian order in 2015 at 35, making her the youngest nun by decades—the closest in age back then was 73. She's smart, dynamic despite having a head cold and funny. When I remark that not many young women join convents these days, she quips, "Yeah, I feel like an animal in the zoo. I tend to stand out." MacDonald has an exacting schedule: in addition to nursing, she's a tour guide at the Catherine of St. Augustine Centre, located on the second floor adjoining Le Monastère; she manages the nuns' website; and she maintains a daily regimen of morning and evening prayers and Mass, plus an hour in personal prayer.

Dressed in her white nursing shift and wearing a large crucifix, Sister Sarah tells me in a hoarse voice that she caught the cold from one of her patients. She works in long-term care with people with Alzheimer's and dementia. Originally from Sudbury, she had been baptized Catholic but rarely went to church, except for the occasional Mass with her grandparents. She earned a degree in religious studies at McMaster University, where she first met women who had dedicated themselves to religious life. This planted a seed. After graduation she worked for Revenue Canada. "I was a tax collector. Any biblical scholars out there will understand the irony."

Sister Sarah arrived on the convent's doorstep seeking a place to stay while she worked at the 49th International Eucharistic Congress, a gathering that attracted thousands of Catholics. Before that she'd served in a Calcutta orphanage run by the order founded by Mother Teresa and visited various North American religious communities. But with the sisters she finally found what she was looking for. It was like falling in love, she says. She took her vows in 2015.

While the sisters value prayer and seclusion, their vow to serve the poor and the sick is also a priority. "We know how easy it is to get caught up in the active world. We can't give what we don't have. So we need to both give back to our community and society, and take care of ourselves," Sister Sarah explains. The sisters build silence into their days, but they also retreat. "Here, our Fridays are always in silence. I also have one retreat day per month, plus one week-long and one four-day retreat per year."

In fact monks and nuns from even the most silent orders take retreats relieved of the responsibilities of everyday life to concentrate on God.

This also applies to the lives of busy secular people, who benefit from learning to balance action with contemplation and to touch on the sacred, she says. "It's a need we've had for centuries: it's who we are as human beings to have spaces or times reserved for something that's greater than we are." This has become increasingly challenging. "We're surrounded by noise and stimulation. It takes a conscious effort to disconnect from everything that's around us, to really listen."

Le Monastère aims to provide people with a taste of healing and silence, a beginning. "Spaces like this allow us to have a profound experience, a special experience of the sacred, but that's really not limited to sacred space. You may experience a mountaintop moment, an insight, a utopic moment, but we need to go down the mountain later—to remember the experience and be able to bring it into daily life, try and find ways to relive it. That's what we do when we retreat: we renew, we remember and take the time. So you don't need a building to create sacred space—you need to find that in your everyday life."

Visitors are welcomed to join the sisters for vespers at 5 p.m. in the church, accessible from the hotel's second floor, and I can just make it before chi kung. I take my place beside two others in a space with room for hundreds in its wooden pews. The sisters file in. Most are slow and bent. They glance up, waiting for one last sister to appear. Finally she parks her walker and leans heavily on the pew backs as she makes her way slowly down the long, empty row. Twelve sisters sit in two short lines in the corner of the capacious church.

The elderly women raise their voices in praise and thanks for the day just past, and it's elevating. The values of the nuns—simplicity, silence, service and devotion—are timeless. I'm no longer certain how I feel about the disappearance of the ancient order of Augustine sisters here, or other such orders around the world. Who doesn't need more prayers? Yet it's true that were the hotel not secular, I wouldn't be here. Perhaps this is the new way, what ancient offers modern: a place where a window is still open to the sacred, however we conceive it. The nuns stop singing and sit a moment in silence, heads bowed. They stir, and then stand up to leave. One walks over and says in French that I'm very welcome. It's touching. We smile and shake hands. As she hobbles away in her sturdy nursing shoes, joining the others in their white shifts, it's as though they're ghosts already.

What a paradox: churches in the West face steep declines in numbers and are closing or repurposing monasteries and convents, while modern-day people are booking up retreats far in advance in these peaceful, spiritual environments, often located in unique historic and natural places. Like the world at large, the idea of retreat, even in religious organizations, has been progressively secularized. Believers and nonbelievers alike are seeking healing spaces and expert advice in traditional religious communities now reinventing themselves—and in the process, defining one of the main ways we retreat today.

Modern people have more retreats to choose from than ever: religious, spiritual, wellness, nature, arts and culture, historical, taster weekends, workshops, longer immersions or self-directed retreats in secular accommodations. Like refugees from the modern world, we're flocking to these places to remember—or discover—how to take a step back. Religious organizations can still provide us with the geography for retreat, and often expert guidance for frazzled souls wanting to experience interiority. For most of us, these communal retreats are far more accessible than finding a hermit's hut, and they come with structure and routine already in place, and gatekeepers who know how to do it.

As noted, while organized religion is in decline in the West, the "spiritual not religious" grouping is growing dramatically. A strong but hidden spiritual pulse was noted by philosopher Charles Taylor, author of *A Secular Age* and professor emeritus of philosophy at Montreal's McGill University. Taylor argues that in the West since the Reformation, traditional religion has not been disappearing, but has become increasingly diversified and personal—an opinion shared by many.

What explains God's enduring appeal? "Religion seems to give meaning to suffering—much more so than any secular ideal or belief that we know of," says Ara Norenzayan, a social psychologist at the University of British Columbia in Vancouver and author of 2013's *Big Gods*. The search for meaning is attractive not just for the traditionally religious, but for people in the "spiritual not religious" category too. "We have one of the least religious societies in North America—almost one in two Vancouverites say that they do not belong to any religion. Yet, a growing number of the non-religious report having spiritual beliefs and inclinations." Many anthropologists, neuroscientists, psychologists and philosophers suggest that humans are predisposed to believe in a higher power. Whatever the case, humans have a clear need to feel connected to something larger, and religion and spirituality offer one channel.

These two ideas—that religion and spirituality are alive and well, and that they are vital to understanding social, political and historical aspects of a complex world—help explain the popularity of retreats to spiritual environments. These notions, it seems to me, have much greater currency in Europe than in North America. Britain's BBC offers myriad programs on religious and spiritual topics that aim to improve spiritual literacy and explore whether ancient traditions have anything to offer modern people. Filming what happens when we retreat, usually an experience that's interior and private, makes for great television, both entertaining and educational.

In *The Monastery*, "Five men, ranging from an atheist in the pornography trade to a former Protestant paramilitary, [find] their lives unexpectedly transformed in the latest incarnation of reality television." The men join a Benedictine community and retreat for 40 days and 40 nights. The edgiest moment isn't a spiritual crisis, though they do occur—it's the grim moment when the brother in charge collects cellphones because everyone is so distracted. It's often hilarious, as when one man says with a straight face, "Applying monastic values to a job in the soft porn industry is particularly challenging." He later changes his profession. In *The Convent*, four women spend 40 days and 40 nights on retreat with the Poor Clare nuns. There's a disillusioned workaholic unfulfilled by success; a woman who is terrified of God who wants to confront her fears; a soul singer and former alcoholic who thinks God is calling her to be celibate; and a free-spirited atheist who hopes to be more at peace. Among other programs are *The Retreat, The Big Silence, The Lost Gospels, Around the World in 80 Faiths, Songs of Praise, Retreat: Meditations from the Monastery* and *The Road to the Camino*.

There's also the incomparable *Extreme Pilgrim*, a reality show/travelogue/documentary I've re-watched many times. The show follows Peter Owen Jones, a former ad executive turned Anglican vicar, as he embarks on three spiritual journeys. He lives with the kung fu monks of central China, gets stoned with mystics of the Himalayas at India's Kumbha Mela—"This is God in colour!" he exclaims—and lives as an ascetic hermit in the Egyptian desert. As the very title *Extreme Pilgrim* suggests, the show is absurd—but it's also fascinating and illuminating. Owen Jones is a long-haired maverick who chain-smokes and leaves behind his clerical collar; he talks openly about the limitations of his church, which he says seeks to actively suppress religious debate. He really does test his physical and mental endurance, which is why the show so interests me. As he prepares to follow in the footsteps of the ancient hermits of the Egyptian desert, who left society to dedicate their lives to the love of God, he admits that this three-week experiment scares him because there will be no escape and no distraction— the most common struggle for modern people on retreat.

The desert hermits gave up mental and material security and comfort to get closer to God. Owen Jones says he's always believed this was an essential part of the religious experience, and he's been waiting for 40 years to do it, to confront his own demons—despite growing misgivings. "I know that their divine knowledge was won by hardship, pain and privation and to learn from them I have to become an *extreme pilgrim*," he intones over dramatic music. Owen Jones was right to be afraid: even for someone with his experience in contemplative life, who is taking part in a reality show, and stocked with ample supplies, three weeks in a remote desert cave is no picnic. His guide to spiritual warfare is Father Lazarus, an Australian who was atheist for 40 years and now sports a long grey beard, black robe and embroidered hat. At the Orthodox Coptic Christian Monastery of St. Anthony, out of more than 100 monks, Father Lazarus is the only cave hermit. He kindly lends Owen Jones his previous mountain cave, right beside the last cave of St. Anthony.

Father Lazarus and the crew leave Owen Jones alone—with a camera so he can film his experiences. This is a reality show after all, but in the modern day, is filming so different from keeping a diary? His pseudo-retreat is nevertheless an illuminating look at the usually private experiences people pass through in their caves, real and metaphorical. At first Owen Jones prays piously. Then he wanders in the rocky landscape. Then he performs push-ups and sit-ups, saying he needs physical exercise: "Otherwise I will go stark, raving mad." He makes friends with a lizard. On day four, as he lights the propane stove, he says it's "like being incarcerated in a French surrealist movie where every single echo, every sound—where they stir their cup of coffee and it takes 15 seconds, all you hear is sugar dissolving and the spoon going around—every sound, especially at night, is utterly magnified, is sharp, sharp." Owen Jones passes through various stages over three weeks: from boredom to defiance—"Why is it always about you?" he complains to an image of Christ on the cross—through abject terror and illness. Eventually, he begins to appreciate the silence and the desert's visual austerity.

Most who inhabit a desert cave at a monastery, or in any isolated place, will have trained first, preparing through prayers, practices and previous retreats. The silence and solitude often start to bring insights only later, after time to adjust. *Extreme Pilgrim* gives a unique glimpse into how taking a step back, far from being nothing, is a transformative experience. On day 21, Father Lazarus returns to give a goodbye blessing and tells Owen Jones, thin but peaceful-looking, "You will go back to the place of things; I want you to carry with you the full emptiness of the desert." Lazarus, incidentally, and ironically, is yet another media celebrity hermit: his fans created a webpage, and he is the subject of various documentaries and articles.

The modern media is simply a stand-in for curious audiences. A celebrity hermit may seem contradictory, but I'd argue this is the modern-day equivalent of word of mouth, which led thousands of pilgrims to chase St. Anthony into this very desert, followers so numerous that hermit communities eventually evolved to become the first settled monasteries in the West.

For most of us today a monk's retreat will be gentler, comfortably communal as opposed to the more advanced retreat to a hermit's cave by the monastery, or alone on a mountain. As more and more people retreat in their hermitages and convents, monks and nuns often say it's because laypeople are sensing the inner void in a materialistic world. Laypeople range from those who think they need to rest, or who want to stay in an affordable natural or historic place and perhaps find something more, to those who are actively seeking meaning in the footsteps of the ancients. In any case it's an exchange made in heaven: with church attendance down, aging communities and bills to pay, the monasteries can earn money while serving society.

The idea of monks and nuns being self-sufficient and making money is nothing new in the Christian monastic tradition. They are not driven by greed or ambition. Their humble work is done to sustain the abbeys where they live and often relates to the environment they live in, and their products and services are sold both online and in monastery-based shops. In Provence monks and nuns sell lavender and honey products; at de St. Benoît du Lac in Quebec, the only monk-run dairy in North America, they make cheese, and at Oka, more cheese is made from the milk of well-loved cows. Kentuckian monks sell fudge soaked in bourbon. The Sisters of the Valley in California sell cannabis, which they grow following the lunar cycle, and meditate while they prepare medical tinctures, oils and salves in the abbey kitchen. Iowan monks make caskets using premium woods from their forest. Other monastic products include fine beer, wine and spirits—think Trappist ales and Benedictine liqueur—musical CDs; butter; brownies; the Pope's cologne, which uses the same essential oils as Pope Pius's with violet and citrus notes; fine soaps and shampoos; and gourmet mushrooms. The Orthodox monks at New Skete, New York, have raised and trained German shepherds for more than 40 years.

With their organic, artisanal products made with care and simplicity, and services provided with love and attention, the monks and nuns are preserving old ways, drawing on expert knowledge gained over hundreds of years. We can enjoy these products whether we agree with Christianity or not, and we can benefit from monastic retreats. Monks and nuns have developed similar patterns and practices the world over for finding God, or Nirvana, or joy and liberation, or peace. Routine, silence and living in community can help us transcend distractions and ego, and experience an alternative state of being, and an "ekstasis, a 'stepping outside' the confines of self," writes author and renowned comparative religion scholar Karen Armstrong, a former nun.

Many Western religious orders still follow St. Benedict's sixth-century rule, ora et labora (Latin for pray and work). Benedict, disillusioned with the city and its licentiousness, retreated to a cave in the Sabine Hills near Rome, where for three years he lived as a hermit, wore a hair shirt and rolled in thistles to subdue his flesh. But he rejected this path and went on to found monasteries that became the centre of Christian monasticism, redefining it as stable, enclosed and isolated. He condemned asceticism and wandering and wrote his influential rule for "regulated" monks living communally under an abbot's authority.

It's amazing to me that Benedict's values and ways have remained constant as the world kaleidoscopes through change. The Benedictines have long recognized that non-monastics need to retreat as well. One of the order's rules is that "all guests who present themselves are to be welcomed as Christ, for him himself will say: I was a stranger and you welcomed me."

At St. Peter's Abbey in central Saskatchewan, the oldest Benedictine order in Canada, founded in 1903, the monks give people a glimpse of monastic life, providing an oasis for prayer and silence to nourish body, soul and spirit, and to help people refocus. They grow their own produce and tend the gardens, orchards, pastures and greenhouses on their 2,800-acre organic farm near Muenster. Nature for the Benedictines is the second book, after the Bible. Aside from offering what's in short supply today, a slow pace, simplicity and natural beauty, the monks' green ways often draw modern people interested in sustainable agriculture and healthy food.

At one point there were 60 monks; today there are 14. With aging residents and a decline in people seeking vocations, St. Peter's adapted for the 21st century by opening a school and later a college. The monks also welcome retreaters and model how to balance prayer and work in times when everyone's life is out of balance. Father Demetrius, the guestmaster, is particularly skilled at this: in addition to five prayers a day, doing prayers on request and working on the farm—he's often in the honey hut, keeping bees—the father hosts 3,000 guests each year, on religious and secular retreats. In this beautiful setting, with its quiet spaces and quiet time, Sage Hill Writing hosts the Saskatchewan Writers' Guild's most popular retreat. Poet Lorna Crozier has said every book she has written over the last 20 years had its start at St. Peter's Abbey: "For me, it's a sanctuary from the distractions of daily life and a catalyst for writing."

Seeking a quiet, affordable place to write, Patrick Leigh Fermor found much more when he entered a world more foreign than the ones he'd been chronicling in his famous travel books. In *A Time to Keep Silence*, Fermor describes his sojourns in some of France's most venerable monasteries in the 1950s, including the Benedictine Abbeys of St. Wandrille, renowned for art and learning. At first he found it hard to adjust, writing: "So much silence and sobriety! The place assumed the character of an enormous tomb, a necropolis of which I was the only living inhabitant." It was painful even to get used to the unfamiliar—a secluded cell, silent meals and solemn rituals, and the company of monks and nuns who seemed joyless and unnatural. Soon this changes, and "the troubled waters of the mind grow still and clear, and much that is hidden away and all that clouds it floats to the surface and can be skimmed away; and after a time one reaches a state of peace that is unthought of in the ordinary world."

A sophisticated Brit who encounters monastic life inadvertently, Fermor describes what we may still find in such settings. On his inward journey his worries "slid away into some distant limbo," he writes. He calls the abbey "the reverse of a tomb . . . a castle hanging in mid-air beyond the reach of ordinary troubles and vexations." When he returns to Paris he experiences this change of perspective in reverse: "The Abbey was at first a graveyard; the outer world seemed afterwards, by contrast, an inferno of noise and vulgarity." A convert of sorts, he wonders with annoyance why we single out solitaries as selfish when social life is not necessarily all service and joy, and solitaries are inoffensive. How is it worse to live in God's presence than in never-ending useless activity? he asks.

Fermor comes to respect the monks. He is moved by their kindness, gentleness, compassion and devotion to saving souls. He admires their capacity for silence and solitude, and their learning, science, beautiful buildings and unparalleled calm, the by-products of their life. He adds that it's "risible" to accuse them of escapism—try living this conviction, he says, confronting "the terrible problem of eternity." When he asks one of monks to sum up his way of life, his reply echoes something Sister Sarah told me at Le Monastère. The monk pauses and then asks, "Have you ever been in love?"

Offering divine accommodation is a common way that abbeys, convents and monasteries survive today, helping modern people to survive in the process. Providing respite to travellers is a centuries-old tradition for many religious communities, so it's not a huge next step for them to begin welcoming secular tourists, or guests who want to retreat, or both. Tourism was invented when religious people wanted to go to the Holy Land and has been big business ever since. Typically, you don't have to be particularly religious, or religious at all, and tourists and pilgrims appreciate the simple, serene, unique and sometimes budget-priced lodging in lovely settings. Going on retreat to the quiet of a monastery, abbey or retreat centre is a common global practice, and many either provide a quiet space for personal reflection, or welcome people to join the community's practices, or provide optional spiritual counselling.

I find the sheer exuberant variety of retreats available to support all manner of retreaters, regardless of slender means, impressive. Worldwide retreats by the hundreds are easy to find: I've spent countless hours combing published guidebooks to lodgings in sanctuaries, monasteries and abbeys and surfing websites such as monasteries. net, monasterystays.com, and the not-for-profit Good Night and God Bless: A Guide to Convent and Monastery Accommodation in Europe (goodnightandgodbless.com). I found Buddhist, Catholic, Hindu, Jewish, Protestant, Quaker, Sufi and secular retreat centres of all descriptions, some overlooking the sea, others high in the mountains, some in mansions with gardens, others in spare Zen temples or simple cabins in the woods. Scholarships, work-study opportunities and discounts are often available for those in need. Armchair retreaters, perhaps people in the throes of family life and counting the years until they can leave the children for a day, a week or a month, will find plenty of dreaming fodder.

A few really stood out for me. New Camaldoli Hermitage in Big Sur, California, founded in 1958 by two Italian hermits and run by Camaldolese Benedictine monks, is built on cliffs with views of the Pacific Ocean. Retreaters are welcome to join the monks for services or not, and there is no proselytizing. Rooms have private gardens, or there are hermitage cabins on the hillside, or for men, repurposed monks' cells within the cloister. There's no cellphone coverage, and no radio, TV or telephones in the rooms. Guests observe silence, and can come for private self-guided retreats, for "preached" retreats on religious subjects or for group retreats where they get a taste of the lives of the monks. At Pluscarden Abbey in northeast Scotland, guests of the Benedictines stay by donation and, similarly, at the Trappist Abbey of Our Lady of the Snows in south-central France, hikers and pilgrims can sleep for a donation in the place where Robert Louis Stevenson stayed in 1878 and wrote *Travels with a Donkey in the Cevennes*. At Nepal's

Kopan Monastery in the foothills of the Himalayas, 360 monks live and welcome outsiders for up to a month for Buddhist study, meditation, retreat and practice for about $20 a day, including three meals.

That a bountiful supply of serene, sacred places already exists hasn't stopped religious orders from constructing new buildings to attract visitors, more quiet oases in a turbulent world. In the rolling green hills near Atlanta, Georgia, the Monastery of the Holy Spirit's 40 Trappist monks took a $7 million calculated risk, breaking ground for a new gathering space and visitor centre with a gift shop, garden centre and bonsai nursery and greenhouse, which opened in 2011. By pulling in more tourists, the monks hope to free themselves financially so they can focus more on living a contemplative life, while offering a sacred space where people of all faiths and no faith can retreat in nature and stillness on day trips, mini-retreats and full retreats.

Still others are inventing contemporary traditions. One of the best reflections of our enslaved times is called Prison Inside Me. In South Korea, hundreds of burned-out workaholics are going to this "prison" retreat to relax. "The true prison is the world outside," says the co-founder of the popular jail-themed retreat- Ji-hyang Noh. The retreat was the idea of her husband, Yong-Seok Kwon, a lawyer who was working 100-hour weeks and suffering the resulting physical and mental toll. Dreaming of freedom, he asked a law-enforcement friend to lock him in jail for therapeutic reasons. "I thought I would feel better if I stayed in solitary confinement. At least there are no people, no phone calls looking for me, no smoking, no drinking," Kwon said. His friend refused so he built his own "jail," a stress reduction centre in a mountain town near Seoul where people can escape manic modern life and go inward.

Paying guests at Prison Inside Me, desperate to de-stress, had to give up their cellphones completely. But the South Koreans, a notoriously connected people, couldn't cope, and the rule was bent so they can check once a day. "People seem nervous without a phone and simply worry too much about an emergency, which seldom happens," said Kwon. "Inmates" put on a regulation uniform and go to one of 28 identical cells. The 60-square-foot solitary confinement lockups have a window, heated wood floors, a tea set, a yoga mat, a toilet, sink and small table, and a panic button. The doors lock, but people are shown how to undo the latch from the inside. Meal delivery is through a slot in the door. Inmates spend time in their rooms, meditating and reflecting in silence, or in private meditation classes, spiritual classes and healing group sessions—for about $150 for two nights. Kwon says he wants guests to pause and find freedom in confinement, safe behind doors locked to the onslaught of modern life. "I only hope that this place offers a chance for visitors to reflect on themselves," he said.

The ancient desert mindset lives on, but renegades leaving society today might head for Slab City in California, which its residents call "the last free place in America." Squatters in this transient desert community are an odd mix of retirees stretching their budgets, snowbirds seeking a free place to park their RVs in winter, and artists, addicts, free spirits, fugitives, modern-day ascetics seeking simplicity and aspiring hobos, young and old. Some don't want, or can't afford, "sticks-and-bricks" living, and come for economic reasons. Here, like-minded souls here can avoid being stigmatized for wanting to live differently or for being poor.

Many of these outsiders are seeking not spiritual revelation, but freedom. You can camp with no rent, no landlords, no property tax and no one to bother you. The community is an off-grid accumulation of RVs, yurts, rusting old buses and makeshift homes of tents and pallets that sit in the empty Sonoran desert among the concrete slabs from Camp Dunlap, an abandoned Second World

War military barracks that operated here until the 1950s on 640 acres of public land.

People eke out a life using energy from generators, propane and solar power, burying their trash and sewage in the ground, and bathing in a single communal shower, nearby hot springs or the irrigation canals. They rely on their own or their fellow Slabbers' ingenuity for most everything in limit-testing desert conditions. They endure shortages of the staples of modern life and learn to live more simply and environmentally responsibly. Self-reliance, sustainability and a "live and let live" ethos are the norm. Numbers can reach 4,000 people in the winter when the temperature drops, but in summer, when it's upwards of 120 degrees, there are only about 200 residents, plus the scorpions and rattlesnakes. Canadians are typically well represented. "Last year, because of the falling exchange rate, a lot of the snowbirds from Canada failed to make it down to Southern California and Slab City's population dropped to under 2,000 for the first time in years," a 2017 article in Britain's *Independent* noted.

The community may not have water and sanitation, but it does have a decent library, a barbershop, churches, nightclubs and Solar Bob's successful company for inexpensive solar-power conversions. There's an Avon Lady, daily news on CB radio and a prom—because most of the people here never went to their prom. There's a pet cemetery and Slab mart—the garbage dump/recycling centre. A tall fork in the road sticks up from the sand beside a sign that explains it's "a replica of the fork in the road that inspired Robert Frost to write the poem 'The Road Not Taken.' The original fork is located in Lancaster, Vermont." There's another sign to West Satan, located next to East Jesus (another way of saying "out in the middle of nowhere"), a thriving artist community with a sculpture garden and works made from trash.

Biblical references abound. Salvation Mountain is Slab City's most recognizable landmark, a massive art installation made of adobe, straw, mud and bright paint, featured in *Into the Wild*, among many other film and photography projects. It's the life's work of Leonard Knight, one of Slab City's most famous residents, who died in 2014. He found it the ideal place to practise his philosophy, "Love Jesus and keep it simple." Slabbers also call the outside world Babylon or, sometimes, the Beast.

Nowadays many tourists visit: you can even do Airbnb in an RV, living side by side with people who like the simplicity and freedom or have fallen on hard times. Or you can show up and take any unoccupied space. Many journalists visit and some Slabbers won't speak to them, giving notice in printed signs in trailer windows that say "Absolutely No Media." As with the Egyptian desert, no one else wanted Slab City's desolate desert land, which is why the squatters were long left alone here. But in 2015 the state said it was considering selling the parcel, 140 miles east of San Diego and about 50 miles north of the U.S.–Mexico border, so some residents organized and applied to buy it.

Builder Bill, who runs the Range, an open-air nightclub, and one of the leaders of the application, worries about displacing the displaced. Many residents have nowhere else to go, he says. Bill himself had been working construction in San Diego when employment dried up. Soon he was living out of a van, with police constantly telling him to move on. "When it's time to get out of Dodge, you have to go somewhere right?" he told a reporter from KBPS, a public broadcaster in San Diego. "You know you can retreat, retreat and retreat, and there's one last little knot on the end of the rope," he said. "That's Slab City."

Builder Bill said the Slabbers embrace radical freedom. "At Slab City you can just sit down and occupy a spot on the planet without any indebtedness or persecution." To prevent outside development and encroachment, the Slab City Community Group and Salvation Mountain Inc. have applied to purchase the public land, while the

Chasterus Foundation of East Jesus bought a 30-acre parcel. Before more land can be sold, complex issues, such as a possible chemical clean-up or disposal of unexploded ordnance, have to be resolved by the state. For this most enduring of temporary spaces, seven decades old, the future remains uncertain.

Along with its positive aspects—simplicity, self-reliance, camaraderie, freedom—Slab City has an apocalyptic feel, with its rusting metal and derelict buses and sometimes extreme poverty. Adding to the end-of-the-world ambience, Slab City is by the toxic Salton Sea that once rivaled nearby Palm Springs and attracted more tourists than Yosemite National Park. The "sea" was created in 1905 by mistake when the Colorado River breached a dike and flooded the desert valley. Now it's dried up again and is lined with abandoned resorts and dead fish, and artists use the derelict Bombay Beach for installations. On the other side of Slab City is the Chocolate Mountain artillery range and a landfill.

In the Anthropocene, rebels who step out of the mainstream— or are pushed out—live not in the pristine desert, but in dystopian ecological wastelands on the edge of commerce. Like the ancients before them, the countercultural Slabbers are seeking a better, more meaningful life. Maybe even waiting for the coming of a new age.

Pilgrim Ways

Traveller, there is no path.
Paths are made by walking.

—Antonio Machado

Since before recorded time human beings have embarked on pilgrimages, travel as transcendence. We're propelled to action by the conviction that larger forces—God, or Shakespeare's lingering presence, depending on your devotion—can influence our lives, and we can touch this power in special places. Pilgrimage is an ancient quest, and I am on a pilgrimage.

I heft my pack onto my back and step onto the sandy trail with a mix of relief and irritation. Relief because it has been a long journey to here, a penance even. For a year and a half I've been trying to enact a walking pilgrimage. Each time, something has gone wrong. I feel cosmically afflicted, yet determined: of all our ways of retreat, literally stepping away from the everyday is one that most beguiles 21st-century people.

This is why I want the experience. Yet I am a reluctant pilgrim. I feel I'm just not a pilgrimage person, though I know journeys have long been foundational practices in most world religions and are still very much in evidence, holding mythic resonance. There's the Hajj to Mecca for Muslims, pilgrimages to Varanasi and sacred rivers and mountains for Hindus, to Jerusalem for Jews and the other Abrahamic religions, to Bodh Gaya and holy sites in northern India and the Himalayas for Buddhists, to shrines across Europe and the Americas for Christians, and for Indigenous cultures worldwide, sacred journeys linked to the seasons, to places of reverence and to rites of initiation. Pilgrimage mirrors the universal human journey—birth, transformation, death.

A red-tailed hawk soars in circles above the clearing at the trailhead, reminding me of how this ancient phenomenon has circled around and revived itself. Modern-day Western pilgrims are flocking to medieval paths in record numbers, for both spiritual and secular reasons. Whatever the stated purpose, on pilgrimage, we're in pursuit of the ineffable, experiences of awe and wonder that can't really be put into words, which are rare in our everyday lives.

Though the sky is grey and the rain is spitting, I feel cautiously optimistic. I'd nearly called off my pilgrim walk yet again—this time because of a domestic tragedy with our backyard chickens. Yet here I am, the air fresh on my face. I've even received an auspicious sign. On the half-hour drive up from Bancroft the taxi driver said that the hunters are depressed because the black bears, fat on abundant berries and crabapples, aren't taking their bait. I'm happy to hear this—partly because I'm rooting for the bears, but mostly because I forgot to buy bear spray.

Being eaten, or shot: however unlikely, such are the considerations for a walking pilgrimage on the Hastings Heritage Trail. This rugged, forested route along abandoned train tracks could hardly be less like the well-worn path of the Camino de Santiago de Compostela, the way of St. James in Spain. That's what I had assumed was *the* model for a pilgrimage: a traditional route that arrives at a set shrine, involving a long physical journey.

We can be forgiven for thinking that the Camino equals pilgrimage: this medieval path has been exceeding historical pilgrim totals each year, and its success has sparked a resurgence of old pilgrim routes around the world. Hostelries closed for hundreds of years are reopening and, to meet demand, ancient routes are being improved, long-neglected ones waymarked and new shrines consecrated. Not only are the devout taking to the road in record numbers, but secular pilgrims on quests outside what's officially sacred have been reframing pilgrimage, improvising on age-old religious journeys and inventing new paths.

In reality only some pilgrimages, such as the Camino, are made on foot. The journey is the vital point, and walking is just one means of personal transformation. Anthropologist Edith Turner calls pilgrimage a "kinetic ritual" in 1978's seminal *Image and Pilgrimage in Christian Culture*, co-written with her husband Victor. We depart "in search of something intangible," writes Rebecca

Solnit in *Wanderlust*. Then there are the destination pilgrimages, such as the Hajj to Mecca, or travelling to Rome to visit Keats's apartment because we love Keats or visiting a site related to a hero or tragedy. This may mean taking an airplane or metro to the holy site. Though the essence is the same as when we walk, the emphasis is on a transformational encounter with sacred energies at a specific place, which elevates and empowers us.

Whether we walk, draw power from the "shrine" at the destination, or both, the pilgrim's journey changes us. Moving through spiritual geography, we travel, and that "travail," that effort, makes us deserving. We advance toward the sacred, or whatever inspires us—the saint's relics, the artist's home, the mountain, Memphis. Then we culminate our journey in arrival, and return home—or in some cases, keep wandering—transformed. Pilgrimage is the physical expression of the intense human desire for meaning, for contact with ultimate reality.

During its medieval peak in the West, pilgrimage was Christian and the destination was holy sites and shrines—and ultimately, heaven. "Europe was born in pilgrimage, and its mother tongue is Christianity," wrote Goethe. After a long post-Reformation gap, the tradition stirred again in the 1960s, when it also began to emerge as a new academic field. Pilgrimage exploded quite recently, in the past 30 years: in 1986, the first year statistics were kept, just 2,491 pilgrim certificates of completion were issued on the Camino—though more may have walked all or part of the route without registering; now records show upwards of 300,000 pilgrims a year.

Each time my walking pilgrimage failed to work out, I became more annoyed, though my knowledge grew. Now, on this journey along the Hastings Heritage Trail, I hope to better understand what compels so many pilgrims to walk away from ordinary life. My "immigrant feeling," which keeps me restless and full of questions, is another motivation. I was born in Scotland and left when I was three. After living most of my life in Ontario, the wild, dramatic lands bordering my cabin are my most beloved geography. Yet I still don't feel I quite belong on either side of the Atlantic. I simply want to walk, touch the land with my feet and consider my relationship to here.

The trail under my feet is the former railbed of the Central Ontario Railway. My route from Maynooth Station, once the railway's northerly terminus, will run about 20 kilometres south to Bancroft, where I left the car. I will walk, sleep overnight near the trail and walk again to the former train station in "Bankies," now a tourist information centre. That a pilgrimage has to involve walking long distances is a postmodern idea, and a misconception: people walk short and long distances, sometimes choosing to visit the shrine only, and they also bike, ride horses, use wheelchairs, and even drive.

The walking pilgrim's path unfolds slowly over days, weeks, months, so we can't see the whole road or know what we will find. Given today's mania for productivity, you'd think this would be a hard sell. Yet worldwide, pilgrims are taking to the road, from vagrants to explorers, religious and spiritual questers, the newly wed or divorced, the grieving, creative spirits, scientists, dissidents, bankers, all walking in search of something. Beauty, spiritual clarity, a relationship, an epiphany; in rebellion, remembrance or penance; or taking a new direction—the purposes are as varied as the people.

Scholars today no longer consider pilgrimage solely religious or historical: it has evolved to mean any transformative journey to a place, or for a purpose, that matters to us deeply. It's a more fluid experience that's open to all regardless of beliefs, and could be to the Ganges or Graceland. It's wonderfully all-encompassing: a voodoo pilgrimage to Haiti brings together Catholic and African practices, a reggae pilgrimage to Bob Marley's birthplace and mausoleum offers optional smoking of sacramental herbs, and virtual pilgrimage is possible for those whose health may not permit a physical journey.

I even found an enviable film pilgrimage curated by Tilda Swinton that gathered together 50 pilgrims from all over the world to pull a blue truck, the mobile 80-seat Screen Machine cinema, from town to town across the Scottish Highlands for eight and half days, showing films about journeys. Pilgrimage is one way of finding meaning while in motion that can be religious, or personal and self-invented. The common notion that religious pilgrims are serious while secular ones are frivolous is one I reject. All of us have beliefs that are unverifiable, and who is to say what's sacred for someone else?

The rain is still spitting, my new hikers are laced up—I know, new boots are a mistake and I've been turning my ankle in these for a couple of days now—and my water-laden pack is strapped to my back—really, one litre every two hours? I'm wearing neon orange, the very shade of Don't shoot. I take out a packet of sacred ash I received years ago from Amma, India's Hugging Saint, whose message is unconditional love. I rip open the brown paper and sprinkle half the ash into the sandy soil, asking for a blessing for my journey. I tuck it back into the bright cloth bag with a shiny black feather, which I then return to my breast pocket. If all goes well—I'm still not confident given my record so far—I'll use the rest of the contents to mark the end of my journey.

Taking a deep breath and summoning all my equipoise I start to walk, worrying about new obstacles, like a sprained ankle. Just as I think this, my foot comes down on round stones that pock the sandy trail and I nearly fall. Cursing, I remember that this will be an easy day, Maynooth Station to Hybla, roughly four hours of slow and digressive walking, based on my estimate of 3.5 kilometres an hour. I intend to take my time. The next day will be longer. Though I couldn't get accurate information on the part of the trail to Bancroft, I'm guessing it will take five hours.

I step and stumble onward with care. It's a vulnerable feeling to head out alone with your pack, carrying all your food and water and clothes and sunscreen and bug spray on your back. The road opens beneath my feet, and I have an anxious yet excited feeling of moving into the unknown. Pilgrimage is a quest over meaningful terrain, both outer and inner. John Muir understood this: "I only went out for a walk, and finally concluded to stay out till sundown, for going out, I found, was really going in." Pilgrimage involves encountering uncertainty and risk, is unpredictable, and unlikely to be a pleasure trip. Typically when we move away from comfort, we're as likely to encounter awfulness as awe. The deer flies, dreadful all summer and which I expected to make my walk hell, have disappeared, so I wear my bug cap with the mesh tucked up over the visor, resolving to stay receptive to the unknown and to "spirit."

I pass the ruin of Maynooth Station, with its caved-in roof. The station was built in 1907 for a railway line that was decommissioned nearly 40 years ago. My pilgrim route, it occurs to me, reverses the original pillaging trajectory: this area was cut up by railways that removed resources, such as then-abundant red pine and white pine, and by north-south colonization roads. In the 1850s the roads sparked the movement of settlers northward. Most became farmers, cultivating small acreages, enticed north by free land. They found themselves stranded in a rocky wilderness. By 1925, the Hastings Colonization Road was described by a land surveyor as "a long trail of abandoned farms, adversity, blasted hopes, broken hearts, and blasted ambition."

Today's maps and histories reveal little of the land's original inhabitants, the Algonquin people, giving the distorted impression that history began with the settlers. This is changing, thankfully: at Eagles Nest, near Bancroft, a sacred place for vision quests, a new interpretative trail and site run by the Algonquins of Ontario tells of early history. Signs along the trail, meant as "an example of meaningful engagement and a step forward in the spirit of truth and reconciliation," explain how the Algonquin in the Shawashkong watershed—the York River—travelled between various encampments by canoe based on seasonal needs, hunting and fishing, and describe the long history of Algonquin families who still live in the area.

Further, in the Algonquin Park region a young archeologist, researcher and cultural heritage consultant, Christine Luckasavitch of the Madawaska River Algonquin people, who belongs to the Crane Clan, has been giving sold-out talks and writing about the roughly 12,000 years of the land's heritage. She covers everything from glaciation to the history of her people—who were displaced by the fur trade, lumber industry, and when the park was created in 1893—to the arrival of European explorers, to logging and the infamous lumber and railway baron J.R. Booth, and the arrival of artists and adventurers. It's heartening that these histories are being restored; it's better for us all to live in reality.

The section of the trail I'm walking is in unceded traditional Algonquin territory and part of a massive land claim process. I know that many of the early settlers who displaced the Indigenous people came from Scotland, my birth country, after being forced off their lands during the Highland Clearances. A pilgrimage here is complex.

The trail is like a ghost railway, with traces of previous lives. Up ahead, an old tree, laden with shining apples, beckons. I pick one, admire its bold red stripes and bite into it. The taste is refreshing, so I pluck two more and stuff them in my pockets. The idea of living off the fat of the land is so delightful that I smile. I tuck a few apple seeds into my breast pocket before hurling the core into the woods. Apples will be my scallop shells, I decide, my pilgrim's badges.

The path winds into the forest, and I feel I've entered a green tunnel. It leads along a raised trestle that must have been pure hell for the old-time surveyors and labourers to build. I'm walking near the treetops of maple, birch, white pine and balsam. Down the steep embankment, streams gurgle. Once in a while I hear an ATV's buzzing approach and stand to the side until it passes. Mostly I begin to get into a rhythm: steps, breath, thoughts.

The path slopes gradually downhill—no more uphill road to transformation for this walking pilgrim?—and descends into the regular landscape, where the earth is more compacted and easier to walk on. As I tromp along, grey clouds morph into white clouds with intermittent sun. Along the way I collect rusty nails, nuts and bolts, relics from the old railway. My mind and body gradually settle and fall into step. Amid recent the busyness, I've had no pause for breath or time to metabolize recent events.

The night before I'd left Kingston to come here, a fox had attacked our hens. Marco heard squawking and ran out to find Princess on the ground, her white feathers torn off and gashes on her neck. The fox was still waiting in the bushes so he put the wounded bird in the house. Hearing a cry he ran out to find Mel, our stylish black Harco, dead on the neighbours' lawn. The next morning as I was about to depart for my pilgrimage, the fox returned, bold in broad daylight. I chased it, squawking chickens in their coop, dogs barking, people pointing. The fox ran up the six-foot back fence like it was a chain-link ladder, leapt into the cemetery and flopped down on a grassy, raised gravesite to look at me, red and elegant in the sunlight. I threw an apple to scare it away, and it jumped up and sniffed as if to say, Is this food?

Vixens, I know, make their kits begin to hunt for themselves in fall. Now as I walk I reflect on the fox's hunger and on why you should never name your pet after a dear friend. Walking and autumn makes me meditative, and I think a long while about what it means when a fox enters your life.

The mid-September trees are tinged with red and my body goes on autopilot, my uptight breath slows and deepens, and my mind gradually empties. By the time I step off the trail to eat lunch, sitting down on a fallen birch looking over a small lake, I'm not thinking of anything. It's as though the logjam in my head has cleared and the thought stream is flowing freely. ATVs periodically whip around the corner, causing a great wind. The peanut butter and banana sandwich tastes divine, and water is extra delicious, quenching thirst while also making my pack lighter.

I continue walking slowly and steadily, hurrying only while I roar at a pack of six dogs, hoping to scare them off. I'd first spotted a little mutt rolling on his back in a shaft of sunlight, legs waving in the air, so it's unlikely they're dangerous. They chase me half-heartedly, barking like mad fiends. Times passes and soon the green tunnel begins to alternate with open swampy areas, where turtle shells are scattered in the sandy soil, and narcotic peppermint scent wafts on the breeze. The slap of a beaver's tail jolts me out of my reverie. "How long have I got to go?" I wonder. I'm starting to feel tired.

Back home I walk most days for an hour or two, but the farthest I've ever gone on foot before today was in elementary school when I was 12 years old. It was a walkathon, terrible—scorching day, blisters, endless tarmac, sticky cream soda for refreshment. I've always been out of alignment on my left side. Like a bicycle with a crooked wheel, one leg doesn't move forward smoothly: I had to stop running at 30, which is why I took up yoga. Long walks and dynamic movement remain difficult. Fortunately so far, the walking has been pleasant, though my pack feels heavier all the time. Jays squawk like squabbling families, and I startle a grouse—a *whoop, whoop, whoop* of slow wingbeats in the bush. Animal shit full of berries is a hazard on the path. Coyote? Wolf? At Graphite Road I find a screwdriver—a fork would have been easier to interpret. I stand at the trail's edge as a side-by-side ATV passes, the driver in a creepy Joker mask and the passenger holding a radio that blasts loud rock and roll. On this peaceful path they seem a study in incongruity. Though as a pilgrim here, I suppose I'm the one most out of place.

Whether it's the gorgeous trees or the fresh, fragrant air, it suddenly strikes me as odd and wonderful to be on a walking pilgrimage. For months friends have been asking with sly grins about my "pilgrim's lack of progress." Among my many attempts that didn't pan out are two religious walking pilgrimages, three modern ones including a water walk, and a number of self-directed treks prevented by unusual obstacles—in one case, a whole road was closed for resurfacing. My quest was under an ill star, everyone agreed. But in my heart I suspected I knew what the problem was: my secret aversion to the walking pilgrimage.

One reason for my antipathy was severe pilgrim fatigue. Pilgrimage is everywhere, and my oppositional nature means I dislike anything that's popular, on principle. As well I've read countless books, from the tedious *Pilgrim's Progress*, incredibly once as popular as the Bible, an allegory of a Christian everyman's struggle for salvation as he leaves the City of Destruction for the Celestial City, to Shirley MacLaine's dippy bestseller *The Camino: A Journey of the Spirit*—okay, skimmed those two. I have enjoyed a great many pilgrim's tales, including Hilaire Belloc's *The Path to Rome*, the chronicle of his Victorian-era pilgrimage from central France across the Alps, with chapters like "The Astounding Wine," "The Erroneous Anarchist" and "The Mount Terrible." I've read poignant novels such as *The Unlikely Pilgrimage of Harold Fry*, and many contemporary true-Camino books, which I loved. But now

I feel as though *I* experienced blisters, sunburn, snoring people in hostels and the desire to put a pillow over their faces. That *I* stayed one glorious night in the glorious hotel with white sheets and towels and had a perfect meal, struggled with my religion or my past, shared the camaraderie of other pilgrims, made fast friendships and saw the censer swinging at the end in the cathedral.

My main complaint, however, had more do with the set route to a set destination, with rote walking pilgrims wearing scallop shells, the symbol of St. James, and carrying credentials, little passports stamped in each village. It seemed to me, in my peevishness, to be overly pious and lacking in imagination. Further, ego-pilgrims get on my nerves, those people in competition to walk the farthest, the fastest, ready to die before sending luggage ahead in a cab, even in dire circumstances. Once, I quietly admitted my lack of enthusiasm for the walking pilgrimage to a friend, griping that it was akin to checking things off a "bucket list," a term I find annoyingly goal-oriented for an adventure. "But why can't it be more like 'a funny thing happened to me on the prearranged path to the preordained destination'?" he protested. We laughed, and though I knew he was right, my obstinacy remained.

Now at least I know I was being unreasonable: I've discovered there are as many ways to walk a modern pilgrimage as people. Up ahead I spot the Hybla crossroads. From there I will call my hosts for a ride to the bed and breakfast. This is another difficulty in doing a Canadian pilgrimage: no convenient refugios to stay in. I had considered a tent by the trailside but didn't feel safe—hunters, bears—and doubted I could carry more gear anyway. I arrive at the road and let my pack slide to the ground with a satisfying thud, have a luxurious stretch and then call for pickup. Predictably, pain now radiates from my left foot up to my sacro-iliac joint. "So what," I think to myself, feeling unfettered and alive, and looking down the trail I'll walk tomorrow, which curves off into the enticing woods. To travel purposefully through the countryside on foot is beautiful, pleasing.

I have a 15-minute wait so I wander down the road a ways to see whether I can find the abandoned Hybla Gospel Tabernacle that I'd read about on a ghost town website. I spot the church nearly hidden by trees, subsumed into the forest. The railway came to Hybla in 1907 to serve a nearby feldspar mine. George Augustus Bartlett founded the once-busy hamlet and "noticing the number of bees around, named the place after the classic Roman town of Hybla which he recalled was famous for its honey." Grasshoppers hop and the odd deer fly circles my head lazily, and a second red-tailed hawk circumnavigates the sky. Basking in the late-afternoon warmth, I look forward to my evening: a hot shower, yoga to straighten my crooked body out, read a bit if I can find a book, eat the beans and rice I'm carrying in my pack for dinner and have a blissful sleep to rest up for day two.

My epic journey toward the Hastings Heritage Trail had begun long before my feet touched the sandy path. It was in the spring of the previous year, when Scottish hermit and author Sara Maitland invited me to explore the pilgrimage route of St. Ninian with her. I jumped at the chance: the medieval era was the heyday of pilgrimage in the West, when fervent pilgrims walked all over the United Kingdom and Europe and to the Holy Land. I wanted to learn about the origins of pilgrimage in southern Scotland's ancient landscape.

This, I felt sure, would help me better understand the role of pilgrimage in our lives today. Maitland and I planned to visit Whithorn and the shrine of Ninian, an early Christian saint who began converting Scotland to Christianity in 397 AD, and walk a popular pilgrim path to St. Ninian's Cave by the sea. Ever since this famous pilgrimage has attracted the faithful from the British Isles and beyond who believed in the saint's power to cure illness and perform miracles.

Maitland lives in Galloway, a place of moors and forests and seacoasts. The train from Glasgow Central made a pleasant clacking sound as it passed towns with daffodils and cherry trees in bloom, and then entered expansive, rolling hills that seemed to call out for you to enter them and walk. The word pilgrimage comes from two roots: per ager (through the field)—and peregrinus (stranger). For centuries, Christian strangers walked through the very fields I saw out my window.

Chaucer's famous *The Canterbury Tales*, written in the 14th century, follows the journey of a group of pilgrims who each tell a story to entertain the others along the way as they walk to the shrine of St. Thomas Becket in Canterbury Cathedral, one of the top destinations of late medieval Europe. This was before his tomb was smashed to bits, and his bones taken to prevent pilgrims from venerating them, an act considered idolatrous during Cromwell's violent Protestant Reformation.

Pilgrimage disappeared for centuries, but it was never quite expunged. Here, the one-track railway south of Girvan begins to shadow the old Whithorn Way, the ancient pilgrimage route from Glasgow. It joins up with the now-signposted Pilgrim's Way, which can be walked, ridden or cycled, and runs from Glenluce Abbey 25 miles south to the sea at the Isle of Whithorn—part of the path Maitland and I plan to travel in our one-day pilgrimage trip to see the "sites" by car.

At Barrhill Station, confusingly not in the village of Barrhill, the train stopped briefly and I leapt off. Maitland and her spirited terrier, Zoe, waited on the platform. Rangy and wild-haired, with red glasses and trousers and wearing black sneakers, Maitland looked like a teenager, though she was in her sixties. We hopped into her gold Suzuki and the dog kindly gave up the passenger seat and curled at my feet. We roared off down the narrow road in pursuit. "I am indefatigable in relation to St. Ninian and much looking forward to this jaunt!" she said as we bumped along.

When the Romans were still in Britain, Ninian was converting the locals, the southern Picts, in Whithorn. He was a healer whose miracles are rooted in the land. For one, during a bad harvest, a monk lamented that nothing was growing in the garden and went outside to find armloads of plants. Whithorn Priory, the oldest recorded church in Scotland, was later built to house Ninian's remains. The town fast became a popular pilgrim destination for those seeking spiritual salvation and healing, and it was also a centre for medieval learning, visited in particular by Irish saints and scholars. The church actively encouraged the creation of cults of the saints to bolster the faith of the newly converted people of Scotland—with a focus on places, on saint's relics and on materials such as holy water, bread, salt and white pebbles.

As we zipped along toward Whithorn, I imagined pilgrims of yore tramping these hills, dressed in rough tunics and heavy cloaks, wearing broad-brimmed hats, carrying walking sticks, a water skin or gourd and a small satchel for food, known as a scrip.

In "The Passionate Man's Pilgrimage," Sir Walter Raleigh, wrote: "Give my scallop-shell of quiet,/My staff of faith to walk upon,/My scrip of joy, immortal diet/My bottle of salvation,/My gown of glory, hope's true gage;/And thus I'll take my pilgrimage." This stanza, written in 1618, is remarkably upbeat considering Ralegh, a renowned explorer, is said to have written it in the Tower of London as he awaited execution for treason.

Some medieval pilgrims on their way to Whithorn would have carried shoes tied around their necks to make the walk a penance— the harder the journey, the better for the soul. Pilgrims believed the fiery pit of hell awaited unless they did something to wash away their sins. By walking, they enacted the desire for heaven and bound the intangible, their faith, with the material of land, body and holy sites. They'd have been full of wonder and uncertainty. For centuries this was the biggest possible adventure: travel was slow, difficult and dangerous, and they might never return home. Leaving everything familiar and travelling light is certainly a good reminder of what's important. "We brought nothing into this world, and it is certain we can carry nothing out," as the Bible says.

Prehistoric sites, standing stones, cairns and barrows, as well as pilgrim places including holy wells and abbeys: this landscape is richly embedded with traces of the lives of ancient ancestors. We pulled over at the ruins of Glenluce Abbey, where Cistercian monks provided hospitality for pilgrims for 400 years until the Reformation—when Glenluce, which means "valley of light," fell into disuse. Set in a peaceful valley close to the River Luce and Luce Bay, it was a convenient stop for pilgrims visiting St. Ninian's shrine. Lepers here were treated with less hospitality, Maitland said: they were driven away to be cared for by nuns in a local place whose name translates as "the women's hill."

We raced on through the glorious early spring afternoon, veering hard left whenever a vehicle appeared suddenly round the blind corners, while Maitland regaled me with pilgrim and other local lore. I'd never met anyone so erudite and energetic—not to mention funny. Not how I'd imagine a hermit at all. The hills soon gave way to pastures and we arrived in Whithorn, where St. Ninian built the Candida Casa, the White House—reflected in the town's name, Whit-horn. Over many centuries, the fame of Ninian and Whithorn spread. The streets would have been packed with pilgrims, and the town full of inns, cobblers mending worn-out shoes and blacksmiths repairing carts.

In the Whithorn Priory and Museum we saw early Christian carved stones found in St. Ninian's Cave—which was perhaps the

saint's hermitage, or a retreat from the monastery at Whithorn—
and the beautiful Latinus Stone, raised soon after Ninian built his
church, and Scotland's earliest Christian monument. Dedications
to the saint are still seen in southern Scotland, Orkney and Shetland
Islands, Ireland and at St. Ninian's Cathedral in Antigonish,
Nova Scotia.

Outside we strolled around the ruined priory, which dates from
the 12th century and is still a place of pilgrimage for the faithful,
and for those drawn to its long sacred history. My Canadian brain
struggled to grasp that Scotland's earliest Christians worshipped
here about 1,500 years ago. And that pilgrims, seeking miracles
and cures, commoners and kings alike, had been coming here since
the seventh century. I was a little disappointed though: I didn't feel
anything special at the site, aside from historical interest.

The afternoon evaporating quickly, we sped toward the sea to
the Isle of Whithorn, now linked by a causeway to the mainland.
Pilgrims would have arrived by water from England, Ireland and
the Isle of Man on this rocky headland where the now-roofless,
13th-century chapel was a stop on the way to the shrine. Further
along the shore is the cave, featured in the "Miracula Nynie
Episcopi," a poem written by an eighth-century monk from
Whithorn: "Ninian studied heavenly wisdom with a devoted
mind in a cave of horrible blackness."

A well-trodden pathway through woods leads to the sea and
along the stony shore to the cave. Pilgrims from all over the world
are drawn here, some leaving messages scratched in the rock.
Medieval pilgrims did this too, carving votive crosses into the
walls. I asked Maitland whether people now are on faith pilgrimages, or walk just for recreation, tourists enjoying a walk. She
shrugged and asked, "Perhaps they're the same thing?"

True, who is to say that recreation isn't spiritual? Old-time
pilgrims weren't only penitents, they were also humans who enjoyed

stretching their legs and getting outside, as we do. The world's first tourists, in fact, were pilgrims journeying to the Holy Land to see where Jesus and the Apostles had lived, and today, religious tourism remains big business. Even in early times, religious motives mixed with other aims: to go on an adventure, see the sights and collect souvenirs such as reliquaries, metal badges worn on clothing to prove where you'd been, or even vials of breast milk, supposedly from the Virgin Mary. It wasn't all piety. London was a gateway for British pilgrims, full of bars, brothels and other temptations outside the city walls, rife with danger from pickpockets and robbers.

With night approaching, we had to concede we were out of time to hike 45 minutes each way to the saint's cave, especially given the spring mud. Darkness fell as we retired to the pub to eat and talk about St. Ninian. I sipped my pint, exhausted by the day's riches. I felt sorry that my mini-walking pilgrimage didn't work out—not yet knowing this was to become a theme—and that the shrine turned out to be more museum than place of power for me. But I had learned more about the historical foundations of our current fascination, the medieval pilgrimage. And I'd seen how ancient pilgrim routes offer tradition and infrastructure to modern pilgrims. Though I couldn't relate to the God motivation, meaningful rituals do attract me—and obviously many others too.

In my imagination everything began to criss-cross: the landscape, old overlaid with new, the interplay between pilgrims' and hikers' paths, the holy places and natural wonders that have so long inspired pilgrims and lovers of the outdoors, the blurry lines between pilgrims, tourists and travellers. Pilgrimage, I saw, is a thread that connects us with our medieval ancestors: we sense more of their lives and what joins us when we walk old paths and visit holy wells, sacred trees and sites such as Whithorn.

This was the medieval end of the unbroken thread. What was happening at our temporal end?

The ancient pilgrim route of St. Ninian had been historically illuminating—and comical, given the high-speed contemporary pace and my longing to get out and walk. Once I walked a labyrinth in Toronto. Instead of stepping meditatively, I found myself running in case I couldn't finish before dark, a metaphor for how I—and we—operate. Despite pushing ourselves ever faster and more forgetfully, despite our disembodied, virtual times, we yearn to reconnect with our bodies, and landscape and nature, and the unmediated world.

Many of us spend countless hours commuting and cooped up in cubicles or offices in front of screens, we find it gives rise to a longing: to feel the earth beneath our feet, the wind in our faces, to be untethered and alive, on the path and with a higher purpose. After a while, a walk around the park at lunch or after work just won't suffice—we crave more. This is surely part of the reason for the phenomenal upsurge in walking pilgrimage in modern times.

Our earliest ancestors were nomads, roaming hunter-gatherers; perhaps it is simply in our nature. We've always been going on quests in search of meaning and our gods. "For in their hearts doth Nature stir them so, Then people long on pilgrimage to go," writes Chaucer in *The Canterbury Tales*. Another famous chronicler of the nomadic urge, writer Bruce Chatwin believed settled civilization was a mistake, and we are bipedal for a reason: "Man's real home is not a house, but the road, and that life itself is a journey to be walked on foot." In *The Songlines*, he describes how Australian Aborigines are called to go "walkabout," dropping everything to head to the outback and visit ancestors, tracing the holy ground of invisible pathways that meander all over Australia. Walking has far more than evolutionary benefits for humans—as worship, for example, and sacrifice.

Freedom of physical movement and freedom of thought and spirit go together, appealing whether it's a religious pilgrimage, or the "Free and Easy Wandering" espoused by Taoist philosopher Chuang-tzu around 300 BC. Also translated as "Going Rambling without a Destination," the aim is to bring people spontaneously into harmony with the natural world. The phrase also implies a going beyond, or wandering beyond, leaving behind the familiar— social roles, values, assumptions—to explore the unknown. Doing this spontaneously is meant to attune us to the natural unfolding of things, of which we are a part.

The primal act of walking connects us with our essential wildness, a wellspring of spiritual energy that's drying up in our technology-addicted, stressful, sedentary society. In his 1861 treatise, "Walking," Henry David Thoreau discusses "sauntering," derived from a word for pilgrims of the Middle Ages. "Children exclaimed, 'There goes a Sainte-Terrer,' a saunterer—a Holy-Lander," he writes. "Some, however, would derive the word from sans terre, without land or a home, which, therefore, in the good sense, will mean, having no particular home, but equally at home everywhere." The saunterer, he emphasizes, "is no more vagrant than the meandering river, which is all the while sedulously seeking the shortest course to the sea."

For sauntering humans, life is a journey, and we walk outer terrain that mirrors inner terrain. We move toward our higher selves, find community and feed the part of us that hungers for the sacred, however we define that. We humans have a foot in two worlds, and as pilgrims bring our embodied, physical selves to meet the other world, the spiritual realm.

Further, pilgrimage holds great appeal in our times of being between narratives—neither religion nor scientific rationalism nor neoliberalism are going to save us, so what now? Being a pilgrim is a simple way to show devotion, do penance, find healing or pursue a personal purpose—without doctrine. Existential questions have not gone away as traditional religion declines. They trouble us as much as ever, and many seek simpler spirituality, often at sites where the sacred existed in the past. In these otherworldly places out of time—islands, abbeys, holy wells—the material and spiritual come together.

Even for secular Westerners, sacred places retain their allure; though more than in medieval times, pilgrimage today emphasizes the shrine within. "Every pilgrimage to the desert is a pilgrimage to the self," observes Terry Tempest Williams. As with other types of retreat, pilgrimage is about personal agency *and* communion. "Pilgrimage to the place of the wise is to find escape from the flame of separateness," Rumi writes.

Recognizing that some things are simply better understood on foot at about three miles an hour, I redoubled my efforts to find myself a journey to embody. In an attempt to overcome my lingering ambivalence I asked myself what appealed, rather than what annoyed, about the walking pilgrimage. My mind leapt immediately to W.G. Sebald's *The Rings of Saturn*, subtitled "An English Pilgrimage" in its original German. The haunting, exquisite book is about a walk through East Anglia—and ultimately, through history and the ruins of civilization after the wars of the 20th century. Saturn is the planet that rules over melancholy, and the work is imbued with a feeling of loss, of living in the aftermath of catastrophe. This is pilgrimage as a deeper form of engagement to map the importance of a particular place, and shows that nothing truly disappears. In our age of displacement, Sebald's pilgrimage is particularly moving. "Any man may be called a pilgrim," wrote Dante Gabriel Rossetti in 1874, "who leaveth the place of his birth"—a definition that encompasses today's migrants, the greatest numbers the world has ever seen, even after the fractures of the Second World War. As well all of us are pilgrims, life to death.

The idea that there can be different cultural purposes for pilgrimage also fascinated me. In a documentary about *The Rings of Saturn*, called *Patience (After Sebald)*, British writer Robert Macfarlane posits a theory. "The British tradition is of walking as recovery and the American tradition is of walking as discovery," he says. The British Romantic tradition is "to strip away the accretions of civilization" while the American tradition, exemplified in the road movie, is "the sense that we travel to liberate ourselves, to discover new ways of being, to acquire methods of life that may become new habits, but don't begin as them."

Pilgrims themselves I did respect: the purposeful journey often appeals to people who resist the barriers and constraints of our consumerist age, who feel, as Robert Frost did, "Something there is that doesn't love a wall, That wants it down." In *Wanderlust*, Rebecca Solnit writes: "Walking focuses not on the boundary lines of ownership that break the land into pieces but on the paths that function as a kind of circulatory system connecting the whole organism. Walking is, in this way, the antithesis of owning." I admire also literary pilgrims such as Frost's friend, writer and poet Edward Thomas—the two were devoted walkers—who notes, "Much has been written of travel, far less of the road," and "The long, white roads . . . are a temptation. What quests they propose! They take us away to the thin air of the future or to the underworld of the past."

As I kept searching for my own walking pilgrimage, I discovered organizations worldwide that are renewing the tradition. Ancient paths in Scotland, England and Wales drew me most. The founders of the British Pilgrimage Trust (BPT), William Parsons and Guy Hayward, are among those leading the resurgence in the

United Kingdom. They have much of interest to say about "why pilgrimage?" Two passionate pilgrims, they are part of a grassroots boom that is seeing ancient routes revived and growing participation by people ranging from religiously devout to committedly atheistic. The BPT website reads: "Rediscover the old way of travelling on foot to holy places in Britain. An ancient tradition refreshed. Open to all (bring your own beliefs)."

Whether modern pilgrims' purposes are spiritual, recreational or other is immaterial, Parsons and Hayward say: "Our core goal is to advance British pilgrimage as a form of cultural heritage that promotes holistic well-being, for the public benefit." Parsons is a wandering minstrel and author who worked to revive wandering minstrelsy in Britain, but found pilgrimage more feasible. Hayward, who confesses to having a "terrible restlessness, physical and mental" all his life, needed release after completing his PhD on how singing forms community: "I was behind a laptop for many years and wanted to get out from [behind a] 13-inch screen and into the world." The BPT has a wide range of supporters, from regular people to the powerful—duchesses, politicians, equity managers, scientists, musicians, artists, literary lights, and reverends and vicars.

An infrastructure of footpath networks already exists in Britain, where the law, the "right to roam," assures passage for walkers, unlike in North America and on the Continent. The BPT is working to rejoin the pilgrimage dots: wells, springs, ancient trees, prehistoric sites, churches and chapels mark the way. What's missing in Britain and many other global centres is the presence of inexpensive accommodation for the walkers. The trust is working with the Church of England to open churches to pilgrims at night.

Once, pilgrimage was Britain's most popular expression of leisure and spirituality, for all classes. The British are inveterate walkers and enthusiastic pilgrims. "For most of our evolutionary history, we were travellers. This is the yoga of the West, about connecting with our spiritual traditions. It's our way to find higher truth, our lineage," Hayward says. Asked why he thinks pilgrimage is so popular, Parsons replies: "Nothing's really changed in terms of peoples' need to connect with themselves, the communities they pass through, with the land, with the spiritual world. Walking to a holy place is and always has been a brilliant way to do this."

The two say they arrived at a definition of pilgrimage, though with difficulty: an unbroken journey on foot to holy places. It's a simple thing most people can do, and it needs to be unbroken as it's about dedication to a destination. "On foot is also essential: it's slower, you see strawberries growing, or stop and talk, get to know the people of the land, find a herb to help your sore feet and learn ways that can help you connect more deeply to your self. You connect with your back and legs: physical things happen, emotional things happen, and it's a way of connecting with forgotten bits of your self," says Hayward.

As for holy, we all have a special place we go to when we need to feel better, Parsons says. Holy derives from the old English halig, meaning wholesome or healthy, though it is not religious specifically. In the 14th century haligdæg meant both "religious festival" and "day of recreation," until these senses diverged in the 16th century. Pilgrimage is more than just going for a walk. "It's a journey into the unknown," says Hayward. "It's a chance to connect to one's self and others and engage big questions, such as, Is there something greater than all of us?—existential questions that are the same whether you are religious or not, human questions."

Setting my quest for a walking pilgrimage aside, I went to visit family in Brazil for Christmas. It turned out I had a tough research call to make: attend an ayahuasca retreat, where you ingest a plant medicine used in Amazonia for centuries for healing and spiritual experiences; or walk as a pilgrim on the Passarela da Fé—the passage of faith—and visit the shrine of Aparecida, Brazil's patron saint. Call me a coward but I decided my hallucinogenic days are long past and opted for the holiest site in the world's most populous Catholic country. European pilgrim traditions are mainly Catholic, and I was curious to see how they transplanted in the Americas.

Brazil is studded with pilgrimage shrines, the most popular being the neo-Romanesque Basilica of Our Lady of Aparecida, Our Lady Who Appeared, the Black Madonna. Not only is this the world's largest shrine dedicated to Mary, the mother of God, it's the world's second biggest church, only slightly smaller than St. Peter's in Rome. Each year, about 12 million Brazilian and global pilgrims descend to venerate "the Black Virgin Mary." Some arrive on foot, but most arrive by car. Even in medieval times in Europe, a pilgrim would hop on a hay wagon if at all possible. A pilgrimage on foot is a transformative process, but so is coming into contact with a destination, such as a saint at a shrine.

On a rainy Sunday morning after New Year's, my sister-in-law Maira at the wheel, we set out from São Paulo for the 170-kilometre drive to Aparecida. A site of pilgrimage for more than 300 years, it's located on the Paraíba do Sul River at the spot where three fishermen had reputedly pulled a statue of the saint from the water. Porto Itaguaçu is marked by a cross and a viewing platform and gets its name from the Tupi-Guarani language: Itaguaçu means big rock, fertile valley or favoured land.

As we passed the Tropic of Capricorn sign the city's concrete began to give way to misty mountains and cows grazing in green fields dotted with red-earth ant mounds. The drive into the Paraíba Valley is pleasant, and we laughed about billboards along the way. One for its odd diction: it featured the photo of a popular country singer with the message "Imprudence causes accidents." The other advertised "Pastelão de Maluf"—Maluf, the ex-mayor and ex–state governor, in jail for corruption, was unlikely to be eating pastelão, which are jumbo-sized fast-food pies.

I read aloud from printouts I'd made from the shrine's elaborate website, available in Portuguese, Spanish and English. The story of the saint began in 1717, when Brazil was still a Portuguese colony. According to legend, when the plentiful river was empty of fish for 12 hours, all but three fishermen gave up and went home. One who stayed caught a headless statue of the Virgin Mary in his net. The next cast yielded the statue's head. Suddenly, the fish became wildly abundant. More miracles were soon attributed to the Virgin, including the freeing of a runaway slave, candles that lit by themselves and, my personal favourite, "the hunter attacked by an ounce." (The translator meant onça—a panther.) People started to venerate the statue, and a chapel was made in 1745. A larger baroque church was built between 1824 and 1888, the old basilica. Construction of the new basilica, which holds 45,000 people, began in 1955, and it became a Pope magnet: it was inaugurated by Pope John Paul in 1980, Pope Benedict came in 2007 and Pope Francis made it a priority to visit in 2013.

In less than two hours we arrived at the giant basilica city, which loomed on a scale sure to impress any pilgrim, part spaceship and part stadium. There was a small fair with old-fashioned rides, a cable car running overhead and a long footbridge. We circled to find parking, passing hotels—Hotel do Papa, Divino Pai Eterno and Sanctuário Palace—as well as tour buses, vendors selling T-shirts, keychains, tote bags. The town had sprung up around the site and relies heavily on tourism.

It was a slow day and we tried to imagine it busy, as when up to 215,000 people attend services to commemorate Aparecida on October 12, a Brazilian national holiday. The parking lot held 10,000 vehicles and was organized by the names of Jesus's Disciples. Somewhere there was a heliport and Cruzeiro Hill, where millions of devotees perform the Way of the Cross. The size of the parking lot told me most pilgrims no longer come only on foot. People have been walking here for 300 years, but only recently a formalized network, the Caminho da Fé, was established.

The Way of Faith, one of the newest and longest Catholic pilgrimage routes in the world, stretches 500 kilometres (310 miles) across southeastern Brazil, has various branches, and foot and bicycle traffic is increasing. In 2003 Almiro Grings, who twice walked the Camino de Santiago in Spain, set about establishing a network of hostels, hotels and homestays catering to pilgrims on the path to Aparecida. Of the 12 million pilgrims who visited in 2014, it's thought that more than 30,000 walked or cycled there along the Caminho da Fé, crossing the endless sugar cane and coffee plantations and making challenging climbs in the Mantiqueira Mountains.

One pilgrim, the aptly named Bob Walker, had walked the Camino de Santiago and found most people he met were not doing it for religious reasons. "But in Brazil it was different," he writes. "I saw macho Lycra-clad cyclists gather in a circle to say morning prayers. And a recently retired policeman from São Paulo told me he was making the pilgrimage to thank God he ended his career without getting shot." Walker, who walked 965 kilometres (600 miles) across Spain without issues, said the hard-packed earth track in Brazil took its toll. He did make it to Aparecida "despite the hills, blisters, and tarantula spiders."

"These same sights greeted Walker," I thought, strolling past the Pilgrim Support Centre with its 400 stores—religious souvenirs and trinkets, pharmacies, a food court with McDonald's. I didn't see the Sanctuary of the Apostles Barbecue and Beer I'd heard about, and somehow missed the aquarium too. The place is its own city, run by 2,000 workers, plus volunteers. People wandered around the perfectly landscaped and organized grounds, unusual for chaotic Brazil—parents with kids in strollers, children, teens, elderly people with canes, everyone with umbrellas. The impressive pink-hued main complex had a high clocktower and many domes.

As a sacred place, surrounded by green hills and mist, it looked suitably mysterious. We passed various chapels. At the sight of one my breath caught; hundreds of tall votive candles flared, reflecting light onto an intricate metal cross that hung from the high ceiling. Ten tons of melted wax, I read, are removed on the average busy weekend. We passed more shops, where you could buy souvenirs and ex-votos to adorn the shrine. Piled up in bins, these body parts made from wax represent what needs healing, or has been healed: hands, arms, feet, livers, left and right breasts, heads. We passed the Aparecida radio and TV stations and magazine offices.

Everything attested to the church's evangelizing success. When it comes to the commercialism of shrines, little has changed in centuries, since pilgrims first went to the Holy Land. Pilgrims have always been tourists too, carrying back souvenirs such as holy water and pieces of sacred ground—believed to hold magic that touches us when we touch them. I was impressed by the Sala das Promessas, the Hall of Promises, where people leave objects and ex-votos at a long counter to ask for the saint's help with hardships or give thanks.

Clerks stand at what looks like the coat check at a large museum and accept 25,000 objects a month. The hall, like an underground shopping mall, spoke of miraculous cures, with photos plastered over the ceilings and glass cases overflowing with offerings. The "work" case held a miniature taxi, a shoeshine kit, cameras and uniforms. Dolls represented babies; piles of gold rings, crosses, antique watches and fine china expressed thanks for marriages and other miracles. I noticed in passing Ayrton Senna's helmet and gloves, Julio Iglesias's outfits and guitars and a plaque with Canada and the CN Tower giving thanks for "one more dream realized" in Toronto in 2015.

Back upstairs in the new basilica we slid into a back pew for Mass, as the huge church was nearly full. Soaring ceilings, gold and works of art—striking blue stained-glass windows, and mosaics of Brazilian scenes: a turtle, armadillo, snake, colourful birds and butterflies, flowering yellow and pink trees, the sea and a child in utero above the door. The basilica was built with donations from the faithful and fitted out with gold, Italian mosaics and fabulous works by sacred artist Cláudio Pastro.

We listened awhile and then slipped out to join other pilgrims and walk the Passarela da Fé. I was bemused to find that the passarela was just a long footbridge that connected the new and old basilicas, the latter located in a souvenir town. Ten minutes later we'd arrived at the old Basilica, with its ornate marble altar and pretty tile floor.

Aparecida, it was now obvious, was all about the pilgrimage to the shrine, not about walking the path, as I'd expected. We lined up to see the statue of Nossa Senhora. When my turn came I looked up at the Virgin's image. She was just over a foot tall, a Black Madonna, wearing a blue cape and crown, her hands in prayer. I stopped a long moment, but I felt no thrill of contact, only a bit let down, as I had in Whithorn.

On the walk back I stopped in one of the tiny shops to buy a saint souvenir from a sweet-faced, elderly vendor who sat surrounded by saint merch and statues of all sizes. I chose one, and asked her about Nossa Senhora. "God is important, clearly. But *She* is *everything* to me," the vendor said with feeling, wrapping my saint in paper. "Each thing I've asked for I received, because of her. She helps people to move ahead." It's necessary to give thanks, she told me, not just ask for things all the time. Looking intently into my eyes she made me promise that I'd go visit the saint's shrine in the new basilica too.

I promised, and on my way back there, I had this strange feeling, as though I was swimming in the waters of an alternative reality, one where believers drew power from Aparecida. Lining up again, this time for the new shrine, I shuffled forward with the others, admiring the main basilica's mosaics of biblical women. The saint was tiny in her golden shrine, and this time she wore a gold crown and a black cape with gold trim. Again, I felt no connection.

What struck me most was that for a Marian shrine, there was so little sacred feminine presence. Yet this Black Madonna clearly meant so much to people here, especially to the working poor and women. She's revered in Brazil and has another syncretized face as the goddess of love and maternity in an Afro-Brazilian religion. Aparecida is known for her power to bridge divisions of race, class, region and religion, and bring people together.

As I stood there it hit me—the power of pilgrimage begins with human ideas. There's little more potent than imagination, which precedes our actions. We go on pilgrimage to a place that represents certain qualities that inspire us, holding the energy of the deity or person we relate to. Mary, anthropologist Edith Turner wrote, is "the most sought-after pilgrimage goal in all Christendom, including God."

I gave up my place in front of the shrine, thinking about the throngs of pilgrims who have come here over the centuries, attracted to the ideals embodied by the Madonna. A sudden thought broke in—we have no idea who is driving this bus, so what's wrong with drawing strength from a benevolent figure? I felt less judgy and glad I had bought a statue of the saint from the sweet vendor. What we believe, what's sacred to us, whether it's bound to traditional religion or not, I realized, is what makes pilgrimage possible.

Back home, I was happy to have gained insight in Aparecida into the power of the "destination pilgrimage" to a shrine. As with the walking variety, the origins of this second main type of pilgrimage predate antiquity. Humans have always been drawn to visit sacred sites as an expression of spirit, as evidenced by Stonehenge (3000 BC)—some archeologists believe it to be a prehistoric Lourdes, a place of healing—and by Indigenous pictographs across the Americas. Ancient Greek pilgrims travelled from near and far to consult the Oracle of Delphi, built around a sacred spring in 1400 BC. Humans thought the border between this world and the next was thinner there so they could communicate with the gods. For the Celtic Christians, a thin place is where heaven and earth are barely separate, a portal where we can draw near and catch a glimpse of the divine. This idea is like that of India's holy tirtha, which in Sanskrit means "crossing place" and refers in particular to pilgrimage sites, though it can be any holy place, text or person. There's the axis mundi of the shaman, the place that is holy above all. Even for modern nonbelievers, these thresholds, doorways and bridges provide a place where we can be jolted out of everyday perceptions and habitual ways of seeing the world and be transformed.

As for my elusive walking pilgrimage, I decided on a new tack: find something closer to home. I was gratified to learn that Canada has many varieties of pilgrim experience. The Catholic shrines of Quebec, founded by French settlers, are our most popular pilgrim sites. More promising for me, I also found new-style journeys that harness the age-old practice of walking for education and social change.

On the traditional pilgrim circuit, more than a million faithful each year visit the national shrine at the church of Ste-Anne-de-Beaupré, about 20 minutes' drive northeast of Quebec City. French pioneers and missionaries brought over a statue of the mother of the Virgin Mary, Anne, the patron saint of sailors, and built a wooden church in her honour on the shores of the St. Lawrence, where they'd established a community. The first shrine was constructed in 1658. When a worker laid the first three foundation stones, his terrible back pain was miraculously cured. Word spread about this and other miracles. Even those who couldn't come in person, such as Anne of Austria, mother of Louis XIV of France, patronized the shrine from abroad. "There, the paralytics walk, the blind can see, and the sick are healed of every kind of illness," an Ursuline nun named Marie de l'Incarnation wrote in 1665.

Now it's become a healing place of Catholic pilgrimage for French Canadians and Indigenous people alike, especially in July, when believers come to the stone basilica to venerate St. Anne, often leaving behind abandoned wheelchairs, walking sticks and crutches. In *The Art of Pilgrimage*, Phil Cousineau writes about his mother's 1946 pilgrimage to Ste-Anne-de-Beaupré, when she was 16. She accompanied her sister and brother-in-law from Detroit to Quebec and at the shrine saw many lame and crippled pilgrims walking and prostrating themselves up a road and the basilica steps. "It was the place to go if you were desperate," she told him, "where Americans and Canadians came for hope and miracles."

Long before Catholic pilgrimages arrived in the Americas, Indigenous people journeyed to their sacred sites, which were often later co-opted or suppressed by colonizers. Given history, and potential turkey-and-genocide associations with the word pilgrim, as in the early settlers in New England, I hesitate to call Indigenous sacred journeys pilgrimages—though both journeys share universal aspects. Edith Turner writes about "substitution shrines, that is, pilgrimage shrines located on ancient Native American sites," which often retain syncretic features from pre-Christian devotions.

This is the case at a special place in north-central Alberta, a small lake believed to have healing powers, where for centuries the region's mostly nomadic Indigenous peoples assembled. Each summer they would come before the buffalo hunt, or gather for fishing, trade and ceremony. The Alexis Nakota Sioux Nation called the lake Wakamne, Holy Lake, while the area's Cree people called it Manito Sahkahigan, Lake of the Spirit. In July 1889 Catholic missionaries founded the mission of St. Anne, named after the grandmother of Jesus Christ—a conversion tactic, as honouring grandmothers is a strong tradition in First Nations and Métis cultures.

As elsewhere, the Christian missionaries grafted their beliefs onto an existing sacred place, renaming the waters Lac Ste-Anne, and marking the beginning of the complex relationship of Indigenous Nations, including the Métis Nation, with Catholicism in the surrounding territory. Each July for 132 years Indigenous people from many Indigenous Peoples across Canada and the northwestern United States have made their way to the lake, often in search of healing and spiritual renewal.

They arrive every third week in July, when the weather is best, and the journey is part of the tradition. Some walk barefoot. Members of the Driftpile First Nation often arrive in a horse-drawn wagon caravan, spending about 11 days on the road. The six-day pilgrimage culminates on July 26, the saint's day, and as many as 50,000 people—few non-Indigenous, though it is open to all—come to pray and bathe in the lake.

Given colonization and the harms that followed, I wonder whether there are troubled waters at Ste-Anne. Is there resentment, a sense that Indigenous spiritual traditions and cultures were undermined on this sacred spot, where ceremonies once took place, and people gathered to trade medicinal roots and herbs? In 1995's *Healing Waters: The Pilgrimage to Lac Ste. Anne*, photojournalist Steve Simon found harmony—though perhaps dissenters stay away, their opinions unrecorded. "The modern pilgrimage is an event in which Native spiritual traditions of many nations coexist within the Catholic faith," Simon writes. Some people go for spiritual tradition and to connect to the past, he adds, and others go because of religious beliefs. Still others combine Catholicism with their traditional spirituality and practices.

The book features striking photos of the gathering—people praying, the elderly wading into the shallow water for healing, a beautiful candlelight procession by the shore—as well as many stories. "The cross and the pipe can come together," says Johnsen Sewepegaham, who was then Little Red River Cree Nation Chief. Others in the book echo his idea, that there is only one God for everyone, and all that matters is that you pray. "I am not praying to a different God, even though other people will say, 'Well, that is a White man's God.' Well, to me, there is no such thing as a White man's God," he clarifies. For First Nations people, historian Dr. Olive Dickason is quoted as saying, various systems, such as traditional beliefs in the Creator and Catholicism, can exist side by side. It may be heresy for the church, but the old spirits endure. "We accept everyone's way," Eva Janvier of the Janvier Reserve, part of the Chipewyan Prairie First Nation in Alberta, says. "But by no means am I here because I am a Catholic. I am here because of my own beliefs in the Earth . . ."

There are signs that the Catholic Church is being converted: Mass is now performed in many languages, including Dene and Cree, and Indigenous traditional practices, such as drumming and dancing, once banned, have been added to the official schedule. Ownership of the pilgrimage site was transferred to a nonprofit organization in 2003, when it shifted to Indigenous control. There's representation from First Nations in Alberta, Saskatchewan and the Northwest Territories and the Métis Nation, as well as the

Oblates and the Archdiocese of Edmonton. In 2004, Lac Ste-Anne was designated a national historic site. Many non-Catholics attend to connect to Indigenous spiritual traditions, or simply to meet up with friends, but at the same time, the pilgrimage is the largest annual Catholic gathering in Western Canada.

Intuitively, all people understand that places have power. This has been recognized even if the places are not obviously marked— or when they have been erased or overlaid. Whether the "dreaming tracks" in Australia or "destinations" such as ancient pictographs and petroglyphs in the Americas, Indigenous sacred places and paths embedded in landscapes are often linked to helping spirits. Early people had waymarkers for their journeys on foot—drawings on the bark of trees, inukshuk. And places of power, as with Christian destination pilgrimages, are honoured in First Nations, Métis and Inuit beliefs.

In Manitoba there is a spiritual place known as the Narrows of Lake Manitoba, writes Robert Houle, a Saulteaux First Nations artist, curator, critic and educator in his essay, "Where the Gods Are Present," published in *The Good Lands: Canada Through the Eyes of Artists*. He says it's "where the water beating against the resonant limestone cliff and pounding along the pebbled shore creates the sound . . . believed to be the voice of Manitou." For the Saulteaux, "It was and still is a sacred place, a power place," and they continue to live nearby and offer tobacco. "Many travel to it seeking renewal, as a Muslim will travel to Mecca. To the Saulteaux, the Narrows are known as the Manitowaban, meaning the 'divine straits.'"

Myself, I have no single obvious place of connection, a feeling likely shared by many who change countries as children. Perhaps this explains why modern, revisionist pilgrimages—especially those that remap obscured histories and paths—attract me the most. Religious pilgrimage was adapted to be political, for change instead of miracles, for the first time in 1953 writes Rebecca Solnit in *Wanderlust*, when an American woman known only as the Peace Pilgrim set out walking, giving up home and possessions, "to remain a wanderer until mankind had learned the way of peace." Using pilgrimage as a way to draw attention to issues is frequently a female-led practice: witness the late Water Walker Grandmother Josephine Mandamin, an Anishinaabe Elder who walked around all five of the Great Lakes to raise awareness about the need to protect water, and the Border Angels, women who walk into the Sonoran desert to leave gallon jugs of water for migrants in the lands between Mexico and the United States.

I'm excited when I discover a walking pilgrimage from the Old City of Montreal to the Mohawk territory of Kahnawà:ke—three days and 36 kilometres. It's the practicum for an annual pilgrimage course called Pilgrim Bodies, Sacred Journeys, offered at Concordia University in Montreal. Students embark on a meditative journey on foot that "connects them with Indigenous culture, with Canada's history of colonization and marginalization of Indigenous people, with their own life histories and with each other." Kahnawà:ke began as a Catholic mission, and Saint Kateri (pronounced "Gateri") Tekakwitha, the first Indigenous woman to be sainted, has her shrine there.

"Sometimes the path to reconciliation is a path," note the university lecturers who designed the pilgrimage course, Matthew Anderson and Sara Terreault. "Because of its narrative and spatial nature, journey (pilgrimage) is a useful and natural way to re-map, re-member, and reinscribe relationships with oneself, one's neighbours and one's physical and cultural environment," writes Anderson. The course and walk, offered through the Department of Theological Studies since 2014, is also a teaching tool.

The idea was sparked at a conference in the United Kingdom, when the two scholars noticed that American and Canadian academics were presenting on European walks. "Why were we not presenting on the pilgrimage routes from where we live?" Andersen wondered. "This question soon led Sara, who is Catholic, and me, as a Lutheran pastor, to grapple with relations between Canada and the First Nations."

Indigenous spiritual journey is distinguished by attention to specific lands and seeking blessing before entering land, from the Elders, the ancestors and the land itself, says Anderson—though there is no tradition of European-like pilgrimage per se, and in fact, as noted, many reject the word. A year after their first class walk, Canada's Truth and Reconciliation Commission published its report, and among its conclusions were that churches and universities should do much more to seek reconciliation with First Nations. Pilgrimage is one way for non-Indigenous people to step toward this.

I contacted Sara Terreault about joining the journey to Kahnawà:ke and was disappointed to learn that for the first time, they wouldn't walk that summer. Her class undertook personal journeys instead, and Terreault, a devoted pilgrim who has travelled with her students to the Camino in Spain, across Ireland, as well as to the Kahnawà:ke Mohawk reservation, agreed to tell me more over supper. How does modern pilgrimage work? I asked. "When you walk long distances day after day, things happen. Your body changes physiologically. Psychologically, the walk slows you down. When you walk a pilgrimage, the journey becomes part of the point, and it provokes existential questions and reflection." Or as her friend once put it, Terreault adds, "Pilgrimage is really an interior journey but it comes in through the feet."

There's no one definition of pilgrimage, Terrault explains, "it's a journey of meaning, or an intentional journey." She asks her students to undertake a personal walk that's meaningful to them, demanding enough to take them beyond their comfort zone. They are to keep journals and afterwards revisit their earlier understandings of pilgrimage based on their own experiences. "The bottom line is pilgrimage is a practice," Terrault emphasizes.

Finally, my fixed idea of pilgrimage shifted. I don't know why I had been stuck in thinking it had steps, was one size fits all, with set narratives and purposes, which made me resistant. I realized it encompasses much more, with key elements such as intentionality, mobility and the alchemy of body and place that come together in fluid ways. One thought led to another, and this was how I finally found myself, newly receptive and walking my own pilgrimage on the Hastings Heritage Trail.

It's day two, walking pilgrimage, and I've just been dropped off back at the Hybla crossroads. It's a relief to throw my imaginary pilgrim's cloak on once more and walk. At breakfast, talk of community conflicts had intruded on my contemplative mood. A pilgrimage is meant to be a transition from the ordinary to the extraordinary, where, away from habits and outside your usual place in the world, you inhabit the liminal space between setting off and arriving, and find something rare—freedom, perhaps, or new perspective, challenge and self-reliance, simplicity, not knowing, surrender, the feeling of approaching something larger, mysterious.

As I enter the green forest's shade I'm thinking of the words of Japanese novelist Natsume Sōseki in *The Three-Cornered World*. The protagonist, an artist on a pilgrimage to the mountains, desires an experience that "abandons the commonplace and lifts me, at least for a short time, above the dust and grime of the workaday world." The book obsessed Glenn Gould—he thought it was the greatest novel of the 20th century, and a copy was found along with the Bible by his deathbed. He described it as being about "meditation versus action, detachment versus duty, Western versus Eastern value systems." A more recent translator changed the title to *Kusamakura*, meaning grass pillow—a traditional literary term in Japan for a journey, a digressive wander rather than a predestined path.

That the path itself can be the destination seems revelatory. Why had I never considered this as a possibility for my own walking pilgrimage? I'd known that for 17th-century poet Matsuo Bashō, the path was the goal, a metaphor for the well-lived life. Off I go down the trail, enjoying this idea, typical of Eastern pilgrimages, which seem to me the best kind. In non-Western cultures, "the ideas of footfall as knowledge and walking as a mode of thinking are widespread, often operating in particular as a metaphor for recollection—history as a region one walks back into," writes Robert Macfarlane in *The Old Ways*. This is also a Scottish way: "the Scots stravaig," he notes, "means to ramble without set goals or destination." No wonder this pilgrim's way calls to me.

While pilgrimage is the universal quest for the self, the path changes in various eras and cultures. The linear paths to Rome, or Mecca, can give way to spiral paths up mountains; or encircling them, as with Mount Kailash in Tibet, where it's considered a sin to set foot on the holy mountain; or also labyrinths, such as the one in Chartres in France. I care little about the clocking of miles or arriving at a particular destination. Maybe one day I'll do an aimless journey myself, I decide, a mashup of the early Celtic and Eastern wandering monks, Sōseki's artist and Bashō. "To wander is the Taoist code word for becoming ecstatic, writes a scholar, but arriving was sometimes regarded with ambiguity," Rebecca Solnit notes in *Wanderlust*.

The sun is hot so I stop to slather on sunscreen, which makes dust stick to my face and arms. I feel dirty, yet strong, and self-reliant. Every conceivable place along the trail there is to rest, every clearing or lake, sports a big No Trespassing sign. Last night I read an old copy of *A Sand County Almanac* by Aldo Leopold, one of the leading thinkers of the conservation movement. He talks of the "trophy recreationist" who to enjoy "must possess, invade, appropriate." Leopold riffs on ideas that apply not just to wilderness, but to our simplistic attitudes about everything on the yin spectrum—emptiness, absence, solitude, silence. "Hence the wilderness that he cannot see has no value to him. Hence the universal assumption that an unused hinterland is rending no service to society . . . to those devoid of imagination, a blank place on a map is a useless waste; to others the most valuable part."

What better way to bring receptivity "into the still unlovely human mind," as he terms it, than walking in the world? Mapping the trail with my feet I repeat a mantra, "arrive home," and feel each step on the earth. I notice each footfall—swing, heel down, forefoot down, push off—and feel the weight transfer up my body. A pilgrim path seems perfect for moving away from wherever we're seized up: physically at a desk, or in an ill-fitting job, or in a constricted family life. When life chafes, or we are disrespected and chained, it's an appropriate response to hit the road, to match our steps to our heartbeat, align the self and the soul's desires as we walk.

I begin to kick a rock along the trail, feeling how different life is when you walk through it with real attention. The land, the sky, the trees, me moving through the scene—I feel like part of a bigger picture. Kilometre by kilometre, however, my erstwhile pilgrim's paradise grows infernal. I catch myself thinking how much nicer it would be to ride the old steam train, just gazing out the window. I pull the big iron railway nails, nuts and bolts from my pack and throw them back on the ground—too heavy. The downhill part of the trail ends and I cross a sunny road, where I'm delighted to find an old apple tree, more evidence of the past.

The apples are the red-striped ones I'd found yesterday. A search I did last night on my phone makes me think they're St. Lawrence apples, an heirloom variety from Montreal. I pick a few and notice they taste sweeter—perhaps because I'm further south? I munch down three apples in a row as I limp along the path.

For ages I keep on going, expecting to reach the highway, the point at which I'll have walked the same distance as yesterday, and where the unmapped part of my journey begins. My feet up to my sacroiliac joints hurt on both sides now, and my steps are minuscule. I keep going, with no more exultations or even thoughts, just one foot after another. I pass a weird nightmare tableau with six gory, life-sized figures, one chained by the neck to a tree, another with a chainsaw, and I barely look up. By the time I reach the hard-earned highway I've developed a sudden interest in all I'd scoffed at before, clocking miles and arriving at my destination. It's 11:30 in the morning so I've been walking four hours. I'm guessing I have seven kilometres, or two hours, to go.

I use much-needed energy to sprint across the highway and avoid speeding vehicles. The flat trail begins to wend behind businesses and houses and then parallel to the highway in the unpleasant midday heat. It's then I enter the piney Sahara: hot, dry, dusty, endless sand. This stretch is the worst yet. I put one foot doggedly in front of the other, stupefied by boredom, hating the soft sand, hating it all utterly, and walking.

Time passes and I become fixated on the York River, where I plan to stop to eat. But it never appears. Periodically I throw myself on the ground in the shade of a tree. I begin to walk on my heels and the sides of feet to avoid my pounded metatarsals, and to alleviate the pain in my hips and back. My hikers weren't broken in after all. I'd probably make more progress crawling on all fours.

The Camino, which I'd equated with boilerplate lack of imagination, begins to make sense: no bears, no need to wear a lurid orange jacket because of hunters or jump out of the way of racing ATVs, many handy refugios to sleep in, bathrooms, gorgeous historical places, kindred spirits, cafés and bars so you can stop to eat and drink and don't have to carry everything on your back. I'm sustained a long while by a fantasy about drinking cava on a patio with new friends and reciting Hafiz: "I fill my glass for you, dear pilgrim/Beneath the luminous leaking barrel."

Flying to Spain now seems ideal: there's an infrastructure, a well-travelled path, which allows you to concentrate on your inner pilgrimage. And there's beauty in the ritual of walking in the centuries-old footsteps of others, something I won't experience, at least not in the same way, on my personal pilgrimage. I'd been wrong about another thing too. I thought I knew all about blisters, sunburn and the other challenges on the path, based on copious readings. It's now painfully clear I knew them only as intellectual concepts, not as the embodied, unmediated experience of sore, hungry, tired, hot, exposed. As life can't be previewed, neither can pilgrimage. And as with all retreats, a pilgrimage is never the way you imagine—because you can't imagine, you have step into uncertainty and give yourself over to the experience.

I do my best to surrender to the long, hellish stretch as part of the transformative experience of walking the path. There's nothing else I can do. Calling a cab does occur to me, but I don't know where I am, only lost in the piney Sahara. I think of those Middle Ages pilgrims, some barefoot. Sore feet and sunburn are nothing compared to old-school forms of penitence, such as self-flagellation, a medieval disciplinary or devotional practice that involved lashing yourself with a whip. Or what about pilgrims in Tibet's high mountains, doing hundreds of miles of prostrations—kneel, lie face down hands pressing the earth, get up, step to your finger marks and repeat, all the while praying. We humans will suffer to approach our places of sacred power.

On a pilgrimage, effort and asceticism can be a means of spiritual development.

I'm no renunciator, so this is little consolation as my stagger through the sands continues to take far, far longer than expected. I have no idea whether the distance is further than I'd guessed, or my pace is to blame. Eventually when I glimpse the river I feel startled. I'm not approaching my lunch stop, I realize, but my destination.

Bancroft. Thank God!

The same sentiment must escape the lips of all pilgrims, religious and secular alike. I limp to a picnic table, pull off my pack and lie down flat, eyes closed. Once I've recovered a little I take out my chickpea stew and water and eat and drink with relish. I'm shocked to see it's just 1:30 p.m.: the past two hours felt like days. The river's smooth surface reflects the green, red and gold of the trees. Beside the path, near the old train station, three tall white pines have survived generations of loggers. A miracle!

I hobble over, sit on the ground with my back against one massive trunk and pull out my cloth bag. At the foot of the big tree I give thanks for my pilgrim journey. I dig a small hole in the earth and tuck in a black feather from my deceased pet chicken. I sprinkle in the rest of the sacred ash and lay a sprig of pine needles over top. I'm happy to end my pilgrimage in this rugged place of forest and rock. And I'm grateful to have tasted the power and possibilities of the walking pilgrimage, which I recognize now is a stellar way to work through our deeper questions as humans. For someone with such low expectations, and on a short, two-day pilgrimage, the wealth of fresh insight I've received amazes me. Insight through experience—pilgrimage lets you touch the things you know in your bones.

I see how pilgrimage is a practice, the symbolic acting out of an inner journey. The path really is the way. This is perhaps why it's so popular a method for retreat: we just step away from the everyday and learn what we need to learn by going where we need to go. On pilgrimage, the hunger for ritual and personal spiritual experience is met in a world that gives little space for either.

My "failed" walking pilgrimages, I see now, weren't a curse but a pilgrimage in themselves, widening my conception of pilgrimage until I hit upon the right path to echo my inner purposes. I walked to connect with here. On one of my perennial immigrant's questions, Who is better off, those who stay, or those who go?, I feel more certain that for me, the answer is those who go. While I love Scotland, this place feels most like home, where I've lived most of my life, where my beloveds are buried and scattered, as I will likely be. On some level I feel less like a displaced interloper—and more as though we all belong on Earth, our home.

I've emerged from my journey with new questions, such as how to "belong" in contested lands. We're all here. If what we *feel* is what's most important—for me, steadfast love and gratitude for the living world—is that a hopeful common ground? Respectful relationships between people and the land, which shapes us all, is a value central to traditional Algonquin ways . . .

Just as I arrive at this thought I glimpse a movement out of the corner of my eye. Ripe apples are dropping from three old trees beside the trail and rolling downhill, the image of abundance. I limp over and pick up a greeny-yellow apple with red stripes, just like the others. At my journey's end the fruit tastes sweeter than ever. If these are St. Lawrences, how did they get here from Montreal? I imagine long-dead travellers picking fruit from trees to eat on their journey and hurling the cores from the train windows miles away. Maybe I too planted an inadvertent tree along the trail? I rummage in my pocket for apple seeds I'd tucked in there, back in Maynooth at the outset of my pilgrimage, and bury them in the ground just south of the wizened old trees.

Fatigue and my aching body mean I'm ecstatic to have reached my journey's end. And yet I sense that tomorrow, my awakened inner pilgrim will have a longing, to walk south along the ghost railway, apples all the way down . . .

The
New
Deities:

Nature and Culture

OF FOREST CABINS, NATIONAL PARKS AND
CREATIVE SANCTUARIES

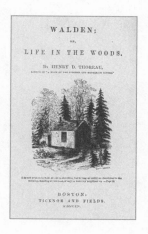

I Will Go to
the Wild Woods

In Wildness is the preservation of the world.

—Henry David Thoreau

One frigid midwinter afternoon I look onto the frozen lake, early for a performance of the Kingston symphony. Unseasonable cold, I worry. Climate change. A huge bird glides past the window. Slow motion, long neck outstretched, black bill, wings extended, body a downy white, with a light tracery of rusty-brown. I've never seen a trumpeter swan before. It's like a mythical creature, dreamed to life by a Cape Dorset artist.

Inside the concert hall, beautiful music swirls, yet my attention stays with the thrill of the swan. Why had this fleeting moment felt so charged? Something resonated, a reminder I was part of the wild world, an animal too. In our times, when humans are in active retreat from embodied life, perhaps this is what the swan offers us—a rare and precious encounter with what is real?

Trumpeter swans were nearly extinct. With conservation efforts they recovered. We think we protected them, but they protect us too. They save us from the impoverishment of a world without trumpeter swans, are a wild reminder of the winged, given world.

On Independence Day in 1845, a young radical philosopher retreated to a one-room pine cabin in the woods near Concord, Massachusetts. At 28 years of age, he was asserting his own independence, stepping back for a time from a society he found offensive and unethical—in its subjugation of enslaved people and Indigenous peoples, and its degradation of the natural world.

"I went to the woods because I wished to live deliberately, to front only the essential facts of life, and see if I could not learn what it had to teach, and not, when I came to die, discover that I had not lived," wrote Henry David Thoreau in *Walden*, the chronicle of his experiment. "I wanted to live deep and suck out all the marrow of life."

Thoreau, a principled rebel, was in pursuit of truth. "Be it life or death, we crave only reality." By the pond and in the forest at Walden, Thoreau came to believe that the path to understanding was to know the natural world we are a part of. "We need the tonic of wildness . . . We can never have enough of nature. We must be refreshed by the sight of inexhaustible vigour, vast and Titanic features." Here Thoreau picks up an eternal thread in the history of retreat: the human desire to connect with what's beyond us, in this case, nature's elemental power, so utterly past our comprehension and control. "We need to witness our own limits transgressed, and some life pasturing freely where we never wander."

Thoreau's writings about his time in the woods—for two years and two months and two days—illuminate the role of nature retreats in our lives even today. *Walden* has been looked at in many ways: as a work of art, as a societal critique, as a manual for a simple life, and as a lyrical love letter to nature. As biographer Laura Dassow Walls writes in *Henry David Thoreau: A Life*, "Thoreau has never been captured between covers; he was too quixotic, mischievous, many-sided." To me, *Walden* is a brilliant account of a consequential nature retreat by an unconventional thinker who continues to inspire us.

Far from being an escape, Thoreau's time apart was a deep exploration of how to live with integrity and how to wake up. "We must learn to reawaken and keep ourselves awake. . . . I know of no more encouraging fact than the unquestionable ability of man to elevate his life by a conscious endeavor." Cultivating oneself, he believed, is what leads to reform in society. "The millions are awake enough for physical labor; but only one in a million is awake enough for effective intellectual exertion, only one in a hundred million to a poetic or divine life. To be awake is to be alive."

Walden was published in 1854, seven years after Thoreau left the woods. It's the story of his own awakening while living in a small forest cabin of white pine he built with his own hands, with the natural world as his teacher. The pioneering naturalist used his five senses and recorded personal responses in communion with the divine, realizing that he was a part, not the centre, of creation. Watching bugs hiding on the forest floor he observed, "I am reminded of the greater Benefactor and Intelligence that stands over me the human insect."

Thoreau's profound gift to us, and his main influence on the history of retreat, is that he inspired us to appreciate the natural world. Giving flora and fauna our reverent attention, he believed, was the basis for loving and protecting it, and for recognizing it as sacred. It's hard to overstate how revolutionary an idea this was: while around him settlers were busy subjugating the natural world, Thoreau was thinking deeply and expressing relational beliefs, ones that sound contemporary.

His work endures as a persuasive and prescient voice for the preservation of wild places. "I think that the genius of Henry David Thoreau is he saw the world whole, even holy," author Terry Tempest Williams said in a radio interview. Though there was no word for ecology in Thoreau's time, *Walden* expresses the understanding that nature is everywhere and not just in "pristine" places. And that humans are part of the natural world, in relationship with it, and not its overlords.

While a retreat can be an act of refusal, it is also a place. Thoreau's mark is obvious here as well. At Walden Woods, the philosophical became the physical: the small cabin has become our proto-nature retreat, the Western version of the ancient Chinese hermit's hut. While there's no evidence Thoreau was familiar with poet Lao-Tzu—though he certainly read many Asian holy books on his mentor Ralph Waldo Emerson's urging—Thoreau's thoughts, about contemplation for example, echo those of this early antecedent.

By Thoreau's time a radical shift in ideas about nature was gaining speed. Wilderness had been for much of history a terrifying and bewildering place, considered "deserted," "savage," "desolate," or "barren," notes environmental historian William Cronon. It was "the antithesis of all that was orderly and good—it had been the darkness, one might say, on the far side of the garden wall— and yet now it was frequently likened to Eden itself." This shift began with the Europeans whom Thoreau is alchemically related to: the metaphysical writers of the 17th century—Donne, Hebert, Marvell and Browne—visionary German naturalist Alexander von Humboldt, and the Romantics of the 19th century—philosopher Kant, and poets Wordsworth, Byron, Shelley and Coleridge, who wrote of "the one life within us and abroad." While some scholars argue the Romantics were more interested in their own minds and pretty landscapes than the objective stuff of nature and the living planet, modern environmental consciousness in the West begins with them. They conveyed a sense of the unity of living things, and they idealized nature, made it sacred. They believed that the best place to glimpse God was in sublime landscapes—mountaintops, rivers, forests, waterfalls, watching the sunset—places where humans experience awe and fear. They encouraged people to retreat to nature.

This was the start of the modern era, when retreat became more relatable, more like our retreats of today. The Romantic withdrawal from human society to commune with nature led us away from the religious retreats of the past, from penance toward joy. Seeking a taste of eternity in the given world, the Romantics believed, educated us in higher spiritual realities, and the imagination could access higher truths than pure reason. The Romantics' retreats were foundational to their new ideas about individualism and political freedom, and as part of this, a startling idea took root: that retreats were not just for the special few, the religious and scholars, but were an essential part of a fulfilled life for all humans.

As well, these nonconformists rejected any mediation of the search for truth by the church, the state or the academy—by retreating, they were seeking beyond received wisdom. The quest was picked up by the Transcendentalists, who drew a line separating religion from spirituality. For his part, Thoreau rejected organized religion, writing, "I suppose that what in other men is religion is in me love of nature." His eclectic spirituality, and personal, experiential sojourn in nature feel modern. "I do not prefer one religion or philosophy to another. I have no sympathy with the bigotry and ignorance which make transient and partial and puerile distinctions between one man's faith or form of faith & another's . . . To the philosopher all sects, all nations, are alike. I like Brahma, Hari, Buddha, the Great Spirit, as well as God."

Thoreau's ideas reflect the philosophy of the American Transcendentalists, which drew on elements of Eastern thought, emphasizing that nature, humanity and God are unified. Poet and essayist Ralph Waldo Emerson founded the Transcendental Club in 1836. Group member Margaret Fuller, a journalist and one of America's first feminists, wrote, "Disgusted with the vulgarity of a commercial aristocracy, they become radicals; disgusted with the materialistic workings of rational religion, they become mystics." When Emerson gave a lecture to Harvard seniors, among them was Thoreau, who became a major contributor to the movement.

Thoreau's background was humble—his father was a not-very-successful pencil maker—but his parents economized to send their intelligent son to private schools, including Harvard. Emerson, his neighbour and mentor, owned Walden, and allowed Thoreau to build his cabin by the pond. By the 1850s the new philosophy, a reaction against the rationalism of the Unitarian Church, had a strong following in Massachusetts, and it influenced intellectuals and writers for generations to come.

The Transcendentalists saw God as both transcendent—or beyond the limits of human experience—and immanent, in every blade of grass and every living thing. This was a fascinating departure for 1830s Puritanical New England. The Hindu and Transcendentalist belief that God resides in each individual leads to the idea that each person can experience the divine within. And, consequentially, they believed one of the best ways to find this unity was to observe nature, in a direct, intuitive way—an idea that encouraged people to retreat.

Thoreau's retreat to live in the natural world at Walden Pond allowed him to attain the Transcendentalist goal, to experience God within. Over and over he writes about this unity of nature, humans and the divine: "I was suddenly sensible of such sweet and beneficent society in Nature, in the very pattering of the drops, and in every sound and sight around my house, an infinite and unaccountable friendliness all at once like an atmosphere sustaining me." Elsewhere he observes, "I was so distinctly made aware of the presence of something *kindred* to me, even in scenes which we are accustomed to call wild."

In "The Bean Field" chapter, Thoreau describes feeling at one with all living things as he works the soil, of fusing with the nonhuman world: "It was no longer the beans that I hoed, or that I hoed beans." Under the influence of Thoreau, Yeats, often called the last Romantic poet, writes of "nine bean rows" in his most famous poem, "The Lake Isle of Innisfree." Predictably, critiques of the poem call it escapist—which, just as predictably, infuriates me, given it's one of the most enduring and beautiful evocations ever written of the pleasures and powers of retreat. "When I was a young lad in the town of Sligo I read Thoreau's essays and wanted to live in a hut on an island in Lough Gill called Innisfree, which means 'Heather Island,'" Yeats explained once, speaking of the poem before a reading.

Thoreau shares insights, practical and philosophical, about his seven miles of beans. He details his earnings from selling the crop. He also notes that the sun and the rain are the true bean cultivators, and says other creatures have as much right to the harvest as he does—an idea that earned him the scorn of the townsfolk, who thought him eccentric. Thoreau lived simply, growing his own food and following a vegetarian diet—though he sometimes ate fish from the pond and, once, an unfortunate woodchuck. Later he regretted this act, and wrote: "The beans have results, which are not harvested by me. Do they not grow for woodchucks partly?" His eco-centric beliefs that humans are part of nature, and that the world is interconnected, animate *Walden*, make it relevant to our nature retreats in the modern world.

For millennia humans have venerated holy places in nature: springs, wells, waterfalls, rivers, forests, valleys, caves, mountains and monolithic rocks. Of sacred geographies the Dalai Lama writes, "Taken together they represent the common need in the human quest for happiness to preserve certain places as sanctuaries, reflecting perhaps each individual's wish for inner peace." And while humans have long been drawn back to wild edgelands for perspective, Thoreau added a modern-day geography of retreat to our repertoire: a wasteland on the outskirts of commerce.

"Walden's general lack of utility made it an 'outback' with an ascetic remoteness that would attract the Transcendentalists, beginning in the 1830s," writes Robert M. Thorson in *The Guide to Walden Pond*. With amazing prescience Thoreau saw the false distinction between "wild" land—uninhabited land and exalted, sweeping landscapes—and "non-wild" land, a way of thinking that has disconnected us from reality, and the natural world. "Far from being the one place on Earth that stands apart from humanity, wilderness is quite profoundly a human creation," Cronon notes in his 1995 essay "The Trouble with Wilderness." Without us to set it apart, of course, there is no wilderness. He elaborates, "Wilderness is not a pristine sanctuary where the last remnant of an untouched, endangered, but still transcendent nature can for at least a little while longer be encountered without the contaminating taint of civilization." Nor is it, I might add, a consumerist "wilderness experience," with its high peaks and endangered animals.

Thoreau's ecological view, that humans are part of nature, meant he rejected the biblical idea—still prevalent today in Western civilization—that humans have dominion over the natural world, which he saw as a kind of hatred for life. In Genesis, humans are told, "And the fear of you and the dread of you shall be upon every beast of the earth, and upon every fowl of the air, upon all that moveth upon the earth, and upon all the fishes of the sea; into your hand are they delivered . . . even as the green herb have I given you all things." Thoreau's step back to the woods, where he noticed the small and particular in nature, was a refusal of this idea, coinciding with rampant industrialization and violent attacks on Indigenous people to force them off their lands. Battles between the army and Sitting Bull, Crazy Horse and Geronimo were daily news in Thoreau's time: he recognized also that lands are contested spaces.

Walden was a new kind of margin for the age, outside the urban and industrial. Before Thoreau came to Walden, when a new road had been built, it bypassed the area. An impoverished village grew up there, where formerly enslaved people, immigrants and day labourers squatted, and no one stopped them because the land was rocky and the soil was poor. Thoreau describes resident Zilpha White, once enslaved, who built a one-room house and lived as a hermit, spinning cloth, for more than 40 years. "She led a hard life, and somewhat inhumane," he writes. White was long gone by Thoreau's time: English soldiers burned her small home and all her animals during the War of 1812.

Thoreau saw the interconnections between nature and historic struggles and inequalities, and his thinking about social reforms considered those who came before: Indigenous people who had lived there for 11,000 years, and the formerly enslaved people and others who had once made Walden Woods their home. In *Henry David Thoreau: A Life*, biographer Laura Dassow Walls observes that the Thoreau who speaks for nature and the one who speaks for social justice grew from the same root: from his recognition of the truth of interdependence.

He went to Walden because he didn't understand why people thought they had no options and resigned themselves to lives of "quiet desperation." He wanted to think deeply about the choices we make and how we live. These choices, however small, he believed, are reflected in the world around us. Now *there's* a sobering thought.

Simplifying life, he believed, frees us to see more clearly, breaking normal habits of perception, which can lead to new ideas and connections. Thoreau wasn't saying we all needed to move to the woods: he aimed to bring us to our own awakenings, which would lead us to act with integrity according to our inner dictates. Before Walden, Thoreau was already a reformer who fought slavery, and also against enslavement to the capitalist economy that alienates us from ourselves, from others and from the land. His solution was to live intentionally, which can be done anywhere. His retreat was not in the old style of a religious hermit in the wilds, but a middle way: a move to the margin, a retreat to the outskirts of town.

Beyond his ideas about nature Thoreau anticipated our modern embráce of Eastern ways of retreat, with yoga and meditation. His readings and dialogue with classical Indian writing influenced much of his work—some scholars even link his desire to go to Walden with these ancient books. The Vedic literature of ancient India reinforced the Transcendentalists in their critique of society's rationalism and materialism, while providing new ideas about love for nature, interdependence and the search for truth. Thoreau used the holy books selectively as instruction manuals and found the Bhagavad Gita meaningful. "Depend upon it that rude and careless as I am, I would fain practise the yoga faithfully," he wrote in a letter to his friend H.G.O. Blake in 1849. "To some extent, and at rare intervals, even I am a yogin."

Thoreau, part forest sage, understood the value of contemplation. "I did not read books the first summer; I hoed beans. Nay, I often did better than this. There were times when I could not afford to sacrifice the bloom of the present moment to any work, whether of the head or hands. I love a broad margin to my life." Often he bathed in the pond on summer mornings and then sat in the cabin doorway, "rapt in a revery, amid the pines and hickories and sumachs, in undisturbed solitude and stillness." He only ended his meditation, he said, when the sun shone through his west window or he heard a distant traveller's wagon.

I love what Thoreau writes next, because he explains the imperceptible change, so difficult to describe, that is a hallmark of a retreat to nature. "I grew in those seasons like corn in the night, and they were far better than any work of the hands would have been. They were not time subtracted from my life, but so much over and above my usual allowance. I realized what the Orientals mean by contemplation and the forsaking of works."

Like contemplatives in all ages, Thoreau became a magnet for curious people. Deliberate at first, and solitary—"I love to be alone. I never found the companion that was so companionable as solitude"—he soon saw his chance to be an educator on a public stage and took to sermonizing. He was very conspicuous, and as many people came to Walden to fish or swim, passersby often saw him from road. People would yell, "Beans, so late?" and family and friends visited often. As well, he sometimes lectured and worked as a gardener, fence builder, stone mason, surveyor and handyman, often for Emerson, but only enough to support himself. He became a celebrity, which led to charges of hypocrisy, because he went home to his mother's to do laundry and eat dinner and, sometimes, to catch up on gossip. In the "Visitors" chapter, Thoreau clearly says he's "no hermit" and describes his three chairs—"one for solitude, two for friendship, three for society"—and marvels that he's had as many as "twenty-five or thirty souls, with their bodies, at once under my roof."

Even in his own circle of iconoclasts Thoreau's act of retreat was too radical to be understood. In 1842 writer Nathaniel Hawthorne began by calling Thoreau "a young man with much of wild original nature still remaining in him . . . He is as ugly as sin, long-nosed, queer-mouthed, and with uncouth and somewhat rustic, though courteous manners." And then, reflecting both the racism of the times and incomprehension about Thoreau's experiment, "[He] seems inclined to lead a sort of Indian life among civilised men—an Indian life, I mean, as respects the absence of any systematic effort for a livelihood."

In the introduction to the 150-year edition of *Walden* in 2004, John Updike writes: "Emerson, like other respectable citizens of Concord, was skeptical of enterprise so personal and quizzical, confiding to his journal that 'Thoreau wants a little ambition in his mixture . . . Instead of being the head of American engineers, he is captain of a huckleberry party.'" Then, as now in many quarters, paying deep attention to the natural world—being present versus being productive—didn't qualify as an acceptable way to spend one's time.

Thoreau, unlike many of the initial Western retreaters, the religious hermits and monks, never planned to leave society forever. He was a social reformer, not a retiring recluse. His political side was expressed in the 1849 essay on protest, "Civil Disobedience," which he also worked on in the woods, a work that influenced Gandhi's nonviolent resistance in India, Martin Luther King Jr.'s during the '60s civil rights movement and countless other dissidents.

In the long tradition of those who retire in order to return, Thoreau's experiment in the woods came to an end and he rejoined society, going first to live with Emerson's family while his friend was away lecturing, and after that, staying mostly at his parents' home. Thoreau turned from questioning everything and observing nature to sharing his findings. He spent seven years on *Walden*. For the rest of his life he was an amateur naturalist, and his formative time at Walden fed his future work. He wrote every morning and evening and walked every afternoon until his early death at 44 of tuberculosis.

In our era of information overload and environmental emergency, Thoreau's wisdom reverberates. That a better life results from cultivating simplicity, solitude and independent thought, and observing nature to gain a holistic view, is an idea that grows in weight with each passing generation.

In *Walden*'s conclusion, Thoreau's discoveries from a small cabin in the woods by the pond evoke how a retreat is always an experiment. "If one advances confidently in the direction of his dreams, and endeavors to live the life which he has imagined, he will meet with a success unexpected in common hours," Thoreau writes. It's about cultivating higher laws and our higher selves. "He will put some things behind, will pass an invisible boundary; new, universal, and more liberal laws will begin to establish themselves around and within him; or the old laws be expanded, and interpreted in his favour in a more liberal sense, and he will live with the license of a higher order of beings. . . ." It's also about action. "If you have built castles in the air, your work need not be lost; that is where they should be. Now put the foundations under them."

Walden was a reflection of the wild inside, and when Thoreau's time by the pond ends, he looks to the future. "There is more day to dawn. The sun is but a morning star," he writes. A deeply philosophical book, *Walden* urges us to apply its findings to our own lives: to explore our interiority in nature, to step back to spark new, ecological ways of thinking and to make the world better.

A retreat to nature helps us fall in love with the living world in times when our most pressing problems are ecological, and we have caused them ourselves. What could be more urgent?

Thoreau inspired generations of literary naturalists and writers who saw Earth as a living temple, and they shaped our ideas about the natural world—in turn, influencing our ways of retreating to nature. Among them, Emily Dickinson, John Muir, Aldo Leopold, Louise de Kiriline Lawrence, Rachel Carson, Wendell Berry, Annie Dillard, Terry Tempest Williams, and Mary Oliver all took a step back from society to the natural world in order to see clearly and think deeply and independently.

Literature has long challenged and transformed cultural narratives related to humanity's complex relationship to nature. From Thoreau's time to now, there's been a continuing shift toward a personal spirituality in nature, which may or may not include God. Many modern people find their sanctuary in the wild world. As well, in the past, with the exception of anchorites bricked into their cells, retreat had been almost exclusively for men. In 2008 Scottish poet and essayist Kathleen Jamie wrote of the tradition

of literate monks and hermits, which she says is "largely uninter-
rogated: the association of literature, remoteness, wildness and
spiritually uplifted men."

From Thoreau's time on, pioneering, self-sufficient and mainly
secular women—poets, artists, explorers and scientists—began to
retreat, ignoring traditional roles. In 1935 Megan Boyd, a famous
salmon fly dresser, moved to a small cottage in northern Scotland
at 20 and lived alone by the sea for 60 years. In 1933 Christiane
Ritter, a painter from Austria, travelled to Spitsbergen, an Arctic
island north of Norway, to join her husband, and wrote *A Woman
in the Polar Night*. Explorer Anne Morrow Lindbergh withdrew
from her busy family life and career to Florida's Captiva Island in
1955, where she wrote *Gift from the Sea*, feeling in harmony with
"the universe, lost in it, as one is lost in a canticle of praise, swelling
from an unknown crowd in a cathedral." Anne LaBastille, a wildlife ecologist and advocate, moved to a remote cabin by a lake in
her forties and wrote books, the most famous being *Woodswoman*,
from 1976, about living alone in the Adirondacks.

Women's historical contributions to our ideas about nature,
and about retreat, are slowly coming to light. One morning,
walking the dog at the lakeside park, I'm startled when my
friend tells me she's visited the spacious gardens where poet
Emily Dickinson liked to wander. I had thought Dickinson was
a recluse shut up in her room, based on a gossipy description
I'd read, written by her neighbour whose letter described her
as "the climax of all the family oddity. She has not been outside
her own house in fifteen years. She dresses wholly in white, and
her mind is said to be perfectly wonderful." In reality, at least
for a time, she roamed freely over 14 acres of gardens, woods
and fields. An avid gardener, she spent countless hours outside
at the family homestead in Amherst, Massachusetts, observing
and working and taking long walks with her big brown

Newfoundland dog, Carlo—whom she called "my shaggy ally" and "my mute confederate."

Dickinson was younger than Thoreau, but familiar with his work and that of the other Transcendentalists. Like him, she was a solitude- and nature-loving rebel who refused to conform to society's narrow expectations. Her view of a woman's fate is declared in this terse line: "Born—Bridalled—Shrouded." Knowing "There is another loneliness," Dickinson retreated. Called "Queen Recluse" by family friend and editor of the *Springfield Republican* Samuel Bowles and "The Myth" by townsfolk in Amherst, Dickinson wrote 1,775 poems she never intended to publish. Few people, even in her inner circle, knew anything about them before her death at 55 in 1886.

Dickinson, like Thoreau, was an early ecologist. Her legacy is that she taught us to see the world. Her subjects were nature, art and spirituality, and she rejected conventional religion for a more personal faith. For her, nature was sacred: "The gentian weaves her fringes . . . / In the name of the Bee—/ And of the Butterfly—/ And of the breeze—Amen!"

Dickinson had an original mind and a strong will. Even though one by one, her family and schoolmates publicly professed their belief in Christ, necessary to become a full member of the church, Dickinson refrained, instead declaring her loyalty to the Earth in a letter to a friend: "the world allured me and in an unguarded moment I listened to her siren voice. From that moment I seemed to lose my interest in heavenly things by degrees." In a letter to another friend Dickinson writes that God's paradise is redundant: "If roses had not faded, and frosts had never come, and one had not fallen here and there who I could not waken, there were no need of other Heaven than the one below—and if God had been here this summer, and seen the things that I have seen—I guess that He would think His paradise superfluous." For her, "Earth is

Heaven," and the house of prayer is her garden: "Some keep the Sabbath going to Church—/I keep it, staying at Home—/With a Bobolink for a Chorister—/And an Orchard, for a Dome."

From Dickinson's time to ours, there's been much speculation about her seclusion. Did she have an illness? Why the nun-like white dress? Why didn't she marry? Did she have a lover? The Emily Dickinson Museum website says vaguely: "As she grew older, she saw people less and less but remained open to visits from close friends and family. Whether she suffered from a medical condition that made her uncomfortable around people or whether she chose to separate herself from society is not known."

This highly unsatisfying explanation fuels much speculation on morning walks with my human friend and our canine confederate in the lakeside forests and fields. Ultimately we decide that Dickinson was simply an uncompromising woman who used retreat as a strategy to live an artist's life—which she then spent mainly out of doors. Her gender meant finding peace to write was hard won. In times when women were expected to marry, and even if single, endure endless rounds of social calls, refusing visitors and invitations sounds to us like a practical decision.

She embraced solitude to go deep to explore "[t]hat polar privacy,/A Soul admitted to Itself:/Finite Infinity." The clear-eyed vision, the passionate, original mind, the blazing intelligence, so obvious from her poems, is at odds with the image of an eccentric recluse—which clings to anyone who retreats, as though stepping out of bounds can't be tolerated by society, and especially not when it's done by a woman. In the light of retreat, I imagine Dickinson differently now: artistically productive, socializing in her own small circle and through letters, giving marriage the slip, walking with Carlo and lowering baskets of homemade gingerbread from her upstairs window to neighbour children below (which she actually did).

Dickinson had an excellent education. She studied botany and was "more widely known as a gardener" than a poet by family and friends, according to author Judith Farr. The family garden and small greenhouse were her paradise, where even in winter she could linger. According to the Emily Dickinson International Society's newsletter, she "cultivated buttercups, ferns, wood sorrel, heliotropes and jasmine, which she quenched with 'a long, slender spout like the antennae of insects,'" recalled her niece Martha Bianchi.

During a New York Botanical Garden show on Dickinson's garden, exhibits director Karen Daubmann described it thus: "Lush, filled with flowers, and fragrant; it includes layered plantings of trees, shrubs, perennials, annuals, vegetables, and bulbs, with a woodland path, meadow, orchard, vegetable garden, cutting garden, and conservatory."

Nature was the sanctuary where Dickinson safeguarded her muse. And the garden was the source of her original and profound insights into the natural world, and of her verse. Her work reflects the relational ethic of today's ecological thinking. A brilliant naturalist, Dickinson not only showed us how to see, but she expressed contemporary ideas—such as extending rights to the non-human world. Reflecting her non-anthropocentric understanding of nature, she writes:

"I robbed the Woods—/ The trusting Woods. / The unsuspecting Trees / Brought out their Burs and mosses / My fantasy to please. / I scanned their trinkets curious—I grasped—I bore away—/ What will the solemn Hemlock—/ What will the Oak tree say?"

Dickinson requested that before her funeral, her coffin be carried around her flower garden, in and out of the family's barn and through fields of buttercups to the nearby town cemetery. She provided a new model for nature retreat: the artist as a woman who steps back to create—not to a room, but to a garden.

The idea of whom nature retreats were for morphed gradually: no longer just for hermits, monks, artists, philosophers or the privileged, the notion grew that it was necessary and beneficial for everyone. Early outliers who took up this idea of democratic access to natural places forever and for all sparked efforts to protect the natural world in the first wave of the conservation movement.

Scottish-American John Muir was a pioneering figure in the preservation of wilderness for the common good and helped create another institution in the way we retreat: the national park. Inspired by Thoreau, his spiritual and literary mentor, Muir lived in a small cabin beside Yosemite Creek in 1869 and wrote a journal that became *My First Summer in the Sierra*. Muir's writing often reflects Thoreau's, such as in the shared belief that in "wildness lies the hope of the world."

Muir saw evidence of the divine everywhere in nature. His religion was rooted in wildness and the worship of God's creation. "If St. Anthony is the prototype of the Christian hermit, John Muir must be the apotheosis of the solitary whose God is nature," writes Isabel Colgate in *A Pelican in the Wilderness*. He had a religious fervour about national parks at the turn of the century, when the word conservation was first coined, a force against industrialization and settlement. Also known as "John of the Mountains," Muir was instrumental in having Yosemite designated a national park, among other acts of preservation, and wrote that it was "by far the grandest of all the special temples of Nature I was ever permitted to enter . . . the sanctum sanctorum of the Sierra."

Muir became an influential naturalist and conservationist, and his ideas spread around the world through his writings: he believed there should be places set aside free from private ownership for all time, so everyone can experience nature and beauty. "Thousands of tired, nerve-shaken, over-civilized people are beginning to find out that going to the mountains is going home; that wildness is a necessity," he wrote.

By the 1860s the American side of Niagara Falls (now public) had been bought by a private landowner who charged people to see this natural wonder. To prevent this happening elsewhere, and to stop development, the public park was born. The Yosemite land grant in 1864 designated the first parkland, protected by the state of California, while Yellowstone, which straddles three states, became the first national park in 1872. Twenty years later Muir founded the Sierra Club for those who wanted to "explore, enjoy, and protect the wild places of the earth," especially those in the Sierra Nevada mountain range. Muir's great influence on the way we retreat is the idea of a preserved park, where the public can step back to the wilds. "Everybody needs beauty as well as bread, places to play in and pray in, where nature may heal and give strength to body and soul alike," he declared.

Before this, Muir's taste for wild country had been whetted in Canada, where he spent two formative years. In 1864, aged 26, he came north with the purpose of "botanizing"—looking for flowers and trees. He spent spring, summer and fall wandering through the woods and swamps of what later became Ontario. Describing it as his "first grand excursion," Muir found a tiny, rare native orchid, the Calypso borealis (also called fairy slipper or Venus's slipper). The discovery, captured in *The Life and Letters of John Muir*, is like a religious experience: "I found beautiful Calypso on the mossy bank of a stream, growing not in the ground but on a bed of yellow mosses in which its small white bulb had found a soft nest and from which its one leaf and one flower sprung. The flower was white and made the impression of the utmost simple purity like a snowflower. No other bloom was near it, for the bog a short distance below the surface was still frozen, and the water was ice cold." And then, surprisingly for a no-nonsense Scot of the mountains, he added: "It seemed the most spiritual of all the flower people I had ever met. I sat down beside it and fairly cried for joy. It seems wonderful that so frail and lovely a plant has such power over human hearts."

That autumn Muir met his brother Daniel and the two set to work at Trout's sawmill and factory, south of Meaford, Ontario. Muir wrote: "When I came to the Georgian Bay of Lake Huron, whose waters are so transparent and beautiful, and the forests about its shores with their ferny, mossy dells and deposits of boulder clay, it seemed to be a most favorable place for study . . . In a beautiful dell, only a mile or two from the magnificent bay, I fortunately found work in a factory where there was a sawmill and lathes for turning out rakes, broom, and fork handles, etc." At Trout Hollow on the Bighead River, Muir lived in a small cabin for nearly two years, working until the sawmill and factory burned down in 1866. Today the Trout Hollow Trail leads to where John Muir lived 155 years ago, and there's a commemorative plaque at Epping Lookout near Meaford. Muir walked much of what is now the Bruce Trail.

Though Muir had studied botany and geology at the University of Wisconsin, he was also known as an ingenious industrial inventor. Obsessed with clocks, he famously made a hybrid alarm clock/study desk that slid him out of bed to the floor in the morning, lit a lamp and gave him a few minutes to dress before it began to pull books out at set intervals so he could study. He also designed water wheels, barometers and an automatic horse-feeding machine. In 1867 when he was working at an Indianapolis carriage factory a sharp file pierced his eye, blinding him temporarily in both eyes. He said if he recovered his sight he was "determined to get away into the flowery wilderness to enjoy and lay in as large a stock as possible of God's wild beauty before the coming on of the times of darkness." After six months, his sight restored, he left his old life behind and set off walking to Florida—carrying only a little money, a compass, a bar of soap and a towel, and a few reading materials, including the poems of Robert Burns, the New Testament and a botany textbook.

The future patron saint of national parks was headed for South America, studying plants and flowers and starting the journal he kept for the rest of his life along the way. He contracted malaria, decided to turn westward instead and walked from San Francisco to Yosemite in 1868. Captivated, he took local jobs—as a ranch hand, at a sawmill and then as a guide—so he could wander and study and explore. He built a cabin over the stream so he could listen to the sound of running water. Later he left in search of glaciers, with no gun and no blankets: he'd make a fire from scraps of wood and sleep beside it in the cold snow of the high Sierra, like some biblical hermit seeking transcendence.

Photos reveal a man with long curly hair and a long beard, very hermit chic: he once called himself a "poetico-trampo-geologist-botanist and ornithologist-naturalist etc. etc. !!!!" and he looks the part. Comically, Muir thought Thoreau and Emerson not "wild" enough: "Even open-eyed Thoreau would perhaps have done well had he extended his walks westward to see what God had to show in the lofty sunset mountains."

Muir retreated to the Yosemite cabin for only a few years, but his time in the Sierra marked him forever. Afterwards he dedicated his life to protecting the natural world, which he saw was disappearing as quickly as the Californian redwoods. A voice in the wilderness, he encouraged others to retreat as he had, and he often went back to recharge in nature.

Viewed from the 21st century, national parks—a modern institution for retreat—are both cause for celebration and change. Muir's desire to preserve natural places has inspired millions, and the preservation of public land from industrialization means these precious sanctuaries endure today. Muir thought of nature as sacred and wrote, "When we try to pick out anything by itself, we find it hitched to everything else in the Universe." And yet he spared no thought for the inhabitants who were driven off these pristine "wild" lands.

Muir's descriptions of Yosemite as a "pure wilderness" where "no mark of man is visible upon it" obscures the long history of those who had lived there for millennia. Back in the 1850s few settlers had even seen Yosemite, but with the California gold rush, explorers and prospectors began bringing back tales of its beauty. Later, military men from the Mariposa Battalion came to dispossess the Indigenous residents and wrongly thought Yosemite was the tribe's name. Scholars learned that the people "called the valley Ahwahnee, meaning 'the place of a gaping mouth,' and that they called themselves the Ahwahneechees."

In Canada Indigenous peoples were forced off their lands to create parks and wildlife preserves, prompting one writer to call them "colonial crime scenes" in a 2017 article. Beginning with the creation of Banff in 1885, early government agencies banned Indigenous peoples, and other authorities had similar policies—Ontario outlawed hunting in Algonquin Park when it was established in 1893, and First Nations people were displaced by the creation of Vancouver's Stanley Park.

Muir's legacy is fraught in many ways: the history of dispossession; problematic "management" practices, such as killing off all the predators in supposedly wild places; and recently overcrowding. Yosemite has more than four million visitors a year. Tourism puts a strain on environments and leads to development, even when it's ecotourism focused on conservation. Terry Tempest Williams, a writer in Thoreau's lineage, writes passionately about America's national parks in *The Hour of the Land*. "We don't need to denounce John Muir's legacy, we need to broaden it," she maintains. Parks are places to fight back against the rapaciousness and ignorance that characterize our relationship to the natural world, she says, and are "the closest we have to sacred space." They "are so much more than a federally constructed reservation for recreation and retail," Williams writes. "They are places of recognition—where we can renew and revive our understanding of what makes us human in relationship to the life that surrounds us."

Parks began as refuges for wildlife, but now they've evolved into refuges for urban, technology-habituated humans for whom placelessness has become a reality. Pollution and climate change don't stop at park boundaries, of course, and yet the natural beauty remains. Muir's words about protected places still ring true and encourage us to go: "Nature's peace will flow into you as sunshine flows into trees. The winds will blow their own freshness into you, and the storms their energy, while cares will drop off like autumn leaves."

What exactly are we seeking, and what are we finding, when we retreat to nature? Peace, perhaps, and awe at meeting forces beyond our understanding, where we can lose our small selves and our sense of separation? For me, being away from society in an environment with trees and water enables me to feel how I'm related to the more-than-human world. This idea clearly animated the life of ornithologist and conservationist Louise de Kiriline Lawrence, whose first words, according to her mother, were *kraa kraa kraa*, spoken to crows. Lawrence, born in 1894 to a wealthy Swedish family—her godmother, whom she is named after, was Princess Louise of Denmark—grew up on a country estate. She reconnected to nature after she moved to Canada, a new chapter in a tumultuous life.

Though her family resisted, Lawrence trained as a nurse. During the First World War she worked for the Red Cross in

Denmark, caring for wounded prisoners of war. That's where she met and married a Russian army officer. In 1919 he returned to northern Russia to fight in the Russian Revolution; she followed, working as a nurse. The Bolsheviks imprisoned them both. Later they were separated and he disappeared, while she, a Swedish national, was released. Lawrence spent four years during a terrible Russian famine searching for him while working as a delegate for Red Cross. She was to learn years later that her husband had been shot. The epigraph for her book about these experiences, *Another Winter, Another Spring*, is from Luis de León, a Spanish lyric poet, Augustinian friar, theologian and academic, and it suits her perfectly: "The beauty of life is nothing but this: that each should act in conformity with his nature and business."

Lawrence, inured to hardship, came to Canada in 1927 to work as a Red Cross outpost nurse near North Bay, Ontario. She was on the front lines caring for injured farmers, loggers and miners, as well as delivering babies and sharing health education. "Depending on the weather and geography, Louise made her rounds by foot, Model A Ford, open boat or dog sled," the *Canadian Encyclopedia* says. She was head nurse to the Dionne quintuplets for a year— and detested how they were removed from their parents and made a spectacle of.

In the 1930s Lawrence wrote a series of articles for *Chatelaine*. "I chose Canada, because she, I knew, possessed the unspoiled soil, the life-giving space, the fresh winds that promote spontaneous growth." In Russia Lawrence had nursed a young Englishman with terrible burns. "He spoke of the small log cabin hidden among the snow-heavy pines in the woods. It squats close to the ground, trustfully and humbly. . . . I caught but a vision of unlimited space and open fresh air, of freedom of movement and freedom of mind." In the prison camp, she and her husband had dreamed of living in Canada.

After she retired from nursing Lawrence married a local carpenter and moved to the woods. She provided another pioneering model of nature retreat for women—as a scientist. She studied and wrote, mainly about birds, when her husband went overseas during the Second World War. He returned from army service in 1945, the same year her first natural history book, *The Loghouse Nest*, came out. Lawrence "retreated to her cabin, a decision that represented the beginning of a remarkable life dedicated to her observations of the everyday in the natural world," writes Amy Wallace in "Barefoot in Sapphires," an essay that accompanied a 2010 exhibition about her life and work in North Bay. Lawrence became a renowned ornithologist and writer, working from her log cabin on a six-acre wilderness plot on Pimisi Bay near Rutherglen, Ontario, where she recorded, banded and collected bird species. "Swedish aristocrat, Bolshevik concentration camp survivor, revolutionary widow, world-renowned nurse, gifted linguist, strict atheist, prolific writer, dedicated conservationist, and friend of the birds, [she] defeats any attempt at categorization," Wallace writes.

Lawrence authored several books, including *The Lovely and the Wild*, which won the John Burroughs Medal in 1969. "She watched the woodland songbirds come, the orioles and ovenbirds, cardinals and cuckoos, finches and crossbills and pine siskins," *Kirkus Reviews* wrote. "She banded birds, fed them by hand, observed mating and nesting habits, fight and flight patterns." About her evolution as a naturalist, the book also registers absences. "Woodland birds still inhabit our forest, but their former profusion is no more," Lawrence writes. "Here is the emptiness. Here and in all parts of the forest marvellous woodland habitats now lie silent and lifeless each spring after the migration of the birds has come to an end, because not enough of these feathered elves still exist to fill the empty spaces." In a line heartbreaking to read now, when bird populations in North America are down 29 percent since 1970, roughly the time she wrote these words, she adds: "Silent spring! Has Rachel Carson's prevision really come true?"

One April, Lawrence finds the first nests of red crossbills, inspiring her to remark that there's nothing better than observing the natural world: "I am aware of new dimensions extending far beyond the limits of the usual familiar very narrow sphere within which I was conscious only of the things directly connected with myself. . . . My own shrinkage brings a touch of illuminating humility that prevents me from meddling with things and from destroying the natural with my clumsy contact."

Early dawns, biting blackflies and deer flies, muscle cramps from staying still, spending the whole day counting the exact number of songs emitted by a red-eyed vireo (22,197) and following birds for hours to find their nests: she was unstoppable. She banded and recorded more than 25,000 birds.

Lawrence was an unusual woman for her day, hunting with a gun, living for a time alone in the bush and conducting science. "The backwoods of northern Ontario allowed her the space to transcend traditional gender norms of her time," note the authors of "She of the Loghouse Nest: Gendering Historical Ecological Reconstructions in Northern Ontario." They add that expertise in "the breeding behaviours of birds, such as courtship, nesting habits, and rearing of the young, [were] areas deemed suitable for women in the first half of the 20th century."

Lawrence was the first Canadian woman elected to the American Ornithologists' Union and is renowned internationally for her rich nature observations and her writing. As well as her books, she wrote many scientific papers and articles for publications such as *Audubon*. Dr. Robert Nero, a noted ornithologist, made her a tribute with his 1990 book of poetry, *Woman by the Shore*. Lawrence died in 1992, and her records, bird skins and nests are held in the Canadian Museum of Nature in Ottawa and the

Royal Ontario Museum in Toronto. Since 2014, the Nipissing Naturalists Club has held an annual Louise de Kiriline Lawrence Nature Festival, and Ontario Library Service–North awards a non-fiction book prize in her honour. She continues to inspire us to step back and experience life in the natural world.

Like hermits of old, generations of literary naturalists considered places—forests, mountains, lakeshores—holy. For Rachel Louise Carson, marine biologist and author, nature was both sacred temple and science laboratory. "Undersea," an early essay in the *Atlantic* in 1937, exhibits the gorgeous writing she became famous for: "Who has known the ocean? Neither you nor I, with our earth-bound senses, know the foam and surge of the tide that beats over the crab hiding under the seaweed of his tide-pool home; or the lilt of the long, slow swells of mid-ocean, where shoals of wandering fish prey and are preyed upon, and the dolphin breaks the waves to breathe the upper atmosphere."

Carson wrote three books about the ocean, and with the earnings from 1951's bestselling *The Sea Around Us*, she bought a small piece of land on a picturesque island in Maine. There she built a small cottage retreat amid the pines, spruces and birches, with windows that looked toward the sea. In this spot on the Atlantic seaboard where the tides rise highest, what was underwater at high tide was revealed at low tide—the pools and the creatures of the intertidal zone she most loved.

I've seen photos of Carson at her Walden by the sea, dressed in a loose shirt and rolled up trousers, puttering along the shore. Amid the periwinkles and eel grass is where she was most content, carrying her magnifying glass, or filling jars with water and creatures to look at under the cottage microscope. "I can't think of any more exciting place to be than down in the low-tide world, when the ebb tide falls very early in the morning, and the world is full of salt smell, and the sound of water, and the softness of fog," she writes. Carson called her retreat Silverledges, and it was an essential staging ground, says environmental scientist Robert K. Musil, who since 2014 has been president and CEO of the Rachel Carson Council. "She identifies with the creatures who live on the edge, this borderland between the power of water that could also crush you and also release life and create new life. . . . Rachel wanted to be still, to feel and to imagine, and this was the place that would allow her to do that."

Carson's contribution to the way we see nature, and the way we retreat, is that she taught us everything is part of life's larger pattern, that each element is connected, and deserves our reverence. Following her sea books, she wrote the work she's best known for in the safe space of her retreat. *Silent Spring* took her four years and dealt with synthetic chemical pesticides, or what she called "elixirs of death," which were contaminating the Earth, killing wildlife and hurting human health. As a storyteller and a scientist, she showed how these chemicals were dangerous and also illuminated larger ideas, such as how ecological systems work, creating a huge shift.

All her life, Carson said, was a preparation to write *Silent Spring*. Far from privileged, she grew up poor in Springdale, a town northeast of Pittsburgh that was set between two huge coal-fired electrical plants. An old photo shows her as a freckled child sitting in the grass, reading to the dog. Carson loved reading, writing and the outdoors: her mother thought children should study nature, so the forest was her main classroom. Learn to love the natural world, the theory went, and you will want to protect it.

At age ten Carson was a published author; at fourteen, she was selling work to magazines. When she earned a scholarship for university, her mother sold the family china to support her. Upon graduation she got a research job as a marine biologist and saw the sea for the first time. It taught her that everything is connected. Carson loved the sea, which seemed beyond the hand of humans. As the sole breadwinner for various dependents— five during the Depression, though she supported some family members for the rest of her adult life—she didn't go on to do a PhD as a marine biologist, and instead went to work in conservation in the fisheries and began to write articles.

By the time Carson quit her job to write full-time she was wholly devoted to ensuring justice for the natural world. From the small pine desk of her seaside retreat, she wrote one of the most consequential environmental books in history.

Carson wrote about the consequences of "the never-ending stream of chemicals of which pesticides are a part, chemicals now pervading the world in which we live, acting upon us directly and indirectly, separately and collectively." *Silent Spring* was released during the height of the Cold War, when the idea that the balance of nature was important to the living world's survival, including human survival, was scorned. People thought human ingenuity had triumphed over nature, and chemicals couldn't hurt anything but insects. At the time, DDT was being lauded as one of the great scientific discoveries of the Second World War that had helped to end the war—along with the atomic bomb—because it was a miracle of public health that had cut down on malaria by killing all the mosquitos. Further, the chemical, which was sprayed everywhere and even available to consumers, was considered the solution to famine and disease, two age-old problems finally brought under human control.

What Carson saw was the collateral damage to wildlife and people. She had collected a dossier of what she called "poison spray material" over a decade. In 1958 when she was told by an old friend that DDT spraying had destroyed a local wildlife sanctuary, killing the birds in horrific ways, she resolved to write about the harmful, often deadly effects of toxic chemicals. "It was pleasant to believe that much of Nature was forever beyond the tampering reach of man: but I have now opened my eyes and my mind. I do not like what I see, but it does no good to ignore it, and it's worse than useless to go on repeating the old eternal verities that are no more eternal than the hills of the poets," Carson wrote.

Silent Spring prompted a revolutionary idea: regulation of pollution. "The number of books that have done as much good in the world can be counted on the arms of a starfish," a 2018 *New Yorker* article observes. The book marked a new chapter in the environmental movement and helped to provoke legislation to protect air, wilderness, water and endangered species, which led to the Environmental Protection Agency's founding in 1970.

Carson's retreat by the sea was a container for rest, renewal, inspiration and deep concentration. "I write slowly, often in long-hand, and with frequent revision. Being sensitive to interruption, I write most freely at night." Without this refuge I wonder whether she'd have finished in time. Carson had adopted Roger, the nine-year-old orphan son of her niece, in 1957, when she was 50. She was single parenting, while writing *Silent Spring* and also under-going medical treatments. After she learned she had breast cancer, Carson kept a sentence from Walden at her bedside, to encourage her writing: "If thou art a writer, write as if thy time were short, for it is indeed short at the longest."

When Carson completed *Silent Spring* she listened to her favourite violin concerto and wept, alone in her study. She wrote to her beloved friend, Dorothy Freeman, who had worried about the inevitable attacks on Carson by powerful interests: "I think I let you see last summer what my deeper feelings are about this when I said I could never again listen happily to a thrush song if I had not done all I could."

It's incredibly moving to watch old footage of Carson speaking out, before Congress, and on television. She's pale and obviously ill. On April 3, 1963, *CBS Reports* presented "The Silent Spring of Rachel Carson." After the interview with Carson was recorded, the reporter told his producer to air the program fast, warning, "You've got a dead leading lady." Carson appears wearing a dark wig—she'd lost her hair. She was seated: the cancer had progressed to her vertebra and her spine was collapsing.

She was dying but she couldn't have been more lucid. "We still talk in terms of conquest. We still haven't become mature enough to think of ourselves as only a tiny part of a vast and incredible universe. Man's attitude toward nature is today critically important simply because we have now acquired a fateful power to alter and destroy nature . . . but man is a part of nature, and his war against nature is inevitably a war against himself," she said with dignity and assurance.

Her words still ring true. "Now, I truly believe, that we in this generation, must come to terms with nature, and I think we're challenged as mankind has never been challenged before to prove our maturity and our mastery, not of nature, but of ourselves."

Between *Silent Spring*'s release and Carson's death in spring 1964, she was granted one final summer beside her beloved seashore. "We live in an age of rising seas," she once wrote. "In our own lifetime we are witnessing a startling alteration of climate." This was Carson's idea for her next book, which sadly for us all, she never had time to write.

Carson made appreciation of nature part of our culture and taught us about the truth of interconnection. In her 1952 acceptance speech for the John Burroughs Medal for natural history writing, she explains why we need to retreat to nature: "It seems reasonable to believe—and I do believe—that the more clearly we can focus our attention on the wonders and realities of the universe about us the less taste we shall have for the destruction of our race. Wonder and humility are wholesome emotions, and they do not exist side by side with a lust for destruction."

The peace that natural spaces and extended silences provide, and the role of nature retreats for modern-day Thoreaus, the planet and deep ecology, are matters of urgency. Poet Mary Oliver's work reminds us of the need to reconnect to nature, and the sacred, in times of climate change. "I could not be a poet without the natural world," she once wrote. "Someone else could. But not me. For me the door to the woods is the door to the temple." Oliver, born in 1935 in Ohio, lived much of her life in New England, the setting of many of her poems. In part, her retreat to nature was to get away from her dysfunctional family, and she often went to the forest. "It was a very bad childhood for everybody, every member of the household, not just myself I think. And I escaped it, barely. With years of trouble," she told Krista Tippett of *On Being* in 2015. "But I got saved by poetry. And I got saved by the beauty of the world."

How do we love a world that's at once terrible and suffering and beautiful? The answer in her work is that we must amplify the poetry, and the beauty. And that attention is the beginning of devotion, and a way to repair our broken relationship with the world. As I was writing this, I learned that Mary Oliver had died. One of her poems seems to contain her epitaph: at life's end, the obituaries noted, she'd always said she wanted to see herself as a bride married to amazement.

Why do we disconnect from nature when it's where we evolved? I'm wondering this as I drive past the Little Cataraqui Creek Conservation Area north of Kingston, where a sign outside says:

"Forest therapy walks." Later I explain to friends that I think this refers to guided walks to reconnect with the woods. One friend's eyebrows shoot up. "People have to be introduced to nature?" she scoffs. Another finds the idea hilarious: "Yes, how will I—*be*—in the forest?" Unsure yet intrigued, I sign up. To me it sounds like an excellent licence to lurk. I've always been a lurker, which I define as lingering in a natural place to look awhile. One of my earliest childhood memories is of lurking under a bush, belly in the cool earth, nose in lily of the valley, watching three huge willow trees swaying in sunlight on the lawn beyond the green leaves of the bush. Needless to say, as an adult, there's never enough time, or opportunity, for this kind of thing.

The conservation area is a place I'm fond of, with limestone and paths through the mixed forest, sugar bush, hemlock and planted pine. I come here also to sit, or think, or write, often on the picnic table by the wind-rippled reservoir. It was here I first began to feel maybe I hadn't made a terrible mistake in moving to Kingston from Toronto.

As the day for forest therapy approaches I start to have second thoughts. Don't I already do forest therapy on my own when I walk in the woods? I have a pile of work due, and I can't really justify three hours to wander. Despite these misgivings I show up at 9:30 a.m., the first cooler day after a scorching summer, though it's late September. At the outdoor centre we meet the conservation educator who is going to lead us. A petite, youthful woman with long dark hair, she wears outdoorsy clothes and a loose-knit hat with a jaunty feather stuck in it, and carries a large knapsack. I'm still fretting about deadlines and praying the experience won't be flakey.

We stand in a circle, ten of us, more women than men, most 50-plus, perhaps because it's a workday, and three people in their thirties. I'm impressed by how the leader moves us quickly past awkwardness and irony and into the experience. She asks us to say who we are and why we're there. A young woman says she's been very poor for a long time, and now that finances have improved, she wants to take better care of her health. Another young woman, a newlywed, says she came because it sounded cool; her partner, a large and loud man tethered to a cellphone, says he's there because his wife dragged him. I need some quiet time, I say, breathing space. Another woman, new to the area, says she's come to meet people and explore—and also, intriguingly, that she doesn't like to touch things and hoped forest therapy might help.

The leader invites us to take a few moments to just notice what we notice. After a while our guide asks us to share, if we feel like it. We say: bird calls, the wind in pines, curious chicka-dees, the shallow pond, the blue sky, the sound of construction far away, the many shades of green. She recites a poem related to the season, Mary Oliver's "Wild Geese," suggesting, "let the soft animal of your body love what it loves." Touch anything you're drawn to, she says as she begins to walk. I stroke the cattails along the boardwalk. A duck lands with its ducklings, and we all watch appreciatively.

"Now pick up anything that speaks to you." I find a sprig of oak leaves with acorns that's fallen on the ground. Soon we stop and choose a place to sit. I lean against a pine, a relief after a long, stiff-ness-inducing car ride the previous day. The leader, who has taken off her boots to stand on the ground, asks us to look around and then close our eyes for about ten minutes. At first I feel impatient, tense, and the carrying construction noise matches my headspace better than the forest. Gradually though, my breathing slows and I start to feel the ground. I start thinking about what supports me.

We continue to walk slowly down the path, while we are given low-key suggestions. One is "notice what's in motion." I go off the trail a little, mostly to escape the young man's constant chatter. In a swampy area I see a few last jewelweeds nodding in the breeze, notice the playfulness of the wind around me. After a while I hear the "coyote call" that's meant to gather us back together. I realize that I'd crossed some familiar paths and didn't even notice, because we're meandering, with no destination. Going slowly, and really looking, I am experiencing the trail differently. Back together we share our experiences. Many people say they feel surprisingly emotional, and some talk about the person who taught them to love the natural world—grandmothers, mothers mainly. Already I've resolved to reschedule the rest of my packed day to not spoil this relaxed and grounded feeling. Breathing space.

Next we all pick up gifts for the forest, a reminder that this is a relationship of reciprocity. Our collage of birch and beech leaves and sticks and cones and pine needles looks like some alternative alphabet, poetic land symbols. My self-contained contribution is, of course, on the periphery. The big guy says he's bored and yawns. This interests me: on every retreat, nature, yoga, meditation, arts, it's common for people not habituated to solitude or slowness or natural environments to get bored or suffer other discomforts while the mind settles. If they can stick with it long enough, they may pass to another state, like diving under the turbulent surface waves to the quiet depths. Another woman looks at our collage on the ground and says it reminds her of transformation. After everyone who feels like it has spoken, the leader smiles and says, "We belong, we are part of this."

She invites us to choose a spot and sit for 15 minutes, after which she will ring chimes to recall us. I wander down the trail to a corner that calls my attention every time I walk by, a few times a week in good weather. And yet I've never stopped before. I sit on a root on a little slope and lean on a sapling. Here beside the marsh I feel at home and sheltered. I notice tiny, delicate white fungus, a companionable frog's eyes that stick out of the water and the wind. A feeling of gratitude washes over me. It's lovely to settle in here, undisturbed. Lurking. I could have stayed for ages, just taking it in. No rush. The chimes surprise me when they sound; it's as though no time had passed.

We gather to sit in a circle under a huge maple tree and speak with excitement. The young man calls his experience "epic," says he'd just rested on a bench and looked at the sky. Others say, variously, they felt grounded, nourished, able to let go. One woman says, with feeling, that moss doesn't get enough credit. We sing a song to the Earth, again without irony, and then we have a tea ceremony. Our leader's large knapsack spills its contents: tea she brewed from foraged plants, cold brewed staghorn sumach and hot white pine, and cups made specially by her friend. The first cup, for the Earth, is poured into the ground, and then our cups are filled. As I sip the warm white pine tea, I'm conscious of taking in the forest.

On the walk back to the outdoor centre—it's 12:30 already?—everything is vivid: the purple asters in tall bouquets, the white asters with fumbling bumblebees, the high, swaying cattails edging the ponds, the chickadees and nuthatches scolding the red squirrels, the silvery blue-grey sky, a slight chill in the air. Milkweed pods—empty, or fulfilled? I feel relaxed, having one thought at a time as opposed to dozens firing off all at once. Breathing space.

Wandering slowly in the forest, awakening your senses, reconnecting with nature in a meaningful way is more than just a walk, it's a small pilgrimage. You are here to immerse yourself, slow down, notice and experience the forest magic with a guide and companions. The experience reminds me we're all interconnected, and of the generosity we experience every moment.

When was the last time I stopped to marvel in beautiful woods? How long do I spend in front of a screen every day? The relief at using not just my eyes and ears, but all my senses, is exquisite.

Being in a beautiful natural place feels good and makes me want to return. Now I get it: the forest is the therapist.

On my way home I hold the image of ten adults sitting on the earth under the huge old maple. Humans are not "stewards." The natural world is larger than us and did better for millennia without our "management." We are part of the living world, a small part, though our powers of destruction are outsized. Why do we forget that we are animals in nature, that we *are* nature?

My sister Kath and I were wild little kids traversing our family's small country property near Woodbridge, Ontario. On three sides were farmers' fields, and out front a dirt road. Across the road was an Arabian horse farm, where ethereal creatures cantered in green pastures. Kath and I trampled down the alfalfa fields, making hideouts, tasted the sweetness of clover and sour rhubarb on our tongues, fled from the loud buzzing of "the Queen bee" in the shed, collected toads in a wheelbarrow, surprised when they leapt out. We climbed the tree behind the shed, out of sight of the kitchen window so our mother wouldn't see, and then slid down the tarpaper roof.

I once stole a robin's egg from a nest in a tree and was puzzled when the bird swooped at me and again later to find pocket-shards mixed with yellow when I went to show my blue treasure. The pungent-sweet smell of manure on the dog. Yellow birds in the willows, how a grasshopper looks like celery when you feed half of it to the cat. Spring chortling sounds after the frozen creeks we'd skated on in winter all melted.

Later I forgot all about this and went to the city, lived in an apartment like a filing cabinet for people and then a house on a small Toronto lot, had a career, lost touch even with the seasons unless they delayed my commute. One time I did drive north to see our old place, near Woodbridge. I was shocked: even the lay of the land was gone. I could find no reference point, not one tree or creek or hill. The land had been bulldozed flat for a subdivision that was nearly complete. We stared in amazement when we found our old house, now the temporary construction office, adrift in this alien landscape. Today, many of our old Edens have been replaced by "developments," the cookie-cutter manifestations of human disassociation from the living world. Placelessness, everywhere made to look the same.

Younger folks may never have experienced much of the natural world in the first place: will they have nothing to reconnect to? Children in the West spend half as much time outside as their parents did. And humans officially became an urban species in 2011, with more people living in cities that outside them, a trend that's accelerating. Cities are now the dominant habitat of our species. Rich, exciting and with many efficiencies for housing large numbers of people, they are also stressful places to live.

The World Health Organization calls stress the health epidemic of the 21st century. City soundscapes are part of the problem: noise increases blood pressure and is bad for concentration and sleep. "Around 80 million Europeans live with noise levels that are judged too high. More than 11 million Americans are exposed to traffic noise so high they risk hearing loss," writes scientist Dr. Qing Li, a leading forest medicine researcher, author of *Forest Bathing* and an environmental immunologist at Tokyo's Nippon Medical School.

Li's science was sparked by the desire to discover what is behind the feeling sunlight through leaves gives us, or a sunset, and how walking in the forest improves well-being. His studies have found that natural killer immune cells, which attack tumours and cells infected with viruses, increased significantly after time spent in the forest. In later research he linked this to scents such as pinenes, limonenes and aerosols emitted by evergreens and many other trees. We all know how good being in nature can make us feel, he writes, like an instinct deep in our bones that's sometimes hard to describe. "In Japanese we have a word for those deep feelings too deep for words—yūgen. Yūgen gives us a profound sense of the beauty and mystery of the universe. It is about this world but suggests something beyond it."

Shinrin-yoku—shrinrin is forest, yoku is bath—is based on ancient Buddhist and Shinto ideas that see the forest as the realm of the divine. The modern practice began as part of a government campaign to save the forests. The idea was that if people were encouraged to visit forests for their health, they would be more likely to want to protect and look after them. Now shinrin-yoku is a common preventative practice in Japan, where many physicians certify in forest medicine, prescribing the country's 48 forest therapy trails to reduce stress and other health problems. The nature cure is an idea that's catching on among doctors in the West.

For most of human existence we've had relative quiet, surrounded by green and natural sounds. And we've known for millennia that nature is good for us: Taoist monks wrote 2,000 years ago about the healing powers of tending gardens. In *Biophilia*, contemporary American biologist Edward O. Wilson wrote that we have a deep primal need to affiliate with nature and the living world. Humans love nature, the hypothesis holds, because we learn to love the things that help us to survive. Hardwired to affiliate with the natural world, our health improves when we're in it and suffers when we're divorced from it.

Our nervous systems are built to resonate with the outdoors— sunlight on water, the sights and sounds of the forest and fresh air give us comfort, ease our worries, let us think more clearly. It's where we feel most comfortable even if we don't realize it, says Yoshifumi Miyazaki, a physiological anthropologist, the vice director of the Center for Environment, Health and Field Sciences at Chiba University near Tokyo and another influential proponent of forest medicine. Our brains are only so plastic. "Throughout our evolution, we've spent 99.9 percent of our time in nature. Our physiology is still adapted to it. During everyday life, a feeling of comfort can be achieved if our rhythms are synchronized with those of the environment," he says.

Being in nature is like going on a mini-retreat—it provides the altered sense of time, a different way to look at the spaces around you and reconnection to the living world. You don't have to have the right gear or resources or go hiking in the distant mountains: it's available to all of us in the park, conservation area, by the lake, at the ocean.

What I'm most interested in is the benefits of full nature retreats—is longer better? Being in nature for several consecutive days, studies show, does yield better health benefits. Writers for centuries have been telling us to spend more time in nature, and they're right, says David Strayer, a cognitive neuroscientist at University of Utah. His "three-day effect" theory holds that in nature the senses, perspective and cognition sharpen over time. Li's advice is similar: "If you want to give your immune system a powerful boost go for a three-day/two-night forest bathing trip."

The average American's screen time is ten hours a day, Strayer says, with only 30 minutes a day spent outside. We multitask, which in 98 percent of people is inefficient and which places many demands on the prefrontal cortex. Our tired brains get worse at critical thinking, strategic planning and impulse control, among other things. Multi-day nature retreats, Strayer found, provide the antidote, so the brain can rest and reset. "The research coming out of my laboratory suggests there is more wisdom to Thoreau's 'why I went to the woods' than most of us will ever know. His insights into the power of nature stand in stark contrast to the exponential increase of screen time we see in businesses, at home, and even schools."

So if we know this, why don't we go to the living world more? For one thing, we underestimate how good it will make us feel. People may stay indoors, Trent University psychologist Elizabeth Nisbet found in a study, "because a chronic disconnection from nature causes them to underestimate its hedonic benefits." Nisbet comments, "We evolved in nature. It's strange we'd be so disconnected." Partially, perhaps, it's a chain effect: as we become more urban and live more indoors, we lose touch, and the living, natural world becomes abstract and seemingly dispensable. While it's innate for humans to want to be in natural places, where we evolved, we also want to forget that we're vulnerable animals and this world is our home. Nature retreats are a reality check, reteaching us about the interconnection of our health and the health of the living world.

Why do we have to relearn over and over the truth of interconnection, that we are part of nature? Years ago performance artist Laurie Anderson commented that people in poor countries are struggling to survive, while people in the West are struggling not to become machines. This rings true: we're in retreat from reality, in denial that we are animals trying to survive like the rest. Machines are invulnerable. "We're becoming unearthly, freed, we like to think, from the physical imperatives of nature by technology, and exiled from its sensuality and immediacy by our self awareness," writes English botanist and author Richard Mabey in his 2005 book *Nature Cure*, about his own lost link and reconnection to the natural world.

As reality gets more virtual there will surely be benefits: technologies can replace zoos, perhaps, or I can experience mountain-climbing despite my dislike for heights. But there's the risk of even further estrangement from reality. Technology is marvellous, but it's dead. The world's alive, and in trouble. Retreat to nature is the opposite of avoidance. It's ever more urgent as we consume the Earth and become more divorced from it. Being in nature for a time teaches us about relationship—with ourselves, others and the planet.

In our anthropocentric way, we tend to think nature needs our protection, but not the other way around. Something important is disappearing—the living world—and we need to restore it for our own sakes, if not for the rest of the planet's.

Spring, the season of renewal, seems a fitting time to visit Walden. The Walden Pond State Reservation is a protected 335-acre park with hiking trails and a replica of Thoreau's cabin, and of Thoreau himself. More than a million people a year visit this international pilgrimage site for conservationists. In the century and a half since *Walden* was published, Thoreau's work has inspired the minds and actions of generations of creators, thinkers and naturalists. The deep pond remains and is still a popular place to swim in the summer.

Thoreau's prescience extends to the meticulous journals he left, noting the first flowering dates for 500 species of wildflowers, when trees were in leaf and the migratory patterns of birds. An acute observer and activist, his observations on Walden now serve as a baseline for current scientific studies on climate change. So far, findings include 2.4°C rise in temperatures and the discovery that plants are flowering ten days earlier. Many species are gone or hard to find now. Researchers say 27 percent of the species recorded by Thoreau and other botanists are no longer present in Concord, and 36 percent of species once common there are now rare.

In our complex and secular world, Thoreau's messages—live deliberately and simply, use only what you need, practise restraint, find spirituality in nature, seek reality—are far more relevant than in his own day. As is his method in an age when freedom to think and be are in short supply: retreat to a small cabin, not necessarily in a so-called pristine wilderness, reconnect to the natural world and repair a broken relationship with the Earth—a disconnection that's killing the planet we depend on for life.

Nowadays, few visitors eat fish from the pond for fear of contamination or dare drink from the pond, as Thoreau did. The shoreline has been transformed, and the pond has been harmed by the effects of pollution and climate change—and of hundreds of thousands of swimmers who flock there each year and urinate in the water. Biology professor Curt Stager, the lead researcher on a study of the pond, was asked, What are people are doing to Walden Pond? "It seems like we may be on the verge of loving it to death, if we're not careful. Thoreau loved it for its clarity and beauty. People love it today for the same reasons, but we're changing the lake." Not very transcendental.

Like thousands of other pilgrims, Stager himself went to Walden—expecting to be disappointed: "Frankly, I was not. It's still beautiful and inspiring. Most of the crowds are on the far end of the lake, opposite the one that Thoreau was on. But there's a footpath you can follow back to the other end of this little secluded cove, called Thoreau's Cove, and his cabin site is right there in a grove of trees. I found all kinds of people enjoying Walden in all kinds of ways—from swimming and fishing, to contemplating Thoreau and our place in nature."

Now there is no place untouched by human activity. At the Art Gallery of Ontario I had the weird aesthetic experience of viewing the devastation in a gallery with crowds of people at a show by the Anthropocene Project, which aims to "evangelize" this term for a new geological age in which humans are the biggest force shaping the planet. The images were beautiful, disturbing and indelible: a mountain of burning elephant tusks and rhino horns, a hell-green dying sea, massive landfills and the people who subsist from them. Outside the exit, a sign anticipated my reaction: "Stay off the Ledge."

Thoreau saw the destruction of Walden even in his own short life—the trees cut down for fuel in the cold winters of 1851–1852, 20 trains a day rattling by, the common spaces of woods, fields, ponds and huckleberry patches shrinking away due to private ownership and development. What would he say to know there are nearly eight billion of us, about the rate and scale of the destruction and climate change?

Writer E.B. White called Thoreau "that hair-shirt of a man." He praised *Walden*, his favourite book, which inspired his own retreat, a boathouse in Maine. *Walden* he described as "the report of a man torn by two powerful and opposing drives—the desire to enjoy the world (and not be derailed by a mosquito wing) and the urge to set the world straight. One cannot join these two successfully, but sometimes, in rare cases, something good or even great results from the attempt of the tormented spirit to reconcile them."

I expect he's right: Thoreau would still try to enjoy the world while setting it straight. To live in harmony with the natural world we must be grounded in the rock of truth, he wrote. "Let us settle ourselves, and work and wedge our feet downward through the mud and slush of opinion, and prejudice, and tradition, and delusion, and appearance . . . until we come to a hard bottom and rocks in place, which we call reality."

His purpose was "profoundly religious," says Laura Dassow Walls, but his temple was made of wood. "He was writing a sacred book for the modern age," she says, "for his age—an age of expanding railroads, and global industrialism, rampant consumerism, mass migration and the exploitation of workers . . . environmental

destruction—in others words, a world an awful lot like our own."
Thoreau knew we each urgently need to find our own Walden Pond,
and he showed us the way.

Artists, Writers, Creative Thinkers, Dreamers

Best of any song is bird song in the quiet,
but first you must have the quiet.

—Wendell Berry

E. Jean Carroll is famous for her impious advice column, Ask E. Jean. From her small cabin in the woods, the former New Yorker dispenses wisdom to society from the margins upstate on questions such as "How do I find my dream job?" and "Can I sleep with my mother-in-law?" She cites Thoreau as an influence.

Carroll's funky retreat, christened the Mouse House because many distinguished rodents live there, is painted with black and white stripes. Inside shelves spill over with all the letters she has ever received for her long-running column, which appears in *Elle* magazine. Every day she gets up around noon, staggers outside and says, "Thank god I don't have children," and then staggers back in to her office to work. "I never thought much went on in the morning anyway," she says drolly. Carroll, who used to write for *Saturday Night Live* and was a contributing editor to *Esquire* and *Outside*, is an elegant woman of the wilds, appearing at home in an *Elle* video wearing a checked shirt with a striped skirt and tossing her cherry-red hair.

Outside, her garden shed is a canvas for the names of writers who influenced her—Jane Austen is writ large—and memorializing her deceased dogs. Rocks and trees are painted blue near the creek from once when it went dry and, horrified, she decided to restore the usual colour scheme and got carried away. Blue dots of the same shade adorn her car. Every day Carroll hikes three miles in the forests of her seven acres with her dogs. It keeps her young in her seventies, she says.

Located in the Wawayanda Mountains near the Appalachian Trail, Carroll's retreat makes possible the clear thinking crucial to her work. "I could not answer the questions coming into the Ask E. Jean column if I was in New York City. You can't think in New York, dating 16 people, which I would be doing if I were in New York. You go to the woods to find out who you are, you find out who you are, and you're even happier than when you came. It's wonderful!" she says.

Retreat is a practice familiar to writers and artists, in whose fields the notion of protected time and space for creation is common and has often been institutionalized—though what's true for artists' retreats applies equally to all creative endeavours. For an advice columnist, as for a sage of old, retreat provides vital perspective. Each day the wise woman of Wawayanda gets 200 letters from readers, asking advice on four main topics: "They want love. They want to be a size six. They want their children to do well. They want to have a purpose in life. They want those same things and that has never changed."

When Carroll needs advice she consults Thoreau: *Walden* is her favourite book. She lives simply, wrote a visiting reporter, describing her as "unmaterialistic and almost transcendental in nature," adding that she stores sweaters and dog food in her oven and shops for clothes at the local tackle shop. Explained Carroll, "I don't need Bergdorf Goodman."

Thoreau, who wrote up a storm at Walden, has inspired all manner of writers, artists, performers, scholars, thinkers and creative spirits to retreat, though not necessarily to the woods, to immerse themselves in their work. These days, when even hermits have websites, people in the arts are expected to be part solitary genius and part self-promoter, and everyone is distracted, a 21st-century stand-in for Walden Pond has become ever more essential. Whether alone, or in community, a retreat offers silence, solitude and simplicity, with few distractions, allowing us to reclaim the extended, elusive peace that for many is a requirement to create, ponder, plan and dream.

From the time of the Romantics on, as religion declined and the industrial age rose, people began to look to culture and nature for meaning—believing like Plotinus that "the soul that beholds beauty becomes beautiful." This led us into the realm of art, poetry and literature, a new focus for our sacred impulse, where we could turn for higher truth. Imagination, people have long believed, expands our sphere, makes us better, deeper, more human. And it consoles and elevates us. "There is no wing like meaning," as poet Wallace Stevens writes. Art can help make our human experience more comprehensible.

While I focus mainly on culture in this chapter, where the idea of retreat is most firmly entrenched, artists and writers here represent anyone who can benefit from creative time apart—philosophers, entrepreneurs, innovators, visionaries, women, scientists. Many today face challenges in finding this space. In physics, for instance, modern forces are working against retreating for "speculative contemplation," writes Felicity Mellor, a lecturer at Imperial College London, UK, who runs the Silences of Science project. Isaac Newton, Albert Einstein (who preferred "to think in apartness," according to a biographer), Henry Cavendish and Paul Dirac, known as a man of very few words, all retreated periodically, she notes in her 2014 article in *Physics World*. "Silence, and its companion, solitude, seems to be a recurring feature in the history of physics. Yet current research policy, in the UK at least, emphasizes silence's opposite." A new focus on communication and "enforced interaction" raises the danger that "an important precondition for creativity in physics could be lost."

Mellor provides highly compelling examples. Peter Higgs, she notes, claimed that he would not have been able to complete his Nobel Prize–winning work in the current research environment: "The peace and quiet that he enjoyed in the 1960s is, he thinks, no longer a possibility." She adds that the Institute for Advanced Study at Princeton was conceived in 1931 to provide "the tranquillity and time requisite to fundamental inquiry into the unknown," and "facilitated collaboration within a context of retreat." However, today in the UK, advanced study centres, like universities, now emphasize "collaboration and social impact over withdrawal and speculative contemplation."

In our busy, social, connected world, where even "successful" professional artists often don't earn a living from their work, threats to finding the time and space for creative practice are multiplying. This makes supportive retreats for working artists more important than ever. They serve as oases, as reminders to culture-makers of Rilke's counsel: "The necessary thing is great, inner solitude. What goes on inwardly is worthy of your love."

Artistic retreats, perhaps more than other types, demonstrate the ways in which retreat is not a set path you follow to a prede-termined goal. There's a misconception that artists are in control of the process and what happens on retreat, but it's more like an off-road adventure, with unforeseen directions, risk, exhilaration, lost weekends and unpredictable outcomes. "Negative capability," John Keats wrote, is being "capable of being in uncertainties, mysteries, doubts without any irritable reaching after fact and reason." It's like holding space for something new to happen— challenging in our productivity-obsessed world. Like God, or Nature, Art is a larger force that can't be controlled. To be an artist you need to be open to this, to be willing to be changed and to cultivate what Keats called "honeyed indolence."

Michel de Montaigne was an early extoller of the virtues of retreat in the 16th century. Against the backdrop of brutal civil wars in France, he wrote about himself in a bid to arrive at universal truths. Of particular note for contemporary people, he reflected on the question "how to live?" in times when the world seemed to have gone insane. Writing what he called essais—attempts, or tries—he created a new literary form, the essay. A nobleman, he had the luxury of leaving politics—"the slavery of the court and of public duties"—at 38 to write and cultivate his inner life. His library was in a tower in his family chateau complex near Bordeaux "to be his all-purpose retreat and centre of operations," writes Sarah Bakewell in *How to Live: A Life of Montaigne in One Question and Twenty Attempts at an Answer*.

The tower library, both a vantage point and a haven, represented freedom. The roof beams were inscribed with philosophy from the Greeks. Thousands of books, papers and curiosities filled the space, which he called his arrière-boutique, a "room behind the shop." This echoes his most famous lines, which offer one key element of what's needed to live a full, flourishing, honourable life: "We must reserve a back shop all our own, entirely free, in which to establish our real liberty and our principal retreat and solitude." For Montaigne, the front shop was for meeting others; the back shop was a refuge for the private self. His essais still influence the ways in which we take a step back to think and write today.

Many artists and creative thinkers value the ability to take interludes away from their regular lives. If poet Mary Oliver is correct that we all have three selves, it's the third self that goes on retreat. The first two, always with us, she says, relate to the ordinary world: the childhood self, and the social self, a "servant of the hours," who has many obligations. The third is a different, more capricious self, where our creative energy resides, and who is "occasional in some of us, tyrant in others," Oliver notes. "This self is out of love with the ordinary; it is out of love with time. It has a hunger for eternity."

Art, literature and other manifestations of culture are for many people sacred, providing a way to touch those larger forces and higher truths I spoke of earlier. Like Creation, human creation is a place of beauty and truth and transcendence. Rufus Wainwright expresses this idea, saying that opera now serves as his "religion in many ways." He told the *Guardian*, "I've often gone into the opera house in quite a state yet come out completely transfigured, so when I gear up to work in that world, it is like I am going into the clergy."

For poet Eileen Myles, "Copying everything in words is a form of loving the world," she says, explaining her devotion. "If I want to sit here and copy all day, that might be the best option available. It's not an antidepressant, and it's not exhilarating, and it's not aerobic, but it's a form of chanting—for religious reasons. I mean, it's my default position." Impassioned people were moved to risk their lives to save irreplaceable artistic treasures from the burning Notre Dame Cathedral. Religious scholar Huston Smith says appreciating art can change us: "Art, when it's great art and it's really working, what it does is transport us, lift us to a different state or consciousness from which the world looks very different." Listening to Bach, reading the poetry of Wordsworth, visiting the Tate Modern's 21st-century art temple, looking at the beyond in the Rothko Chapel: for many, these are transformative, numinous experiences.

Every great work of art and all beauty has a quality of mystery, and creativity is a force you have to give yourself over to. Yet there's a modern expectation that all artists must pivot easily between the sheltered place of deep reflection and surrender and the limelight for a little self-promotion. Today, the Brontë sisters' publicist would have insisted on a book tour, Emily Dickinson would likely be diagnosed with an anxiety disorder, and W.G. Sebald would have been pressed to be a little more upbeat to promote *The Rings of Saturn*. The whole idea of going deep, being vulnerable, becoming a receiver like a plant to the sun's energy, and creating art seems out of date and at risk in times that are all about speed, sociability and superficiality.

Though not everyone needs to withdraw to create, the idea that "solitude is the school of genius" is well established, and for centuries, artists and thinkers have retreated. While some may prefer to work at the kitchen table like Kazuo Ishiguro, who wrote his first two novels there, others, like painter Agnes Martin, require a studio without gadgets where one is "to be disturbed only if the house is burning." Time apart in retreat can be especially important to nourish developing artists, thinkers and dreamers. In *The Cloister Walk*, poet and essayist Kathleen Norris writes about two extended retreats, when she lived with the Benedictines at St. John's Abbey, Minnesota. There are no prodigies, she observes: "I have come to see both writing and monasticism as vocations that require periods of apprenticeship and formation."

Religion is full of meaningful rituals. I see retreat as an equivalent, a way of marking sacred time and space for art, or deep thinking, or for any creative purpose. Poet Meena Alexander was once asked at a public talk, "What use is poetry?" She lamented the struggle in our times for the poetic voice to be tolerated, much less fully heard. "Most of the forces in our ordinary lives as we live them now conspire against the making of a poem. There might be some space for the published poem, but not for its creation: no ritualized space is given where one is allowed to sit and brood."

A retreat serves as this ritualized space, and its imaginative hallmarks carry forward from the earliest retreaters in the West, the desert hermits and monks. In *Pilgrim at Tinker Creek* Annie Dillard describes her own step back. "I am no scientist," Dillard writes. "I am a wanderer with a background in theology and a penchant for quirky facts." She tells us she lives by a creek: "An anchorite's hermitage is called an anchor-hold; some anchor-holds are simple sheds clamped to the side of a church like a barnacle to a rock. I think of this house clamped to the rock-bottom of the creek itself and it keeps me steadied in the current as an anchor does, facing the stream of light pouring down." Dillard's is a very contemporary-style retreat, characterized by purposes that overlap rather than traditional religious ones—a time away for focusing on spirit, nature and art, in various measures.

For each kind of retreat our spirits seek, humans either go solo, or to institutions we've created so we may withdraw: hermitages and monasteries for the spiritual and religious; small cabins and protected lands for those who find divinity in nature; and arts colonies and residencies, which reflect what we consider the optimal conditions for artistic production. Many residencies open their doors more widely in recognition that creative people who aren't writers or artists also need to retreat.

Artists and thinkers have long engineered the degree of solitude that best suited their needs. Many produced their greatest works in time apart from the world, including notable self-directed retreater William Blake, who wrote, "Great things are done when men and mountains meet / This is not done by jostling in the street." He spent three artistically fertile years at a patron's cottage retreat, writing of the haven near Bognor Regis, where he and his wife stayed from 1800 to 1803: "Away to sweet Felpham, for Heaven is there; / The Ladder of Angels descends thro' the air." There he also wrote the timeless first words of "Jerusalem," "And did those feet in ancient time," a poem that later became the first line of the famous hymn that introduced the words "dark Satanic Mills" into the English language.

Ludwig Wittgenstein, one of the 20th century's most influential philosophers, was an inveterate solo retreater. He began to live in extreme isolation periodically in Skjolden, Norway, in 1913. His small cabin, halfway up a mountain and called "Little Austria" after his native country, served as his retreat throughout his life. Wittgenstein's longest stay was 13 months, when he went there to confront his own thoughts. "Whoever is unwilling to descend into himself because it is too painful," he wrote, "will of course remain superficial in his writing.'"

A remote farmhouse with no electricity on the island of Jura in the Hebrides is where George Orwell retreated in 1946, desperate to finish his novel. "Smothered under journalism," he told one friend, "I have become more and more like a sucked orange." The success of *Animal Farm* had added to the pressure. "Everyone keeps coming at me," he complained, "wanting me to lecture, to write commissioned booklets, to join this and that, etc.—you don't know how I pine to be free of it all and have time to think again." Already ill with tuberculosis, he fled London for creative freedom, accompanied by his young son and a nanny, to complete *Nineteen Eighty-Four*. By all accounts, the effort killed him.

Swedish filmmaker Ingmar Bergman wrote and storyboarded most of his scripts on the small island of Fårö. The year he released both *The Seventh Seal* and *Wild Strawberries*, 1957, he ate only yogurt and Marie biscuits and drank buttermilk—partly for simplicity's sake as he worked with great intensity, and partly due to an ulcer. Bergman had found the island while scouting for a film, and later retreated there for good, from the '60s until his death in 2007. Recently a rich Norwegian inventor and archeologist bought the house and turned it into the Bergman Estate on Fårö, a retreat that welcomes artists, scholars and non-fiction writers to come and work.

North American artists, likewise, devised the means for retreats of all descriptions. Painter Emily Carr bought the Elephant, her "grey and lumbering" caravan, in 1933. She'd have her moveable retreat hauled to a solitary place in the woods to work under huge cedars, or by the Esquimalt Lagoon, with its "wide sweeps of sea and sky, drifts galore, and hillside and trees, and great veteran pines," she writes in *Hundreds and Thousands*. Accompanied by her four dogs, Woo the monkey and her rat, she set the caravan down in a patch of daisies and wrote in her journal, "It's fine here. Nobody pesters you. The great wide beach is yours for the taking, its lapping waves and its piles of drifts all yours. The roses on the bank, bursting in a riot of cool pink from the piles of deep green leaves, toss out the most heavenly perfume."

Later Carr came to think of the Elephant as "a motherly old hen. Towed out, she meekly squats, fluffs out her flaps on all sides and encloses us. There's always room for another beast and we never seem crowded." Though it wasn't all bliss: on wet days Carr laments the primitive stove and having to lug water from the spring, "this pattering through puddles in a cotton nightgown and rain boots and pleading with the wet wood while hunger and hot-drink longings gnaw your vitals."

Carr's retreat allowed her to step back to the woods for weeks at a time in the summer to paint alone and explore her passion for the forest, like an ecstatic of old. Her work was a spiritual quest, and her approach to these retreats, writes Susan Crean in *The Laughing One*, "was to see them as both liberating and demanding; demanding of serious discipline and some physical hardship, and liberating spiritually as well as literally from the oppressive domestic routine back home."

Carr, a resilient fringe dweller, had a passion for the woods and, like many artists of her time, was influenced by Transcendentalist beliefs. Her success came later in life, after the Group of Seven discovered her and encouraged her work in 1927. Against the odds she became a pre-eminent painter, one of few major female artists working in North America or Europe. Before her resurrection she had done little painting for 15 years, caught up in the endless work of running a boarding house, breeding English sheepdogs and rabbits and making rugs and pottery to earn a living. Though she had produced a distinguished body of work, in conservative

Victoria she was viewed as an eccentric old spinster, a failed artist who had refused marriage because painting was more important.

Her newfound success allowed her to buy the Elephant, to take to the woods and commune with trees, and create some of her most powerful paintings. "What do these forests make you feel? . . . How absolutely full of truth they are, how full of reality," she writes in her journals. "Why is it that I feel that things are clearer when I am away from people in the woods? Whatever the reason, it explains my affection for the wild. If one's place of worship is that place that allows you to draw nearest to the universal spirit, then the forest is that for me. It is my church, my tabernacle, my refuge."

Notably, in *Places of Their Own*, organized by the McMichael Canadian Art Collection in 2001–2002, Carr's work was exhibited alongside that of two artists who worked—and retreated—at roughly at the same time: Georgia O'Keeffe, who withdrew to the Taos desert for part of each year, and Frida Kahlo, who began painting in enforced solitude, rather than voluntary retreat, after she was impaled in a tragic bus accident and left bedridden.

Among the most envy-inspiring retreats of all time is the Group of Seven's railway boxcar, specially outfitted with bunks, a stove and water tanks. Funded by Lawren Harris, scion of one of Canada's wealthiest families, the boxcar enabled the painters to take off in solitude together into the wilds of northern Ontario. "A car to live in, eat in and work out of," Harris wrote with excitement to J.E.H. MacDonald, imagining the train driver taking them to their muse. "They will move us about as we desire and leave us on auspicious sidings that we may proceed to biff the landscape out of a cocked hat at our sweet will." Though I don't quite know what "biff the landscape out of a cocked hat" means, his boxcar elation is unmistakable.

For pianist Glenn Gould retreat was more than a practical need to go deep into his work—it was a compelling artistic theme. After retiring from the concert stage at age 31, already an international virtuoso, Gould found himself drawn to the North, its isolation and its creative possibilities. He made the Solitude Trilogy, three hour-long documentaries about "withdrawal from the world." Gould believed "isolation is the indispensable component to human happiness," and that the ultimate goal of art and creativity was "the gradual life-long construction of a state of wonder and serenity." Gould's idea about solitude and society makes perfect sense to me, though each artist, and person, will have a different equation. "I've always had a sort of intuition that for every hour you spend with other human beings you need X number of hours alone," he says. "Now, what that X represents I don't really know, whether it be two and seven-eighths or seven and two-eighths, but it's a substantial ratio."

Six acres of boreal forest in Newfoundland is both retreat and subject for environmental artist and poet Marlene Creates, who won a 2019 Governor General's Awards in Visual and Media Arts. She says the ecosystem of the patch of forest, where she has lived since 1985, "has become the basis and the focus of all my work." At first she struggled to work in a studio, thinking that's what artists do. Eventually she decided to work outside. "Everything changed after that and the whole world became my studio . . . then I found I could work anywhere. I could use the whole planet and all its weather systems and celestial overhead—it all became material that I could use for my work instead of just sort of sitting in a room and trying to imagine something."

While many artists are aficionados of the self-directed solo retreat, akin to hermits, others prefer to be "alone together," more like monks. Formal artistic retreats gained favour in the late 19th and early 20th centuries, when progressive patrons sought ways to shelter high culture from the forces of the marketplace. Many of today's retreat-offering arts institutions in Europe and North

America grew out of this notion, also influenced by the Arts and Crafts movement that was led by architects, teachers and crafts-people working with patrons in a reaction against the soulless, machine-made products of the Industrial Revolution. The movement promoted the idea that beautiful, handcrafted everyday objects related to a good society and enhanced the lives of citizens and makers alike.

Places such as the Banff Centre for the Arts in Canada, the MacDowell and Yaddo colonies in the United States, Tyrone Guthrie in Ireland, the Arvon Foundation retreat centres in Britain and Skagen's Klitgaarden—The Dune House—in Denmark are among long-established residential arts retreats. Much lore is associated with such places—sex, drugs, clashing egos, wild imaginative flights—which I'll soon discuss. For now I'll describe a recent writing retreat I attended, which in my experience is more representative of the modern-day, cleaner-living norm. For many of us, a retreat is the best way we can access the deep privacy, free of family obligations, cooking, cleaning and juggling paid gigs. What feels most voluptuous is simply to be left alone to work.

In a courtyard enclosed by a 15th-century ruin and perched on a limestone crag above the River Esk, I admire the square tower of the castle's ancient keep, which now houses a library. I've carried my Fortnum & Mason wicker basket outside to eat lunch on the grass beside a deep well that descends to Bronze Age caves in the cliff below, and to pore over articles about my mysterious literary patron. Three short weeks ago, she died here at the castle, at age 103.

I'd hoped to thank Drue Heinz, heiress to a vast ketchup fortune, in person. For three decades she'd been married to tycoon Jack Heinz, who died in 1987—the same year she transformed her estate into the Hawthornden International Retreat for Writers. The castle, fittingly, was once the retreat of 17th-century poet William Drummond, sometimes also referred to as Hawthornden.

Mrs. Heinz, as everyone here refers to her, had a special affinity for literature: speaking about dying to a friend once, she'd remarked, "It's rather disconcerting to realize you can't take even a book with you." That friend, Darryl Pinckney, wrote about Mrs. Heinz in the *New York Review of Books*. While she'd rallied at the end, he said, "this weird and wonderful woman finally passed away, peacefully enough, they say, after a few weeks of decline, of talking to the radio, asking for her ski boots, and seeing a man in a cloak. She died at Hawthornden, the lovely castle nestled in a glen in Scotland that she was proud of having made into a writers' retreat."

The obituaries for Mrs. Heinz give me the impression of a fabulous yet difficult woman, a figure from a bygone era. Apparently she could spin a fiction herself: she told people she was an orphan cared for, variously, by lawyers, at a girls' school in Ireland and by spinsters in Norfolk. Other reports say her parents were from Norfolk, her birthplace. Doreen Mary English was her original name, she didn't go to college, had a brief film career under the names Drue English and Drue Mallory in 1950, and then married Jack Heinz, her third husband, in 1953. She liked to collect art and houses, lived in the United States and Europe and was known for her lavish parties.

Mrs. Heinz was also a chronic insomniac who spent nights between the covers of books and used her riches to become "the great literary philanthropist of our time," as Jonathan Galassi, president of the publisher Farrar, Straus and Giroux, described her. The publisher of the *Paris Review* for 14 years, Mrs. Heinz also co-founded Ecco Books in 1971, named for a beloved dog. She was a generous patron of the arts in both Britain and the United States. Magnanimous, yes, but she could also be menacing. Writes

Pinckney: "She was a nightmare to work for, her friends observed. One story has a guest at Hobe Sound, her house in Florida, opening the kitchen door to see Drue hitting the cook over the head with a leg of lamb"—or a frozen salmon depending on the source. Her husband called her writer friends "your crazies," which became a social category—"Drue's crazies." She loved writers though she rarely mixed with her creative guests at Hawthornden. But you might bump into her literary friends, as one young playwright did, starstruck to meet Tom Stoppard, who was just passing by.

I study the photographs of Mrs. Heinz: red hair, strong posture, spirited looking. At her retreat writers receive the kind of care usually only bestowed by kindly friends and family. It's as though a rich comrade has invited me to stay and work, giving me the run of her 120-acre estate and all I need to fill the cup.

In the lovely courtyard I thank the late Mrs. Heinz vigorously for these 30 days to write without distraction: for my sweet garret, three meals a day, laundry service, towels and a dressing gown, three libraries, the expansive grounds. Anyone with a published book can compete for a spot at Hawthornden. Learning in November I'd been granted a spring fellowship, I dreamt about it all winter long: a romantic castle, effortless writing, long walks, new literary friends. The fellows' guide was especially delightful: "Sherry is available for 50 p a glass in the Garden Room . . . fellows should keep a tally of their own consumption and settle up with the Director before leaving." Very notably, the guide also said there would be no cellphone or wireless signal: "You are strongly advised to make arrangements to forgo Internet access." Mrs. Heinz had specific ideas about how the writers must work. No gadgets—she thought the Internet was sinister—and silence from 9:30 a.m. till 6:30 p.m. This, my idea of unimaginable bliss, is not for everyone. Not all writers, or people, like the idea of retreat. Many wonder why go to a quiet place when they're looking for stimulation and might prefer a writers' retreat in Las Vegas, worry about getting bored or fear unravelling when faced with no distractions.

Hawthornden's unplugged aspect, in times when even yoga retreats and national parks usually have wireless in main buildings, doesn't suit everyone's work habits. I concede it makes research harder. Such a short time ago we went everywhere without our technology. Now, it seems impossible to manage one's life without it: opportunities missed for not answering in time, annoyed friends and family, inability to find your way without Google Maps. The idea of all-day silence is so unfamiliar it makes people agitated. The fellows' guide explained, "The idea is to provide a refuge free from the distractions and duties of daily life, where people can concentrate wholeheartedly on their writing," without obligation "to be sociable or do anything that will interfere with the business of writing."

When the time came to head for Scotland I was horrified to discover Mrs. Heinz's obituary in the *New York Times*. No one said otherwise, so off I went to Edinburgh. On an unseasonably hot April afternoon the director pulls up at Waverley Station, and hurriedly heaves my bag into his blue Subaru—do I note a disapproving look? I get in the back and a poet from Romania says hello from the front seat. A Russian novelist, who lives in Berlin, smiles as I buckle my seatbelt. Our questions to the director are met with extreme brevity, so we settle into our thoughts. We pass Arthur's Seat, an extinct volcano that looms over the city, and wend our way into the countryside. The director provides need-to-know information: he points out the village, the Paper Mill restaurant, which has Internet, and the bus stop in the small former mining town that we can walk to.

After about a half hour we pull up in front of a metal gate. The director tells us to note the password: magic, the keypad numbers to the kingdom. The gate swings open and we sweep down a drive lined by mature trees. The tires crunch to an abrupt stop on pebbles in front of the castle, our first sighting. It looks like a smallish castle from this angle, where you can't see the sheer drops to the river on three sides. An old door with a shield on it leads through the archway into the courtyard. We pass life-sized roe deer sculptures and enter a door into the modern house, attached to the ruins of the old castle. I have an impression of lots of tartan and hunting paintings as the director helps us drag our suitcases up three spiral staircases, each one narrower as we go. Now I see why he may have looked askance at my bag.

On the top floor, the servants' quarters, the rug is a shade of green I've only seen in photos of dying seas. Down at the end of the hall, I'm in Jonson—named for Ben Jonson, a guest who over-stayed here, I later learn. A fireplace! A hot water bottle. A pine desk and lamp. A tartan bag on the doorknob. My laundry day is Monday, and I just leave my bag in the hall for the housekeeper. A window that opens above the courtyard. The other rooms are Boswell, Evelyn, Herrick, Brontë, Milos and Drummond, poet and previous owner of the castle.

I meet a novelist from Boston coming out of Brontë, and take a quick walk along the steep, wooded banks of the river. The small chapel cut in the rock, which Queen Victoria visited in 1842 after stopping at nearby Rosslyn Chapel, of *Da Vinci Code* fame, is now off-limits due to a landslide. That evening when we gather for sherry before dinner, everyone else is dressed in finery, especially the fifth writer, a poet from Israel who has just arrived. I sport purple flip-flops. There are no sherry glasses, just wine glasses of various sizes, some cracked, and the garden room, which opens into the courtyard, is freezing cold. Next door in the dining room the décor runs to old portraits, stag's horns and a chandelier. A fire roars in the grate, rain patters against the window, and on the long wooden sideboard there's vegetarian haggis, mashed potatoes and turnips, and Gruyère soufflé for dessert and wine. The professional chef, a gem, has worked in many big houses. The conversation feels curiously stilted, I find, as though people are trying to score points and get one another's measure. I snort mentally, for instance, when the Romanian fellow says his favourite poet is Bukowski.

We ask the director questions. We ask when we can see the ancient Pictish caves under the castle. "Later—too soon, and you'll become jaded." I ask about Scottish poets. "Oh, that's not really my thing," he says vaguely. I ask about his poetry. He shakes his head, says he doesn't "go in for that," though we all know he's published, from our collective pre-arrival Internet searches. I ask about Mrs. Heinz. "She was a very formidable woman," he says with the practised delivery of a politician. After a little wine, he makes a Star Wars reference—something about Darth Vader? And Gorgons?

The writers retire to the drawing room, where we poke around in the adjoining library. It has a long, vertigo-inducing view down to the river gorge, and contains volumes about the castle, books by Hawthornden Prize winners, such as Tessa Hadley, Hilary Mantel and Graham Greene, and works by and about William Drummond. After Drummond's fiancée died on their wedding day in 1615 he spent years travelling, and then successfully married and retreated to Hawthornden. It's been more than 400 years since his *Poems Amorous, Funeral, Divine, Pastoral, in Sonnets, Songs, Sextains, Madrigals* was published. He addressed poems to the woods and loved his retreat, called it "sweet, solitary place." He rarely left until his death in 1649.

It's beautiful to think that this place has offered solitude and inspiration to writers since the 17th century. (There was a gap— apparently the last Drummond died in 1970 and gave the castle to his butler-chauffeur on a whim, and eventually, Mrs. Heinz bought it.) In the drawing room, portraits of Mrs. Heinz's friends Truman Capote and Aldous Huxley gaze down. We notice coffee stains on the reputedly Laura Ashley décor and worn and threadbare patches, dust on lampshades, a plug-in fire. None of us could care less, grateful for this gift of time and "decent ease."

For 30 days, time stretches ahead with nothing else to think about except writing. The staff—the enigmatic director, plus the brilliant professional chef and two kind housekeepers—support us in getting our work done. Over breakfast, a simple buffet in the Hearth Room where we usually also eat dinner, whoever shows up might talk about the relative merits of Pushkin and Chekhov, or the delights of the Scottish Poetry Library and thrift stores in Edinburgh, or the best walks by the river and along the old railway tracks. Then we fill in our lunch menu slips, ticking off choices so we can receive our baskets, left outside our room doors in the attic. The housekeeper asks us to let her know if we won't be there, as this is also how they keep track of us, make sure we're okay given the intensity of it all. They even know all about our staring into space trying not to panic, the supercharged imaginative particles colliding in our heads.

Then for the day it's silence. I usually work upstairs in my room until I hear my basket arrive around 12:30, a moment of huge significance. I sometimes photograph my lunch and send the images to friends, having discovered a cell signal on the driveway where the trees were trimmed. Most days, I have vegetarian soup in a thermos with a cup, a tuna sandwich with coleslaw, carrot sticks and Babybel cheese, which I eat in the courtyard, or the drawing room when it rains. I borrow boots and walking sticks and umbrellas as needed and walk along river paths above a gorge, with its spectacular views—one leads to Rosslyn Chapel, though now it's too muddy. Or I hike the old railway line path, or go the back way to the Paper Mill for coffee, or to Lasswade, where

William Drummond is buried in the cemetery, or march on paths alongside pastures with horses and farmers' fields to get to the bus stop or the town's library. When I return, I work some more, often in the castle's main library. Most days I do yoga in the adjoining conservatory, and lead classes for whoever wants to join me, with spring bees abuzz and apple trees blossoming. The estate's woods—ash, hazel, hawthorn, wild cherry and Scots pine—and gardens are flourishing.

After the first three days of terrible tech withdrawal, I become more grateful each day for the absence of Internet. Back home I sometimes write and research at the same time, which ruins my concentration, given the infinitude of the Web. Once, while writing the hermit chapter, I decided to check something I'd read. "Did hermits wear hedgehog skins?" I typed in. Three hours later, after reading about the many uses of animal skins and hair, and watching *Cave in the Snow*, a documentary about a British hermit who slept in a three-feet-square traditional meditation box for 12 years, I still hadn't written one word. But here, the muddy waters of my thought processes are settling into blessed clarity.

Without any distractions, technological and other, small events such as meals begin to take on enormous significance. We're expected to dress and show up for dinner, which is great because as the days go on, I get ever more dishevelled and unused to speaking. I enjoy our dinner talks, the only time we're all together, and learn how it is to be a poet in Israel and Romania; the secret of the group's two most prolific writers, both novelists, who say they work to reach daily page counts; about other international residencies to try and much else. One evening I mention a community of Trappist monks who, forced by new health regulations to shut down their egg business, had to find new work light enough for elderly men. "Sperm donors?" someone guesses. Gourmet mushrooms, actually. Another night the director tells me a hair-raising tale about Armand Jean le Bouthillier de Rancé, founder of the Trappists, who found religion after seeing the decapitated corpse of his mistress. Each night when the director blows out the candles to signal dinner is over, we disperse. We're monkish and rarely meet after dinner, instead heading back to our rooms. I read and am in bed most nights by 10:30 p.m. When I discover I get a cell signal in my room, I watch *Extreme Pilgrim* and other spiritual reality shows on my phone, wondering whether the BBC has ever done a program on arts monastics.

My inner contrarian always acts out so that on a writing retreat, I never work on the project I've brought with me. Or maybe it's just that the unplanned slips in. At the castle to advance my poetry manuscript, instead I become obsessed by hermits and monks, and read and write prodigiously. In the flow of the days, under the spell of the river below, time glides by and we all begin to lose track of the days and feel reluctant to leave the peace that enfolds us. It's glorious: the spring flowers and trees in bloom, birds singing. I spend sunny hours reading outside, one book about the pleasures of being alone and free, another about a modern-day sojourn to monasteries in the Holy Land. I wake up earlier and earlier each day, at dawn and before, and soon, by breakfast I have worked for hours.

As time goes on, we all begin to visit Edinburgh for a needed change of air from our intense little community. One day I walk in the ravishing botanical garden. I'm amused to realize I'm lingering in the Native Woodland area, which feels most like home, and in front of an Andy Goldsworthy sculpture made of flat stones called *Cone* that reminds me of a Celtic monk's beehive hut. That evening at dinner, the Israeli poet, passionately engaged in the conflicts of home, asks how long I stayed in the gardens. When I tell her she says, "Yes, three hours is enough—you can only stay in a garden so long." The conversation moves on, but I'm still wondering, "Why?" Must we limit our intake of peace and beauty? What about "gather your rosebuds while ye may"? Gardens, like libraries and art galleries, are sanctuaries we can access easily in our everyday lives. And given that we *are* nature, visits can't really be of a prescribed duration. We humans tend to focus only on the dark, on conflict and action; but isn't this what makes amplifying the light, the peace and deep reflection we ignore, of such relevance?

About midway through the retreat the director, ever strategic, shows us the ancient caves. He offers to lock me in if I want to experience hermit life for my writing. I decline, feeling panicked. We also visit the medieval dungeon. It takes two to pull open the heavy trap door in the courtyard. Everyone descends, but I feel it may not be a good idea to step down with the others in case the director is finding us tiresome—especially now I've learned the story of Ben Jonson, my room's namesake. The poet laureate of England, a former bricklayer, he walked for a month from London to Edinburgh to visit Drummond/Hawthornden, who later slagged his new friend in a private journal. The insult got around, however: "He is a great lover and praiser of himself . . . oppressed with fantasy which hath ever mastered his reason—a general disease in many poets." Sir Walter Scott later commented that conflict between them was likely as the two men were so dissimilar: "one, a genius and man of the world, 'risen from the ranks' having a long struggle for intellectual superiority—the other (who did not exceed a decent mediocrity) living a retired life, and, therefore, cautious and punctilious, timid in delivering his opinion, apt to be surprised and even shocked at the uncompromising strength of conception and expression natural to Jonson."

Wild connections, such as linking an unwanted guest more than 400 years ago to the director potentially locking me in a dungeon, are rife among us by now. Odd imaginative states are common on a month's retreat, and being thrown up against your own work for an extended time sparks both joy and terror. Annoyances are also common. Week three I write in my journal: "This morning A ate ants with his Cheerios. I had a little sprinkled on my muesli and likely ate some too. People are in revolt about the old Victorian toilet that trickles for ages before you can flush. No fires in the grates, cracked panes, frayed carpets, faded grandeur, a kind of rote quality about things." The next day I write: "It doesn't matter at all: gratitude that someone would support our efforts like this. It is so heartwarming. I feel buoyant."

On our final morning I sit in the courtyard thinking about arts patrons. Over the past hundred-plus years, retreats were often founded by the rich philanthropists of the industrial era. Hawthornden has hosted hundreds of poets, playwrights, novelists, short story writers, biographers and essayists from around the world over the past 33 years, playing an essential role in literary production. For me, periodical retreats were how I became a writer, stepping stones that led away from the swirl of a busy everyday life focused on other things. These precious pauses from the everyday were, and are, my lamp, lifeboat and ladder, in Rumi's words. Retreat remains my method to make space for creative work, and for my yoga life, as I'll get to soon.

The motto of Hawthornden is etched in stone on the wall beside me, taken from the inscription with which Drummond venerated his house in 1638: "ut honesto otio quiesceret," to be in peace and decent ease. In the modern world, "peace and decent ease," the notion of deep absorption necessary to create art, is at risk. Do most artists even want that now—and do audiences want what comes from that uninterrupted space? I wonder whether havens like this are fading out, much like the castle's old carpets.

Mrs. Heinz truly loved books. I'm gratified that she saw fit to redistribute her condiment wealth by making this oasis for writers—though the rich arts patron model of retreat is often repellent. The early departure of a writer at the highly sought-after Santa Maddalena in Tuscany, a by-invitation-only retreat, is described in a 2007 article in *New York* magazine. The writer, it seems, "was breaking the code that defines the artist-patron relationship: The artist is to be charming until excused." Baronessa Beatrice Monti della Corte von Rezzori, the article adds, is "an impatient, charismatic, preternaturally controlling woman." Santa Maddalena is her home, which she converted into a retreat after the death of her husband, the novelist Gregor von Rezzori, in 1998. When the bell rings for lunch, writers "descend from their respective studios and join the baronessa and her pug, Alice, on the poolside patio. Hostess to a breed not exactly known for their extroversion, Beatrice is fond of turning meals with writers into impromptu seminars on etiquette." Santa Maddalena has no endowment, and its future is uncertain. It sounds like a holdover from the past, when the rich wanted to be associated with literature and writers for prestige—a role more often fulfilled, perhaps, by movie stars and celebrities today?

Oftentimes, however, what began with a patron evolved into a sustaining institution: two of the leading retreats in North America—the MacDowell Colony, founded in Peterborough, New Hampshire, in 1907, and Yaddo, founded in 1926 in Saratoga Springs, New York—were created by wealthy lovers of art. Both retreats still perform their mission—to give the gift of time and space to artists so they can further their creative process and work without interruption in a supportive community. Both provide room and board for about 30 artists at all stages of their careers, including writers, visual artists, musicians and composers, who apply for free residencies of up to two months. Like many colonies, both are now nonprofit organizations funded by private philanthropic largesse. Over the years they have hosted thousands of artists and writers, playing a vital role as a retreat for the likes of James Baldwin, Leonard Bernstein, Saul Bellow, Flannery O'Connor, Truman Capote, Jacob Lawrence, Henri Cartier-Bresson, Sylvia Plath, Carson McCullers and, more recently, A.M. Homes, Amy Tan and Michael Cunningham, to name a few.

The MacDowell Colony was founded by pianist and philanthropist Marian MacDowell and cultivates a New England work ethic and simplicity. It has 32 cabin-studios in the woods and one strict rule: it's forbidden to interrupt other artists while they're working. This is wise considering that you might find someone weeping, disinhibited and dancing around, or sleeping at odd hours. Michael Chabon and his wife, the novelist Ayelet Waldman, take turns going on retreat here annually for two weeks. "For me there's no substitute," Chabon told the *New York Times* in a phone interview as one of his four young children screamed in the background. As well, these artist sanctuaries are often socially responsive. Yaddo housed many writers during the Great Depression, and today, MacDowell has doubled endowments to investigative journalists, explaining, "In this era of fast news and free content, a new model of support is needed for journalists who dedicate their lives to telling complex stories that have the power to change our lives and make our society better."

Yaddo, as one might expect from an over-the-top imitation of an Austrian castle with 55 rooms on a 400-acre estate near the Saratoga racetrack, has a totally different atmosphere than the woodsy MacDowell. It is perhaps most storied of all American retreat centres, founded by Katrina Trask and her financier husband, Spencer Trask.

Yaddo, meant to rhyme with shadow, was named by their four-year-old daughter, who, legend has it, saw shadows cast by her recently deceased brother amid the trees of the estate. "Call it Yaddo, Mama, for it makes poetry!" she said. Tragically, the child and another brother soon after died of diphtheria. Then an infant daughter died, and after that, Yaddo burned to the ground. The grieving Trasks rebuilt and opened their artist's colony. Katrina imagined artists who were "thirsting for the country and for beauty, who are hemmed in by circumstance . . . creating, creating, creating!" In *Yaddo: Making American Culture*, Micki McGee writes that it was conceived for those "gifted with Creative power"— "a place of respite for creative workers whose labours were not likely to be supported by the mechanisms of an expanding market economy that had so generously rewarded the Trasks' own undertakings."

The idea that high culture needed to be protected, uncontaminated by popular culture, had taken hold by 1900. "With this new cultural stratification came the idea that an elite culture, one that would uplift rather than pander to popular tastes, would require new, non-market driven forms of patronage. The ideal of culture as a gift to be protected from the exchanges of the marketplace emerged," writes McGee. "The Trasks shared an abiding faith in creativity as a transformative force that would necessarily improve life for mankind."

Early on, Yaddo was praised by the *New York Times* as a "new and unique experiment, which has no exact parallel in the world of fine arts." Katrina's vision went like this: "Some of them will see the Muses. Some of them will drink of the Fountain of Hippocrene, and all of them will find the Sacred Fire and light their torches at its flame." Hedonistic drinking, legend holds, and other sacred fires were also in evidence: John Cheever, inebriated, once slid down the grand staircase on an ornate ice sleigh, a gift to the Trasks from the Queen of the Netherlands. He boasted that he had enjoyed sex on every flat surface in the mansion, not to mention the garden and the fields. Yaddo, he declared, attracts "all kinds—lushes down on their luck, men and women at the top of their powers, nervous breakdowns, thieves, cranky noblemen and poets who ate their peas off a knife."

Yaddo is where, in 1940, Carson McCullers developed an ardent crush on Katherine Anne Porter and lay in front of the older woman's bedroom, hoping in vain for some attention. Porter, annoyed, stepped over her, and rushed off for dinner. Yaddo, known for its bats—there's a policy against killing them—made Truman Capote complain in a letter, "I simply can't stand that cheep-cheep crying as they circle in the dark." Poet Elizabeth Bishop, who called herself "three-quarters Canadian" and lived as a child in Nova Scotia, the setting for various poems, once wrote that everyone needs a long period of solitude at least once in their life. (Elizabeth Bishop House in Great Village, now privately owned, was for decades a retreat and place of pilgrimage for writers.) Yaddo wasn't the place for Bishop. Her witty, often anguished, accounts of her time there feature in *One Art*, a fat volume of her letters selected by her long-time editor, Robert Giroux.

At Yaddo, where she was twice, in 1949 and 1950, she spent most of her time at the racetrack drinking coffee and eating blueberry muffins. "The auction of the yearlings was fun and very beautiful—particularly the chestnuts under the bright lights and against the bright green grass." Or getting terribly drunk and feeling second-rate and lonely. "I've mixed about like a drop of oil in water," she writes to one friend. She tells painter Loren MacIver: "There's not much point describing this place. It would take forever and was obviously all the dream of mad millionaires with high ideals, etc."

The mad millionaires' room was to be hers. In a 1949 letter to poet Robert Lowell, she writes: "I have that huge room with 34 windows—bloody hot—but very grand. I haven't been able to 'work' at all so spend most of my time very pleasantly sitting on my balcony blowing bubbles. There is something a little sinister about the place, though, don't you think? I keep getting bats in my room and even met one in the woods in broad daylight—and then all those awful scummy ponds. But I think what is really the source of the trouble is the *smell*—old lunch boxes, I guess."

Bishop veers between desperate and charming. "In fact I JUST DON'T KNOW anything except that I'd like to die quite quickly," she writes at one point. And then, "It has been a tough stretch but the agony has abated, as Macaulay said at the age of nine when he burned his finger & someone asked him how it was." Years later she described this time at Yaddo as "the most wretched and unpleasing stretch" of her life. By November she was 40, falling apart and spent Christmas in hospital to dry out. She stayed at Yaddo until March, when she received the Bryn Mawr fellowship that changed her life. She decided on "a crazy trip" and found her perfect retreat in Brazil, where she did her best work, for which she received a Pulitzer Prize. Her small studio was in the garden of the house in the hills near Rio she shared with her beloved Lota de Macedo Soares, an architect. The house, Samambaia, which means "fern," in Portuguese, inspired her luscious poem, "Song for the Rainy Season," and much else.

At Yaddo today the mission is unchanged, though the range of artists eligible is wider: writers, poets, painters, sculptors and composers, choreographers, film and video makers and performance artists, says president Elaina Richardson. "But now we operate in a deeply changed landscape, where—thankfully—residency opportunities have increased dramatically for contemporary artists, but paradoxically, financial support for individual artists (of all kinds) has diminished radically. Thus the role of a place such as Yaddo in the ecology of artistic production has shifted." Arts retreats now too often face financial challenges: Yaddo's endowment doesn't cover its expenses so it began opening its doors to the public in 1993, hoping to inspire further gifts.

Complete artistic freedom, like water in the desert, is what the Banff Centre for Arts and Creativity aims to give performing artists, visual artists, writers, film and new media creators. Recognizing the difficulties faced by artists today—and everyone who needs time and space for creative work—Banff recently offered a retreat that's about retreat. In the Art of Stillness residency with Pico Iyer, people from various disciplines reflected "on artistic practice in an accelerated world," exploring "what this increased speed of life means for practising artists and what value we can gain in slowing down."

In times when financial support for artists has plunged, as have incomes in a "free content" digital world, the chance to experiment and work free of everyday concerns is rare and precious—as is meeting passionate others who have accepted the absurd and insolvent artist's life, because there's nothing they'd rather do. Artistic people find ways to retreat, even in hard times, cracks in the pavement where their work can take root. Sheds have been frequent retreats—Dylan Thomas's "word-splashed" writing shed at Laugharne, Virginia Woolf's shed at Monk's House where she wrote in summers, Philip Pullman's garden shed. Cabins in the woods are common too, and today one can add myriad quirky retreats. Low-rent storage spaces frequently serve as studios in places with decent weather, and a garbage dump program in San Francisco has been offering selected artists studio space and "scavenging privileges" since 1990. It was the idea of an artist trying to normalize recycling, writes Amanda Petrusich in the *New Yorker*—and a sign of our times. "The symbolism of sequestering artists to the garbage pile is perhaps too hilarious and heartbreaking to ignore," she notes.

True, artists are squeezed hard and a proliferation of off-beat residencies can be seen as an indicator of how difficult it has become to maintain any sort of creative practice. But I can't help thinking it also displays the resilience of creators, who refuse to cede their marginal space, in which they make what has no utility—which is their strength. "To paint now is an act of resistance which answers a widespread need and may instigate hope," writes John Berger in the conclusion to his brilliant essay "Steps Toward a Small Theory of the Visible." In the past, painting was an affirmation of what exists, the visible, he says. With technology this has changed: no longer real, or an encounter with what's real, virtual images abound, and technology refracts them in instants. Berger relates this to the system's need for consumption, our appetites, which created a shift from the real to mere spectacle. Existing outside convention and the commercial, artists traffic in the genuine and heartfelt.

Writers today can find their muse on an Amtrak train residency, and Container offers 12 artists the chance to spend a month each on board a huge cargo ship on worldwide routes. "Artists require solitude, beauty, the natural sublime and global travel," the administrators write. "They crave extended stretches of time, free of any interruption, in order to create new work. All of this can be found on a container ship." Dune shacks by the ocean; a residency at the Large Hadron Collider in Geneva; farm retreats where you can choose to exchange work for room and board; Land Art Mongolia 360 for site-specific land art that reflects the biodiversity of the Gobi Desert—the possibilities for retreat, paid, unpaid, subsidized, are endless.

All creative spirits can emulate artists' imaginative ways to find islands of time and space. I was charmed by an artist in Valencia who takes retreat to new heights: he built a tiny urban hut under a concrete bridge, suspended 20 feet up in the air, to claim the solitude to work. Fernando Abellanas's retreat, which took him two weeks to make, is simply but beautifully decorated, with a chair, desk, duvet and cushions. The traffic, he says, provides just the right amount of white noise. To get up there he steps onto an accessible platform on the low end under the bridge, and then hand-winches it across. Abellanas, understandably, won't reveal his retreat's exact location, but says he will "enjoy it as long as it lasts." He emphasizes that urban environments are full of small, unnoticed quiet places we can adapt for our purposes.

His hut under the bridge and his remark stir my imagination. Abellanas echoes the call to retreat, noting that space is every-where if we have eyes to see it. His actions also underline why retreat matters: so we may pay attention, step past what we already know and move from the authorized into new ways of being. The marginal, liminal space his hut occupies under the bridge reflects the way artists and writers, not to mention hermits, monks and pilgrims, and lovers of nature, occupy threshold space. In self-exile in a quiet retreat, outside the everyday hustle and bustle, we preserve an inviolable place for original thinking and for a kind of divinity that makes life worth living.

May Sarton speaks to the deep engagement, transcendence and wholeness to be experienced in such sanctuaries of retreat—whether we are making art, appreciating it or engaging other creative purposes, alone or alone in community. In *Journal of a Solitude*, published in 1973 and still in print, she evokes this state of union beautifully: "I have a fire burning in my studio, yellow roses and mimosas on my desk. There is an atmosphere of festival, of release in the house. We are one, this house and I, and I am happy to be alone—time to think, time to be."

Light
of the
East

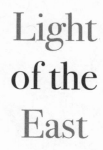

OF YOGA ASHRAMS, MEDITATION HALLS
AND BODY AS TEMPLE

*In a place helpful to the mind and pleasing to the eyes,
in a hidden retreat, let the aspirant cultivate spirituality.*

—Svetasvatara Upanishad, fifth or sixth century BC

The Inner Temple

The wind howls but the mountain remains still.

—Eastern proverb

In India, the decision to step back to a sacred grove, mountain cave or ashram by the river has long been encouraged and respected. Of all the Eastern traditions that reached Western shores in the 20th century, yoga and meditation—which both value retreats and teach that fulfillment can be found within—have been the most ardently adopted. These aren't New Age fads, but ways to rediscover the much-needed wisdom of an earlier age, to cultivate peace and equanimity amid ceaseless change. Moderns by the millions have embraced these ancient paths, learning how to *be* versus *do*—by looking inward and periodically going on retreat.

I always roll my eyes at the misconception that a yoga or meditation retreat is all bliss and butterflies. Consider the experiences of Jodi Ettenberg, a writer from Montreal who attended a vipassanā retreat in New Zealand—never having meditated before. "I need to defrag my hard drive. It isn't running efficiently," she told a friend, comparing the retreat to hiring a personal trainer to help her at a first-ever session at the gym. Her friend replied, "No, it's like running a marathon having never run before. . . . *What* are you doing to yourself?"

Ettenberg signed up for ten days—no talking, no interactions and no eye contact—"in a moment of quiet desperation" after nearly a year of insomnia and chronic pain. At the retreat she suffered mightily, afflicted by perfectionism, panic, pain, silence, spiders. Yet her experience overall was positive: "I emerged from the course a calmer, temporarily less anxious version of myself. I started to sleep again. The relief of rest was palpable." A year afterwards she added that the retreat had "calmed me at a deep and inexplicable level . . . imbued me with a sense of perspective I now maintain and am deeply grateful for."

Yoga and Buddhism have overlapped significantly in our spiritual but not religious times, and we often draw on both. Retreat is integral to these India-rooted systems, which share the same ancient source, the Vedas, the world's oldest sacred texts. The rise of yoga and meditation in the West—and along with it, the practice of retreat—resulted from a surprising alchemy. Who could have predicted that when the vast wisdom of the East's spiritual heritage—which shaped the great civilizations of India, China and Japan, and Southeast Asia—reacted with the materialistic West, the result would be a yoga and meditation revolution?

These imported traditions have shaped how we retreat today, guided by a lively array of gurus and their countercultural students, and spiced with many East-West collisions. Yoga and meditation have also penetrated deeply into our culture, seeping into religions, as well as scholarly work, civil rights and protest movements, health care and psychology. First seen as religious practices, they appear in many secular contexts such as schools, workplaces, hospitals and gyms; yoga studios and meditation centres are nearly as ubiquitous as corner cafés. This familiarity is why today Westerners willingly face the rigours of retreats in groups or alone, choosing from thousands of options on websites like retreat.guru and learning to find sacred space inside. "It is through your body that you realize you are a spark of divinity," said esteemed Indian yoga teacher B.K.S. Iyengar.

From the start, yoga and Buddhist meditation suited the Western temperament. Both offer freedom of thought and worship, as well as personal pathways to the divine or the infinite. For secular people, no need to believe in God—more of an impersonal intelligence—though it's no problem if you do. No need to separate intellectual and spiritual enquiry—it's about consciousness, one of the great mysteries, which some scientists call "the hard problem," also a concern of Vedanta yoga philosophy and Buddhism. With no need to wait for the afterlife, these traditions also offer techniques and benefits that appeal to Westerners' pragmatic love of provable results, such as better health and happiness.

As organized religion declined, these traditions filled a vacuum for people who "found a vision of possibilities that seemed not only sublime but rational and attainable," as Philip Goldberg puts it in *American Veda*, about how Indian spirituality changed the West. "What some saw as theology, others saw as testable hypothesis. What some viewed as spiritual practices, others viewed as therapies."

Matthieu Ricard, deemed by neuroscientists to be the world's happiest man, is a Tibetan Buddhist monk and geneticist who has spent years in solitary retreat. When researchers monitored his brainwaves as he meditated on compassion, he produced brain gamma waves never before reported in neuroscience. The waves are linked to consciousness, attention, learning and memory. Ricard credits meditation, which he calls weight-lifting for the mind. Anyone can become happy, he adds, by training the brain. As with yoga, all that's required is the lab of one's own body to apply the techniques and experience what happens.

As with everything else you do consistently, the more you practise the easier it gets—though habit energy is strong and it takes time and focus. In general, yoga and meditation, which come in myriad varieties, teach that the way to a clear, calm mind is to pay attention to the body and the breath—the basis for touching the infinite. "Tell me, what is God? He is the breath within the breath," writes 15th-century Indian poet-saint Kabir.

Simple, and yet to stop and focus on what's happening in the moment is a radical act that may involve breaking a lifetime of habit. Paying extreme attention is where retreat comes in: in a distraction-free setting that fosters our ability to go deeper, certain insights arise naturally—that the body and mind are one, for example, and that everything is interrelated and connected at a deep level. The idea is that retreat helps us get beyond the ordinary, conditioned self, with its concepts and endless discursive thoughts, to another, embodied way of being in the world.

Tellingly, body-centred ways of retreat—the pilgrimage, getting outside in nature and yoga and meditation retreats—are the most popular in our deskbound, virtual, breathless 21st century.

Retreating is a bit like learning to drive: at first, you don't want to go on a busy highway; you take a wide, quiet road. Once you've mastered the basic disciplines of yoga and meditation, you test your newfound attention and equanimity in challenging places, like everyday life. Far from being individualistic, yogic and Buddhist retreats aim to promote self-development that will create a more positive world. They relate to deep ecologies, and movements like the "socially engaged Buddhism" of Vietnamese activist and teacher Thich Nhat Hanh, who emphasizes if there is to be peace in the world, there must first be peace in the heart. Personal insights ripple into the political. By replacing our usual obliviousness with mindfulness, we slow down, settle and begin to understand ourselves and the impact of our own thoughts and choices. From there, we can try to create the kind of world we want to live in once we return from retreat.

Modern-day commercialization has diluted Eastern spiritual traditions—I thought a yoga and pole-dancing demo on *Oprah* must be the final low, but that was years ago, and now these practices are being used to sell everything from hamburgers to wine. At the same time it's amazing to see that fuller spiritual systems continue to gain currency—as with yoga's "eight limbs," which extend beyond the familiar physical postures and breathing practices. And study retreats are more widespread than ever.

Vedanta yoga has proven so popular, writes Philip Goldberg in *American Veda*, in part because it satisfies conditions that were by and large not emphasized in organized religion in the West: transformation and transcendence, or "the yearning to enlarge the perceived boundaries of the self, touch the infinite, and unite with the ultimate Ground of Being."

What are we in search of on retreat? Contemporary Buddhist teacher and filmmaker Khyentse Norbu articulates the purpose of the path of meditation in the entertaining documentary *Words of My Perfect Teacher*: "When you don't have obsessions, when you don't have hang-ups, when you don't have inhibitions, when you're not afraid you'll be breaking certain rules, when you're not afraid you won't fulfill somebody's expectations, what more enlightenment do you want? That's it." Being free from neurosis, basically. Sounds like nirvana indeed.

The transmission of yoga and meditation retreats to the West was led by an army of pioneering teachers who, especially since the 1960s, popularized Vedic and Buddhist ideas and practices and awakened millions to the power of retreat for inner transformation. To deliver their teachings these yogis, acharyas, monks, bhikkhus and Zen masters began moving into former Catholic seminaries, summer camps and prisons, where they built new learning outposts in the forests, mountains, cities and suburbs. The idea of retreat gradually became commonplace.

There have always been people in history who show their warriorship through peace and gentleness. Among them is Swami Vivekananda of Kolkata, often credited with bringing yoga and meditation, and retreats, to North America. Vivekananda, "clad in gorgeous red apparel, his bronzed face surmounted with a huge turban of yellow," appeared at the World's Parliament of Religions in Chicago in 1893. The handsome, dignified monk was an instant celebrity, drawing large crowds, writes Rick Fields in *How the Swans Came to the Lake*. A perfect envoy for Vedanta yoga in the West, he'd attended a college founded by Scottish missionaries, where he studied Western philosophy, logic and history. And he was a devotee of Sri Ramakrishna, "probably the first well-known exemplar of religious pluralism . . . famously declaring that all traditions can lead to the infinite," writes Goldberg in *American Veda*.

Swami Vivekananda set a pattern many later gurus were to emulate: he spoke English, knew the ways of the West and made practical adaptions to his approach to suit his new audience. He evoked the Bible, talked of religious unity—kicking off the modern interfaith movement—and admired science. Notably for the progress of the practice of retreat in the West, he also founded the Vedanta Society to disseminate his teachings. Still highly influential today, the organization has about 20 retreat properties and centres worldwide, including one of historical and spiritual significance not far from my home in Kingston.

Vivekananda Cottage, on Wellesley Island in the St. Lawrence River, is known to millions of followers worldwide as the place where the guru reached enlightenment while meditating in the woods in 1895. He'd been at the summer place of one of his wealthy New York students, leading a seven-week retreat. The property was acquired in 1946 by the Ramakrishna-Vivekananda Centre in New York City and has been the site of an annual spiritual retreat for devotees ever since—including J.D. Salinger in the '50s, before his unhealthy reclusion set in and he put curtains on his car windows. Today pilgrims from India and all over the world visit the Victorian cottage, open in the summer months, often attending arati, the singing of devotional songs and meditation.

Vivekananda adapted ancient ideas to the conditions of modern life, with a focus on meditation and mantras, rather than movement, and on Vedanta philosophy. The first wave of yogis who had come to North America from India at the turn of 19th century, including Vivekananda, were "hatha-haters" with a legacy of "yoga from the head up," writes Robert Love in *The Great Oom: The Improbable Birth of Yoga in America*. They scorned yoga's physical poses, influenced by British colonizers, their Indian sympathizers and Christian missionaries who saw the physical practices as "the embodiment of heathenism." Vivekananda attracted Western followers from diverse backgrounds, including inventor Nikola Tesla, and he had many influential friends—notably William James, the father of modern psychology and author of *The Varieties of Religious Experience*. From this time on, many leading Western thinkers were to be influenced by Eastern teachers, both Vedic and Buddhist. And for advanced learning, they attended retreats.

After Vivekananda, Eastern teachers began arriving in waves, bringing new traditions, publishing books and opening retreat centres and ashrams—taking their place in a lineage of mavericks of retreat in the West that stretches from the early desert fathers and mothers through the Romantics and Transcendentalists. The first superstar guru, Paramahansa Yogananda, whose name means "supreme swan" and signifies someone in a state of union with God, arrived in the United States in the 1920s. He introduced millions to yoga and meditation over the next 30 years, founding the Self-Realization Fellowship (SRF) retreat in an abandoned hotel on Mount Washington that overlooks Los Angeles—a city he called the Benares (Varanasi) of the West, after India's holy city and pilgrimage site.

The quiet and disciplined world of the SRF retreat, which is now its international headquarters, drew worldly celebrity students who helped to spread the word. Elvis visited often during his Hollywood years, once supposedly telling a monk, "Man, you made the right choice." He also frequented the serene Lake Shrine at the Pacific Palisades retreat, a ten-acre campus where George Harrison, another follower, held his funeral. The Hollywood Temple on Sunset Boulevard was founded in 1942, and the Lake Shrine in 1950; both are still open to the public as sanctuaries for contemplation and meditation apart from the smog and noise of the city.

Yogananda's profile skyrocketed when he began going on lecture tours and filling halls, and after he released his modern spiritual classic, *Autobiography of a Yogi*, in 1946. He wrote the book in a hermitage that overlooks the Pacific Ocean at Encinitas, California. There, he also started the SRF retreat program, which he called "a dynamo of silence where [you] may go for the exclusive purpose of being recharged by the Infinite." Until his death in 1952 he continued to open retreat centres, often with donations from affluent disciples like George Eastman, founder of Eastman Kodak.

The SRF offered "happiness now" and advocated for world peace through kriya yoga for mind, body and spirit. Yogananda appealed to spiritual and secular students alike with his practical approach, calling chakras "centres," rejecting dogma and embracing universal principles: he revered Jesus and praised scientific rationalism. His various temples and monasteries drew laypeople wanting to retreat and also housed monastics. All lived simply in cell-like rooms and spent days in meditation, prayer, doing yoga postures, working to support the community and in spiritual study and silence. Like Vivekananda, Yogananda helped set the template for retreat in the West; today he has millions of followers and myriad retreat centres worldwide.

At first, yoga and meditation, ancient spiritual disciplines, were considered dangerous and corrupting by the Western mainstream. One early stumbling block was that we have no tradition of living with your teacher to study on retreat. Westerners struggled with the teacher-student relationship in general, which required a different level of trust, perhaps similar to the way you believe in your doctor's desire for your well-being, and in their prescriptions. Conflicts resulted when Eastern tradition met Western student—and many gurus were to fall off their pedestals for abusing spiritual authority. Over the years, countless high-profile scandals have exposed the sexual and economic exploitation of students.

Rigorous discipline and unquestioning obedience were not very Western, and the style of Eastern teachers was also a departure:

to quote Tibetan-Bhutanese Lama Khyentse Norbu once again, a teacher "is the assassin you have hired to dismantle you" with the goal of ridding you of qualities, such as greed, that stand in the way of your enlightenment.

One of the earliest tales to emerge from this cultural encounter, and the most vivid, is *My Guru and His Disciple*, a spiritual autobiography written by Christopher Isherwood in the 1930s. Best known as a novelist, Isherwood describes his unlikely monastic life in retreat with his Bengali teacher, Swami Prabhavananda, a pioneer sent to continue Vivekananda's work. Isherwood captures what he calls "the inconsistency of my life as a demi-monk": as a worldly gay man known for his sophisticated works of fiction who is newly dedicated to the study and practice of Vedanta, his worlds collide.

The extraordinary book, which is based on old diaries Isherwood revisited after the Swami's death in 1976, is a relatable look at a mystic's life that makes the spiritual path seem understandable, as well as precious. This is quite a feat. For one thing, inner life is difficult to write about. And because materialists consider mystics flaky—while mystics think materialists are missing the big picture—it's not easy to write an account with such wide appeal.

On Isherwood's first visit to what was then a sleepy, leafy, flowering Hollywood Hills neighbourhood, he discovered the gates to another world. He describes a "squat Hindu temple with white plaster walls and onion domes" next door to an ordinary wooden bungalow—the ashram, where students lived with their teacher. The retreat centre is still headquarters today, established in 1938 to promote harmony between Eastern and Western thought and to recognize the truth in all the great religions of the world. Of the temple, with its images of Krishna, Jesus, Buddha, Confucius and leaders of other world religions,

Isherwood writes: "I was immediately aware of the feeling of calm in this room, rather uncomfortably so. It was like a sudden change of altitude to which I should have to get accustomed."

This is a perfect way to evoke the movement from the everyday world to the world of a retreat. A shorter retreat, say for a weekend or a week or two, may well turn out to be peaceful and restorative—important in the scheme of yoga and meditation as a prerequisite for going deeper. But just as often, you might find you sleep for a week, get a headache, become terminally bored or desperate to flee your own thoughts, or actually flee—all part of the process of settling, of acclimatizing.

Isherwood writes elegantly of common obstacles that face secular Westerners encountering Eastern spiritual traditions. The swami—whom he describes as "charming and boyish, although he is in his middle forties and has a bald patch at the back of his head"—speaks to Isherwood about the search for God. "I said I hated the word 'God,'" Isherwood writes. "He agreed that you can just as easily say 'The Self' or 'Nature.'" It amazes me that nearly 100 years ago, the swami foresaw today's "secular sacred"—that self-development and the natural world would become new temples for meaning in the West. Religious or not, the deeper human question of retreat hasn't changed, the one the whole world asks: what is the meaning of my life?

In another typical negotiation, Isherwood wants to know whether one can have a spiritual and a worldly life. Specifically, he lusts after men. The problem is not lust for a man, or a woman, the Swami replies, just that it impedes one's progress, because celibacy allows sexual energy to be stored up for spiritual life. It's a response Isherwood likens to a coach who tells his athletes to avoid certain things—such as smoking, or overindulging in food, alcohol and sex—because they aren't good for the training, not because they're inherently bad. The idea that we're born divine and there's no such thing as sin was highly appealing for many Westerners who encountered Vedanta. Me included—a welcome reversal of the Calvinistic "You'rrrrre all DOOMED!" of my Scottish forebears.

Convinced that you can't go deep by attending sporadic teachings, as his friend Aldous Huxley did, Isherwood decides to commit, Eastern-style: he moves into the ashram, cohabiting with a dozen other people, giving alms in exchange for his live-in studies and pondering his guru's teachings. Aside from curiosity, the other reasons he gives for retreating with his teacher preview what the counterculture would soon be seeking. Isherwood was attracted by his teacher's sanity, honesty and intelligence, his faith and love, and he wanted to seriously pursue spiritual truths in an increasingly baffling, violent, war-prone world. The goal, he said, was to accept with compassion that there will continue to be good and evil in the world, but that he can change himself, wake up to his divine nature and be an agent for greater peace, love and understanding.

Predictably, Isherwood's monastic path is rocky, especially when his habits begin to erode and his ego rebels. "It merely wanted to maintain the usual messy aimless impulse-driven way of life to which it was accustomed. It would actually rather wallow in 'lazy black misery' than be interfered with by Prabhavananda," he says—capturing a typical dynamic of retreat. On good days Isherwood might write, "The desire, the home-sickness, for sanity, is the one valid reason for subjecting oneself to any kind of religious discipline." Even after an exhausting day, spent mainly doing prostrations and sitting in meditation, as well washing dishes and working on translations for the Swami, he exclaims happily, "And this is what they call an escape from the world!" Or he experiences peace and vows to stay forever: "To learn to be alone and at home inside myself—that's what I'm here for." He also confronts his inner Puritan and his outsized ego, not just with the disciplines of introspection, but with help from his guru. "Once fishing for a compliment, I asked Swami why he so seldom scolded me. He answered, 'I don't scold for the big faults.' He gave no sign of awareness that this statement had crushing implications."

On difficult days Isherwood longs for his lovers, loathes the rules and whines about being sick of pujas and sitting cross-legged in the temple three times a day. "This weekend has been stormy, unexpectedly so. We had a puja and there's nothing like good puja for stirring up lust." He often fantasizes about escape from the retreat. "I long to get away from this place. And yet, if I do manage to wriggle out somehow, I know that, in two or three months, I'll pine to get back in again." And later: "My day of silence. Eight hours in the shrine. Boredom. Blankness. Storms of resentment . . ." He regularly complains about the misery of the discipline, often while carrying out monastic duties with a "fair share of diligence." Pleasure-seeking interludes punctuate his practice. "Then, on September 20, I went to lunch with the Viertels in Santa Monica and had another sex encounter on the beach." Feeling "ten times more disagreeable" than he has ever been before in his life, he asks his teacher to explain why he isn't more peaceful. "Swami says it's like cleaning out an inkwell which is screwed to the table: you keep pouring in water and nothing comes out but dirty old ink—at least, not for a long long time."

Ultimately, Isherwood leaves the ashram when he falls in love in 1945, but his time of living with Prabhavananda influenced his life profoundly. He got the idea for his first religious novel after going with his teacher to Belur Maṭh, the headquarters of the Ramakrishna Math and Mission founded by Swami Vivekananda—and where his relics are enshrined. Isherwood's final novel, *A Meeting by the River*, is the story of two brothers, the elder a worldly hedonist, the younger a novice about to take his vows as a monk. They meet at a monastery on the Ganges after a long separation. Scandalous for the times, the novel dramatizes the conflict between sexuality and gay identity and spirituality.

Returning periodically to the Vedanta Centre for spiritual retreats and teachings, Isherwood continued to work on translations with the Swami. He was always considered family there, though he was sure the monastics had heard the "lurid and no doubt fairly accurate rumours about my life." Asked in the *Paris Review* in 1974 about his relationship with his guru, he attempts to explain the unexplainable: "It's made a very great difference, but I couldn't exactly describe to you what the difference is. I could say what, so to speak, I've got out of it. I simply became convinced, after a long period of knowing Swami Prabhavananda, that there is such a thing as mystic union or the knowledge—we get into terrible semantics here—that there is such a thing as mystical experience. That was what seemed to me extraordinary—the thing I had completely dismissed."

Like many of us today, Isherwood was seeking meaning, retreating and then testing out Eastern philosophy in the workshop of modern life. When the Vedanta society began to ordain American monastics in 1946, monasteries and convents branched out from the main Hollywood Temple, and Vedanta societies opened in cities worldwide, including in Canada.

Living with one's teacher to study was integral to Eastern yoga and meditation traditions; curious Westerners began to retreat more, and the ancient practice adapted. The presence of women was one major change. Also, in contrast to living at a monastery, retreats were redesigned to accommodate laypeople, who had to fit yoga and meditation retreats in between jobs, studies and family life. Now, the metaphorical cave *and* the hearth were possible, allowing householders to practise as monastics by going on retreats from time to time.

In the 1950s the Zen meditation boom hit when D.T. Suzuki arrived from Japan, and among those inspired to retreat were artists, thinkers and other influential followers who turned many others on, including musician John Cage, who shifted to making music "that was as strict as sitting cross-legged, namely, the use of chance operations." Bestselling author and Trappist monk Thomas Merton was also captivated and observed that, despite differences, the contemplative traditions of East and West both aimed at the transformation of consciousness using spiritual disciplines.

Zen retreats proved difficult for Western students, who were puzzled by the lack of conceptual explanations and unused to sitting cross-legged on cushions for hours. While in Japan new students might sit seven days by themselves, with breaks only for meals; in the West, retreats were often cut down to three or five days. As well, the idea of a few months in retreat followed by a few months out was introduced as an alternative to the usual method: years of uninterrupted retreat in isolated places for the serious practitioner.

Again students struggled when Tibetan Buddhist meditation arrived after 1959, the year the Dalai Lama, disguised as a peasant, fled through mountain passes to India. One hundred thousand others had followed him into exile by the time the Chinese sealed the borders, and soon Tibetan teachers began spreading West, fulfilling Padmasambhava's ancient prophecy: "When the iron bird flies, and horse runs on wheels, / the Tibetan people will be scattered like ants across the World, / And the Dharma will come to the land of the Red Man." Om mane padme hum entered Western vocabulary, along with another new tradition of retreat.

One of the first Tibetan teachers to arrive in the West was Tarthang Tulku, whose strict meditation disciplines tested his early students: even the introductory practices, usually done on retreat in Tibet, were gruelling. Imagine performing 100,000 full prostrations—to honour Buddha, and as a purification practice to cut through false pride—by stretching out full-length on the floor, getting up and repeating, for hours, while also reciting mantras and doing complex visualizations.

Western pilgrims also began to travel East, visiting sages in caves and meditating in jungle monasteries, boosting interest in Eastern teachings and practices when they returned home. By the '60s and '70s, times of great social upheaval, yoga and meditation were everywhere in the West, with retreat centres dotting the landscape—even more true today.

I have observed that with yoga or meditation retreats, the longer the duration, the greater the intensity and challenge—and the more likely that the secret curriculum will come into play. By that I mean experiences you don't expect or want, but in retrospect may find priceless. Now, for your edification, or perhaps your recognition, I'll share the story of two yoga retreats. In one, most goes well; in the other, all goes terribly, terribly wrong.

In the busy port of Nassau I slip through a gap in the chain-link fence and walk toward some industrial warehouses, searching for Mermaid Dock. Squeaky cranes move shipping containers on and off cargo ships, workers banter and sway to calypso that blasts from the radio—and this has got to be the wrong place. I'm about to leave when I spot a small, hand-painted sign with lotus flowers and people doing handstands.

I sit underneath the sign on a shaded wooden bench to wait for the boat to Paradise Island. Blue Bahamian water shines and dazzles my winter-weary eyes. Off the edge of the pier discarded conch shells by the hundreds tint the depths a delicate pinky-cream. February heat seeps into my body along with relief that I chose this ashram in Nassau rather than the one in wintry Quebec, a few hours' drive from home. I'm here for a month to learn to teach yoga. I've fallen in love with this ancient practice, which helps me to breathe freely and inquire more deeply. Now I want to share its benefits with other frazzled, fast-moving people.

I pull a notebook from my knapsack. "Now it will be no tobacco, caffeine, alcohol, drugs, eggs, meat, fowl, fish for a month," I write. "Not even garlic or onions, which make one 'rajasic' and create agitation in meditation. Worst is no wine." I remind myself that I'm tired of my own habits and want to try something new. I see a speedboat approaching, and think of all the inner journeys launched from this dock in the past 50-plus years. I'm one of thousands from all over the world who have come to study at the yoga school's five acres between the bay and the deep blue sea.

The tossing boat pulls up, I step onboard, and we zoom across the choppy channel to the ashram side. Disembarking beside the main temple I follow a path fringed with ferns and tropical flowers—red, orange, pink and white hibiscuses, bougainvillea. A large sign with the heart chakra painted on it declares "God is one. The names are many." Other signs in the foliage read "Unity in Diversity," and "The highest religion is love." I follow the path all the way to the sea, a calm turquoise stripe between white sand and blue sky. A large yoga platform encircled by swaying palms faces the water beside the beach. This, I decide, is an enchanting place to learn more about yoga and its ancient philosophy, Vedanta.

Once the retreat gets underway I start to question this as a suitable locale for a yoga school. The island is overrun by tourists: Club Med is right next door and Atlantis is down the beach, a coral-pink monstrosity with the biggest casino in the Caribbean and bars, lounges, waterfalls, pools, a faux Mayan temple with waterslides and "the largest man-made marine habitat with eleven exhibit lagoons, home to more than fifty thousand sea animals." We're told sternly that impersonating holidaymakers is grounds for "immediate expulsion from the yoga retreat." Rumour has it that developers have tried to buy the ashram's property, even offering a private island in exchange, but the senior teachers refuse to move. Their guru, who died in 1993, blessed this land, making it the abode of divine qualities such as peace, bliss and wisdom.

Not that you'd notice: in the busy channel between the ashram and the mainland, yachts proliferate like seagulls and noisy float-planes take off and land in the water gaps between vessels. Each day, many times, a powerboat roars up, cutting its engines just off the windy campsite where I've pitched my tent. On board, a man with a megaphone waves his arms at the tourists who crowd the deck as he delivers his script.

"This here is the Port of Nassau. And this here is a yoga ash-ram," he says, separating the word in two. "They don't eat meat, they don't drink, and they don't have sex." There's a calculated pause before he yells: "I guess they ain't our kinda people!" The tourists laugh, the engine revs, and, cocktails aloft, they speed away. Every night the squawking cranes load and unload shipping containers on the docklands, and music blares from the speakers of the cruise ships in the port. Every night, as we sit down in the temple and close our eyes to begin silent meditation at eight precisely, the opening guitar riff of "Sweet Home Alabama" twangs across the bay.

In stark contrast to "the good life" all around us, at the yoga retreat, we focus on simplicity, peace and interiority. Our routines are strict, anchored in meditation and yoga. I'd heard that this month-long retreat was intense, meant to purify students through the path of yoga so they may reach god consciousness—whatever that means. A Sunday school dropout, I prefer the practical website blurb: "The teacher training course is a profound personal experience, designed to build a firm foundation of inner discipline and provide the proficiency to teach others." My fellow students come from many parts of the world and include models, engineers, lawyers, financial wizards, aging hippies, biodynamic farmers, psychiatrists, psychics, fitness instructors, musicians and artists of all kinds.

Early on, one of the senior teachers tells us how our teacher-trainee retreat is going to unfold. The first week, he says, we'll feel adrenaline and energy in the air. The second week, people will get tired. And the third week, the food and postures will have changed us, our egos will kick up to put on the brakes and people will get upset. He doesn't say anything about the fourth week. "The retreat can be really hard," he cautions. "But I advise you to stick it out and see what happens." He emphasizes, "Yoga philosophy asks you not to believe someone else, but to explore and experience for yourself and then decide."

We realize quickly that this is not a relaxed place to do yoga and eat vegetarian food. It's yoga boot camp. Wherever you are in the world, Sivananda yoga ashrams, outposts of transplanted India, follow the same 5:30 a.m. to 10:30 p.m. timetable. The physical poses are just one element of the wider system of classical yoga, which includes breathing practices, meditation, chanting, philosophy, community service and more. Each morning and evening, about 200 of us, including trainees, residents, teachers and guests, descend on the temple for satsang, a lecture, followed by silent meditation and chanting.

We teachers in training are subjected to attendance, which along with our uniforms—two yellow T-shirts and two pairs of white cotton pants—makes us feel like schoolchildren. We sit on the hard temple floor for an hour and a half twice daily, the air redolent of tiger balm. Also twice a day we have a two-hour yoga class: Sanskrit chants followed by breath of fire and alternate-nostril breathing, and then sun salutations and variations on 12 poses: headstand, shoulderstand, plough, fish, seated forward bend, cobra, locust, bow, spinal twist, crow, standing forward bend, triangle. At the end we sink into savasana, the corpse pose, to relax and integrate the effects of our practice.

Twice a day, we gratefully eat, at 10 a.m. and 6 p.m. We also receive our "karma yoga" assignments. Doing an hour of daily "selfless service" is meant to help students "eliminate egoistic and selfish tendencies." A Greek man says his army service was much easier. Alice, one of the Irishwomen I scrub pots with for karma yoga, says she sometimes feels like she's in prison. "No, prison is nicer," she corrects herself, giving a massive soup tureen some elbow grease. "You don't have to get up at 5:30, and you get coffee and three meals a day."

As time passes, I notice how small things become magnified. I keep on obsessing about my headaches, though it's likely a simple case of caffeine withdrawal, and buy up all the chocolate kisses at the Health Hut, administering them like aspirins. My mind grasps at dramas and fights going inward. With the usual distractions gone, the "monkey mind" tries to manufacture new ones—according to the "mind balks at discipline" section of my training manual. Staying distracted is easier than being quiet, a hedge against emptiness that prevents uncomfortable questions such as "What am I doing here?" and "What is the meaning of life?"

Week three arrives, and, as our teacher predicted, the counsellors, who sit at picnic tables at designated hours, get busy. People cry and want to drop out. A British man says he won't be controlled in this way and stomps off to pack his bag. From my perspective, regular life requires far more conformity. Yoga and meditation are about freedom and transformation, so I'm willing to stick it out.

It is true that we all struggle—mainly to get accustomed to the exacting schedule, which leaves only about two hours a day free in which to do homework, eat, shower and do laundry. The latter is becoming a real flashpoint. There are only two machines, so it's a fight to keep our two uniforms clean. As an added challenge, the shop, which sells tokens and soap, isn't open at the same time as the laundry room. Then the rain begins. It lasts three days. One man has a meltdown and insists he *must* do his laundry. He's yelling, irrational. People feel sorry he's distressed and two guests, both former yoga teacher trainees, put his clothes in the dryer for him while we're in yoga class.

After what feels like countless sunrise-to-sunset replays of the same day in dreamlike succession, the mysterious final week arrives, the one our teacher didn't describe. To my surprise suddenly everything feels harmonious. During final relaxations at the end of yoga classes, I get this cosmic perspective, thinking how all my cells work together as a whole in my body, though I don't consciously experience it that way. And about the beauty of the night sky here, and how the Earth is a tiny speck amid millions of worlds in the darkness. I also experience a deep, felt, bodily sense of being part of a vast larger intelligence, a unity. Thirty days is a fairly typical time span for a retreat—long enough to let the experience change us and to begin to absorb what we're learning. My classmates and I have lived a yogic lifestyle, experienced its supportive routines, and we can feel the benefits in our own bodies. We'd grumbled, even despaired, but most of us now say we wouldn't have missed this for the world.

On the last afternoon we sit in the temple, listening to our orange-robed teacher's lecture. A moving tableau of pleasure boats cruises behind him. Cross-legged on the hard floor on our yoga mats, we fidget less than before. We all want the same thing, the teacher says—some call it happiness; others, peace. We run after worldly pleasures because we're seeking happiness, not the objects themselves. These things are fleeting, which is why we are perpetually looking for something more. As he talks, a massive cruise ship, ILLUSION painted on the hull, coasts up, disappears behind him and coasts out the other side. In a flash I realize this is actually an ideal place for a yoga school. The ephemeral pleasures the swami is talking about, Nassau's "high life," are constantly on display. Where else can you find such a perfect vantage point for seeing the "ordinary" world in such stark relief?

Clearly, the swamis have a different vision of paradise than their neighbours—and most people. It's not that worldly pleasures are bad, they say, just that they're fleeting. Inner life is the honey, they say, but everyone thinks it is the powerboat and bank balance, and that there is no transcendental realm beyond the senses. This is maya, illusion, our teacher tells us. Paradise Island ashram: the ultimate nature-of-reality show.

Our other teachers take turns on the dais, their voices competing with sirens wailing across the bay. What we've received on retreat are seeds, they say: we may not understand at first but when we practise and gain experience, they will sprout. They reiterate that we should never accept anything we can prove to ourselves by our own experiments. Just follow the ancient yogic map and see for yourself, they say. There's no need to seek freedom in distant lands: it exists within, in our own bodies, hearts, minds and spirits. Inner space offers realms as vast as external geographies to explore.

Next morning as I pack my bag and fold up my tent, which I have no memory of having slept in because I have been so exhausted every night, I feel markedly stronger. I'm also more centred, and purposeful. As I step onto the tossing boat that will take me back to Mermaid Dock, I wonder about my new life as a yoga teacher and the after-effects of the retreat. What will linger like the mud stains on my white yoga pants? What will fade like my tan?

Years later my experiences on this "north star" yoga retreat still guide my steps. Alas, the wine never lost its appeal, but I did gain a little discipline, and clarity and perspective about what's healthy, and what's important to me. I also found that yoga connected me to an experience of harmony, no beliefs required. That's why four years later, wanting to delve deeper into yoga, I retreated again. This time I went to India, to the source.

We climb into the white Hindustan Ambassador and luxuriate on the sofa-like back seat. Instead of his usual pink sweatpants, Mani is wearing a saffron lungi—a South Indian sarong. After our 36-hour trip to Cochin, Marco and I are grateful to see our friend. Mani is a little brother of a man: small, sweet, with a quick laugh. Dear to everyone. He's also one of the first yoga teachers I studied with in Toronto. Mani's charm, gentle wisdom and devotion to the path of yoga have kept me in his orbit.

We speed away from the airport in a melee of other Ambassadors, black-and-yellow autorickshaws and motorbikes that swerve around goats and cows. A grape-purple bus thunders by, festooned with marigold garlands and stickers of Jesus and Ganesha, the elephant-god. Destroyer of obstacles. We're a long way from Mani's yoga studio in Toronto and our home in Kingston—15,000 kilometres away. Yet I feel certain that this three-week "yoga intensive" in his home village, where his family lives, will deepen my understanding of stillness and help me to become a better yoga teacher.

After driving through a busy town—the closest one to his village, Mani says—we enter the green countryside, where we wind through palm groves and over small canals. Water buffalo, ropes looped through their noses, watch us pass. Bumping onto a red-earth track that cuts through emerald tapioca fields, we reach the village and pull up at Mani's yoga school—at first glance, a graceful, two-storey house ringed by tall coconut palms.

We hoist our bags out of the trunk and onto the wide verandah. Garbage is piled high. Inside, everything looks dirty. "I wasn't expecting this," I think groggily. Mani shows us to a room with a mattress on the floor. He hands us bedsheets and two bottles of water. "You can rest here for now," he says.

That's when I notice the noise. Mani explains that unexpectedly a brickyard has opened up next door. It sounds like they're sawing cement, and a radio blasts vertigo-inducing music I've only ever heard in Bollywood movies.

The room spins now that we have finally stopped our perpetual motion. I dig out the construction earplugs, hand a set to Marco. "Let's try to sleep. Things will seem better when we wake up," I say.

I think back to our flight from Dubai to Cochin, a bright moon floating in the dark blue sky. An auspicious sign; I had read that the moon rises during meditation when one attains a deeper level of calm.

Right now, earplugs firmly intact, I can still hear sawing. "What kind of sign is this?" I wonder, plummeting toward sleep.

When we awaken a few hours later we see white walls stained with monsoon rot, dust layering every surface. Mouse shit is abundant. Mani says he tried to pay someone from the village to clean up, but no one would. The place had been closed for nine years.

The retreat starts in four days.

That evening, Mani leaves to stay with his parents. Marco and I are alone in the silent ashram. The long trip and searing heat leave us thirsty, but we have little fresh water, and there's none here. Should we go out to buy water? And where exactly would we go?

A droning engine approaches around 9:00. An autorickshaw lurches up out of the night, and two laughing women descend with bag upon bag of purchases. I watch them from the upstairs balcony with relief. Merry people! I rush down to meet them.

"Come and see what we bought," Maya calls as Dorothea waves us back upstairs. Their room has a pretty paper star hanging on the door. The bed is decorated with a pink mosquito net. I watch as they pull out cotton housedresses—"You have to get some when we go to town"—and display new cotton bras with freaky missile breasts. Marco and I gratefully accept a bottle of water. Dorothea encourages us to move upstairs and away from the brickyard. Upstairs, she says, "the noise sucks less."

Our new room has a large ceiling fan, a cement shelf built into the wall, a window with iron bars and a heavy wooden bed frame. This room's been cleaned, colourful straw mats adorn the black polished cement and there's a bathroom. Perfect, we agree, as we drape our mosquito net over the bed.

Next morning, we help Maya and Dorothea clean up, while Mani visits relatives. They had been travelling in France and Holland together, and had just recently arrived themselves. I jump as hand-sized black spiders scuttle out from behind whatever object we move. "That's nothing," Maya says. "We found the mattresses all piled up in one room. When we pulled one down, dozens of mice came leaping out." Marco and I groan. We drag our bed outside, douse it with DEET, and leave it baking in the sun.

That afternoon, we take a break and ride the bus to town, where local people stare and smile. We are celebrities, of sorts. An old lady with no teeth comes up to Kevin, Maya's 22-year-old son. She's laughing, motioning to his lungi. It's on backwards.

Signs advertise "unlimited free STDs." This, Maya explains, is where you go to use the telephone—standard trunk dialling. We learn how to cross the street: walk into traffic quickly and pray that vehicles swerve around you.

The sun's incessant beating, combined with car fumes, gives new meaning to the word "exhaustion." Sitting on a curb to drink a reviving chai, I try not to think about unpasteurized milk or hepatitis. The other customers use this technique for drinking so their lips never touch the cup—they pour the chai into their open mouths, straight from above. When I try this, the liquid curdles down my front.

In a futile attempt to cool off, I buy some talcum powder. "A mist of hypnotic charm," the label says. "Mind-blowing & alluring aroma. An unforgettable experience enriched your feelings."

Slowly, other yoga students arrive until we are 12 in all. Canadians. The group includes a carpenter, two university professors, a public health nurse, a student activist, a graphic designer and a fitness instructor. Dorothea is a film editor, and Maya owns the gas station where Kevin works. All but one person has studied with Mani in the past. Many of us are also yoga teachers.

The night before the retreat begins, spirits are high. We chat on the balcony upstairs, looking out at the green mountain. Mani notices that we've been taking turns reading a book we'd found while cleaning up. It's by the guru of his teacher's guru.

"Don't look at what it says about women," Mani makes a face.

"Too late, we've read it," I say. "So sexist."

"Even gurus mess up," he replies with a shrug.

I'm relieved when the retreat gets underway. At first, we all focus on yoga and fall into the ashram rhythm of full, structured days, beginning at 5:30. The faraway sound of drums and temple song carries, otherworldly, on the wind. We gather for satsang from 6 to 7:30, and then for yoga class from 8 to 10. Our yoga room is in an unfinished building that will eventually serve as the kitchen for Mani's brother's catering business. I don't envy those who didn't bring their own yoga mats as they perform headstands on thin rush mats atop the lumpy concrete floor.

After class, we walk up to Mani's mother's house for breakfast. Then it's a little time to wash clothes, nap or read—despite the brickyard racket—until the two o'clock lecture. Then yoga again, from 4 to 6, followed by dinner at 6:30 at "Mum's" and satsang from 8 until nearly 10:30.

All day, one moment flows effortlessly into the next.

In the "never hurry, never stop" tempo of our days, Marco and I have the most contact with the other upstairs dwellers, especially Maya and Dorothea. They have a shelf stocked with cookies from Holland, chocolates from Paris and Greens Plus supplement; they also have every medical remedy known to humans. The women share generously.

Maya even bought an electric burner so we could make coffee—and boil drinking water. She creates a sense of community, and Marco and I are grateful. At dawn, we sit on the upstairs balcony with our cups of instant coffee, gazing wordlessly out at the mountain.

Dorothea, who is constantly saying lewd things and swearing in Dutch, keeps me laughing. She bellows silly lines from *Young Frankenstein*—"It's Fronkon-steen"—an old film we both love, and tells disgusting stories about parasites and chilling tales of being sexually harassed in Varanasi, where she spent three months learning to play the sitar.

The downstairs dwellers are another story. Two laid-back profs in their fifties, a new student who left a course at another ashram

IN PRAISE OF RETREAT

to join ours, two thirty-something women. Mani. Some have rooms. Others have pitched tents beside the ashram.

During our yoga classes with Mani, I'm impressed once more by his skill in teaching asanas, the yoga postures, and by the way he connects with students. Watching the advanced yogis twisting into poses I've never seen anyone perform, I'm inspired to try new ones myself. Being a student again, taking a break from yoga teaching and my other work, I feel free.

The village's eternal rhythms induce peace. Tall coconut palms sway, fronds clacking in the wind. Kingfishers flash electric blue in the treetops. Out back, a woman in a sari leads three goats on strings. Other women in bright turbans work the tapioca fields. White egrets freeload on the backs of grazing water buffalo. Time slows. Once in a while, things feel so harmonious that I think I could even live in a crazy little community like this one.

Then come the irritations. People struggle with wicked colds, insomnia and constipation. The South Indian diet is unfamiliar. Although it's vegetarian, it's high on rice and low on fresh vegetables. There is little drinking water. There is 40-plus-degree heat. One day, Mani announces he will collect money to buy water. This does not go over well, given we all paid a fair sum to attend the retreat. Eventually, he purchases an electric burner like Maya's, so the people downstairs can boil water too.

The day we do kriyas, cleansing practices, there's little water, as usual. For this exercise, we are going to drink eight cups of salt water each and then throw up. The last time I had done this, years before, I'd felt weak and dehydrated. I pass on the practice.

I tell Marco about my previous ashram experiences. Normally, day-to-day concerns about living space and meals are well organized so that students can focus on learning. Why is Mani so unprepared? There's litter everywhere. Out front is a canal that's full of eels. People and water buffaloes bathe in that canal—our water source, we realize. We've been taking showers in that water, boiling it to drink. The public health nurse develops a tic under her eye and insists we all accept bottles of hand sanitizer.

And the explosions. Over the sawing of the bricks, we hear repeated explosions. Maya says they come from where the mountain used to be, out back. The mountain is no longer visible; it's been mined away completely. Mani is also disappearing—into one young woman's tent. They giggle together, like kids. Someone asks me if they are lovers. I dismiss this as a silly notion. In the mornings, Mani is often late to lead the 6:00 silent meditation.

When not feeling at one with everything, I also notice how distracted I am getting. My mind wanders ceaselessly during meditation. That floating moon I'd seen on the flight, my bright omen of deepening calm? It's definitely not rising. Instead, I'm caught in wave after wave of resentment toward Mani. I'm troubled by the upstairs/downstairs rift, with the malcontents upstairs, the keeners down.

Maya and Dorothea quit smoking. They start again. They try to hide it from Maya's son, Kevin. Mani is smoking too. One day, he gives a rambling lecture about the difference between yoga and Vedanta—which, translated, means "the end of knowledge."

I'd been looking forward to this, one of the main topics to be covered. The ancient sage Adi Sankara, an adept of the Kevala Advaita Vedanta path—the pure, non-dualistic school of Vedanta—was originally from South India; he had summarized the essence of Vedantic teachings in three statements: God only is real. The world is unreal. The individual is none other than God.

But as Mani talks, clarity does not come. I wonder, "Is it just me? Or do all his lectures seem less focused than usual?" I'm more interested in Kevin's efforts to find a loophole in the laws of karma. He's started speaking with an Indian accent that makes him sound like Peter Sellers in *The Party*. Maybe he has the right idea. During lectures he stretches out on the ground, appears to be sleeping. Once in a while, Mani asks, "Right, Kevin?"

"Right," Kevin says.

The questions I thought I'd be engaging on retreat have been replaced by "What's biting me?" "Where can I get some water?" "What the hell is going on?"

Early the first week, Swamiji arrives. Mani explains that they had studied together for a decade in the ashram when they were in their twenties, and that Swamiji will teach a few classes. His car, a black Ford with blacked-out windows, looks like a yogi-pimpmobile. It features a fancy "Om" symbol in orange on the windshield. The car seats, Kevin tells me, are covered in fake fur.

Swamiji's classes run as follows: "Sit down. Sit straight," he orders. He instructs us to question him in order to draw out his "deep knowledge," but when someone does ask, he barks, "I already told you." He rambles nonsensically in poor English or replies with a kingly air, "You can't possibly understand." At one point he says, "Ask Mani about yoga, and ask me about spiritual matters." He talks about using yoga to gain powers to fight enemies, to walk on water. What about seeking truth, or perhaps becoming a more peaceful, sane person?

One night, he tells us that the best way to sit in meditation is on the skin of a deer or a tiger—but only one that died of natural causes.

"Have you experienced this?" Maya asks with a devilish grin.

"Yes, I had a tiger skin."

"The animal died of natural causes?"

"Yes, the tiger was electrocuted when it touched an electric fence."

We all exchange looks, laugh out loud, when Maya says under her breath, "So how exactly is electrocution 'natural causes'?"

"I sat on the skin a few times and it was powerful. I gave it away though," he adds. "I didn't want animal rights people saying I was killing tigers or something."

We tell Mani that we don't want any more classes with "Ji"—the diminutive means "little"—but Mani insists that he wants us to see "how yoga is taught in India." Ji has been sleeping in his car, trying shamelessly to snare some Western students of his own—us.

Yoga teachers often emphasize how the physical practice of yoga—hatha yoga—is not as important as its wider philosophical and spiritual foundations. "It's level one, please go beyond and bring yoga into your life," Mani says.

Here, for me at least, the poses are by far the most fruitful part of the day.

Walking along the canal after class one morning, a yoga insight arises out of the stillness. My steps feel heavy. I think of Mani, and the words form: "This is your disappointment to bear. Let this experience be what it is," I think. Accept it.

For a little while, it's a relief to let go.

The upstairs/downstairs split continues to deepen: skeptics on the top floor, acolytes on the bottom. Two young women from downstairs chant nonstop, "Vande gurudev, jaya jaya gurudev." We mimic flinging things at them from the balcony.

The skeptics are giving up on the retreat. Marco reads the Krishnamurti books he brought from home, meditates on the roof and joins us only for yoga class and meals. Kevin practises "naked yoga"—likely a few poses and a nap—up on the roof or hangs out with his friends. Young men from the village sit with him on the bridge in the evenings. I love Kevin's reports of these conversations. "They say we are like animals with clothes," he tells me one night, referring to Western sexual practices. His friends will have arranged marriages, most likely when they're in their twenties.

I skip classes too. In the village, the tailors play chess outside, and I have chai or buy beets, beans and lentil and jaggery balls for dinner so we won't have to eat with the group. I take an autorickshaw into town to buy water. I do anything to avoid Ji's Bhagavad Gita classes. He takes this spiritual gem, this masterpiece of Sanskrit poetry and world literature, and tortures each sutra. There are 700.

Mani's lectures are growing worse. Someone—a devotee from downstairs—comments on how his discourses are spirals, how he adds a new piece of information each time. I once thought that too, I realize. In addition to lectures, Mani has now asked Ji to lead evening meditation. Mani complains that he doesn't have enough time to teach and to see his relatives, the retreat is *a lot of work*. The course is 15 days long, minus three days off. Twelve days of teaching.

Seven days into the retreat Ji starts leading evening satsang. I give him a chance, but after the fourth time, I stay in my room. One night, he comes upstairs to round us up, calling, "Students, come."

On day eight, Mani announces that Ji will also take over afternoon yoga asana class. This means we'll be with Ji from 2:30 onward, through the evening. And where will Mani be? People complain, yet Mani gives Ji more and more to do. Mani persists, says Ji is an Ayurvedic expert who knows all about plants, and we should take advantage of his knowledge. Soon he is giving treatments, going in and out of rooms and tents.

Carol, a beautiful blond fitness instructor, has a skin condition on her scalp. She gets an hour-long treatment that involves a head massage. It also involves taking off her top. I hear Dorothea, who has a similar problem but is less conventionally pretty, say that her treatment lasted all of five minutes, scalp only.

Still, some sensible people from downstairs, men and women, have been having treatments, and I too have a skin condition—for which, I hear, tulsi leaves are excellent, so when Ji asks, I agree to a treatment. I lie naked on my sarong on the floor as he plasters green paste all over me. He tells me I can wash it off in half an hour. I feel uncomfortable, but I tell myself that he's okay—he's Mani's friend. They studied together for ten years, didn't they?

One morning during his lecture, Mani tells us that people either love or hate India. I'm not sure where I fit just yet. I vacillate. Mani says to try to drop our expectations, learn to relax.

"India will give you nothing if you come to see old buildings. You need to relax yourself when frustration arises, and it's the best thing for you in those moments."

He says if you learn to relax here it's a gift, as India can be crazy and maddening. So far, what I'm finding crazy and maddening is Mani.

Our day off arrives. We are grateful, and go to visit a local waterfall, returning that evening to good news. Ji, Mani says, has gone because of our feedback. "I understand that you came to India to study with me," Mani says.

In my journal I write, "I hope this improves the focus and depth of the retreat."

The next morning's scuttlebutt is that Ji's departure is due to his behaviour with two female students during "Ayurvedic" treatments. In one case, he had dropped his lungi during a massage and started talking about tantric sex. Oh, and there was something about a camera hidden under a cloth. And drugged tea.

I feel sick—as does everyone else, especially those of us who had skin treatments with Ji. I tell Mani that I'm angry, trusted this man because he was his friend. Why did Mani ignore us for over a week when we said we didn't want Ji here?

"Do you think I would invite someone here to exploit you, my family, on purpose?" he retorts. He complains that we should have told him if something was wrong because he has lots on his mind, adds that Ji is gone and never coming back, all in a "so drop it" tone of voice.

Mani becomes more organized and focused. He does not apologize, but says "the worst has happened."

"Is there anything else that needs to be said?" he asks.

No one speaks: a few of us have conversed with him already. And it's odd—the woman who says she was molested, who says that Ji had tried to film and drug her, has shrugged it off, saying, "It's his karma." Another woman Ji touched sexually during a massage says she "handled it."

One night, near the end of our final week, I hear a rickshaw engine's approaching buzz accompanied by wild laughter. Marco and I watch from the upstairs balcony as three yoga students tumble out of the back seat, drunk.

They try to creep upstairs quietly, but when they see us, they crack up. "We had 17 beers," Maya shouts, awakening everyone in the house.

I go to bed, my head spinning. In the past, Mani taught me valuable, even life-changing lessons. In India, I'd hoped to move to the next level of yoga knowledge, which he certainly possesses.

How then did I end up in a yoga cliché, replete with fake gurus bent on power and sex, tiger skins and befuddled seekers—including me?

Next morning. Six o'clock meditation. Afterwards, Mani says, "This is not a holiday camp but a serious retreat centre." His voice is stern. The miscreants are still asleep upstairs. After all that's happened, his words sound preposterous.

Today, mercifully, is the last day of classes. Tomorrow's have been cancelled because we've been invited to a Hindu wedding and Amma, the famous "Hugging Saint" of Kerala, will be giving blessings nearby. Marco and I will then leave for Cochin, and soon head back home.

In the afternoon, we write a test for our yoga intensive certificates. It's a charade, but I'm in this to the end. At least it's the kind of learning I can relate to. I decide to complete the test with the serious intent that I brought to the retreat.

That night, we gather on the roof of the ashram, in a circle. The sky is dark, black, the stars in unfamiliar southern constellations. There's a big full moon. We are all strangely quiet, Mani comments.

I stare at the tall coconut palm silhouettes swaying in the breeze. Mani continues to talk about how he thinks it was a good retreat. We all sit silent. A huge lump rises in my throat.

I'm sad about my friend and teacher. And about my lost hope of learning, transformation. All retreats hold the potential for a touch, a look, a realization that will change you forever. When we came to study in India, yoga's birthplace, this is what I both feared and hoped for.

I look at that moon and learn what there is to learn: that no matter what I expect, life will be what it is. Which in this case, I decide, means the same old shit with an Indian flavour.

In the past, Mani's teachings had been exactly what I'd needed, and for that I remain grateful. But now? I might get to a place of understanding, grasp the secret curriculum, what I'm learning but don't realize I'm learning. But at this moment, I am angry and disappointed.

The retreat officially over, we all lie back in the darkness and gaze at the sky. I think about another yoga teacher of mine, someone back home. Once she had advised: "Trust the path. Trust yourself. Trust the teacher." Then she'd laughed. "No, forget about that last one."

I ponder this awhile. My mind turns to Wallace Stevens. Was he the poet who said that the last illusion is disillusion? The moon glimmers, golden in the dark.

In Canada, our pioneers of yoga and meditation founded retreats coast to coast in the late '50s and '60s, as in the U.S. and Europe. One of our first yoga teachers was Swami Sivananda Radha, who established the Yasodhara Ashram in 1963 on the shores of Kootenay Bay, British Columbia. Swami Radha was also one of the first Westerners, and the first women, to be initiated as a spiritual teacher by an Indian guru.

Born Sylvia Hellman in Berlin to a well-to-do family, she became a writer, photographer and professional dancer, and immigrated to Montreal after the Second World War. She had lost two husbands, the first killed by the gestapo for helping Jewish friends leave Germany, and the second to a stroke. A vision of her guru appeared to her in meditation, and she made a pilgrimage to the foothills of the Himalayas in 1955 when it was unheard of for women to travel in India alone. She found Swami Sivananda in Rishikesh on the banks of the Ganges and became his disciple.

In *Radha: Diary of a Woman's Search*, she chronicles her life-changing retreat, which included mundane troubles from hungry bedbugs to self-doubt, as well as transcendent experiences. I was so refreshed to find an early female exemplar of retreat that I read her book twice in rapid succession, studying the rare historical photos with pleasure: Sylvia meditating on the roof of her apartment in Montreal; Sylvia sitting beside the Ganges with her guru, who is wearing a cross she brought him as a gift; and the newly ordained Swami Radha, in the ornate dress and jewellery of an Indian dancer, performing on the steps of the temple.

Swami Radha's descriptions of an Indian monastery, the dwelling place of the spiritual teacher, were not what I'd imagined, and bear little resemblance to her own orderly, graceful retreat centre. Ashrams, she writes, are happy, busy places without a Western equivalent. "Catholic monasteries all over the world are established for the purpose of attaining God-consciousness by means of perfect discipline," she observes. "This is carried out in the small details of everyday life. In complete obedience, punctuality, cleanliness, tidiness, orderliness. On such a foundation, in time, will be laid the spiritual discipline. Not so here in the ashram . . . In fact there is no discipline at all."

She details her struggle to find a quiet place for meditation and study, the constant noise, the need for "immunity to insects and vermin of all kinds"—she puts the legs of her bed in tins of water to evade bugs, except the ones that drop from above—and says the spiritual aspirant has to "be able to drink water from the Ganges without shivering at the things floating in his cup." She wonders whether or not such "chaotic conditions are more effective in producing saints than the methods of the West." Her words are not a criticism. "Certain things exist only under certain conditions, come alive only under certain conditions," she notes. She's wary of her own preconceived ideas and talks about the need on retreat to give ourselves time for development and understanding, about how our senses are the organs of our perceptions and are limited, which is why we indulge in oversimplifications—something any retreater will do well to remember.

Swami Radha's time in India ended when her guru asked her to open an ashram in Canada and spread yoga in the West. "You teach them only the practices—the way yoga is used by many religions. It is not itself a religion, but a scientific way of life," he instructed. Swami Sivananda also told her to live on alms; in India teachers charge no fees, but students take care of their needs, giving financial contributions and/or service. "When you go back to the West," he said, "do not work anymore for money." She told him this was impossible. "When you go back, just await developments," he insisted. "Everything will fall into place."

For more than 50 years now, Yasodhara has been holding space for people to retreat in search of meaning—including me. The dreamlike natural beauty of the setting, evident from the ferry boat as I approached the ashram, brought to mind the guru's final directive to his new disciple: "When you leave here, go where you have mountains in the back, water in front, and trees all around," Sivananda told her. "The mountains will give you strength and energy, the water will calm the mind, and the trees will offer you protection."

Many improbable events later Swami Radha found this place, which she called Yasodhara, the name of the wife of the Buddha, thus recognizing the feminine principle in spiritual life. From here she shared her distinctive synthesis of yogic teachings and Western psychology. Swami Radha died in 1995, but her presence is felt throughout the flourishing spiritual community, and through her teachings, which stress that we each need to cultivate our unique inner "Cathedral of Consciousness."

Distracted, thinking about Swami Radha's influence, I bumped into a tall, blue-eyed swami in the hall on the way to dinner. She put a hand on my shoulder, smiled, inhaled deeply and said, "Breathe." Meals at the ashram were eaten in silence, which I loved. Silence except for a chant that played over and over, hari om in a high voice: I found it eerie so I went to sit outside. It turned out to be a recording of Swami Radha, and now I often play it in my car. At Yasodhara my room was simple and comfortable, and I felt I'd landed in a supportive, caring community.

The gardens of the radiant natural campus have flourished, and its graceful buildings are full of art. Fittingly, images abound of Saraswati, the patron deity of the ashram's lineage of teachings and a symbol of art, music and wisdom. Swami Radha also had a literary bent: she wrote more than a dozen books and founded Timeless Books, the ashram's publishing house.

The modern way of retreat is often multi-faith and multi-purpose, where East and West have come together in a weave of yoga and spirit, nature and environmentalism, art, and personal and professional growth. Individual and group retreats are offered, and there's a residential karma yoga program—like a work-study in integrating work and spiritual life. In exchange for discounts or full room and board, depending on the program, people can do groundskeeping, make meals, or otherwise support the community.

Around the same time as Swami Radha was planting the seeds of retreat out west, another, sent by the same Indian teacher, arrived in Montreal. Swami Vishnu-Devananda was charismatic, with a flair for publicity that helped propel yoga, and the practice of retreat, forward from the fringe. In quick succession he founded nine international Sivananda ashrams, named for his teacher. In 1963, he opened the organization's worldwide head-quarters retreat centre near Val-Morin, Quebec, followed by other ashrams in India, the United States and Bahamas, where I did my teacher training.

Notably, Swami Vishnu was an early influence on the most famous spiritual retreaters of their generation, the Beatles. He met the Fab Four near the Bahamas ashram when they were shooting the 1965 film *Help!* The band was approached by a "swami in orange robes," according to the *Beatles Anthology*, who gave them each a signed copy of his *Complete Illustrated Book of*

Yoga. Ringo reportedly said he couldn't stand on his legs, let alone his head, while George asked intelligent questions. The Beatles' subsequent extended retreat with their guru, Maharishi Mahesh Yogi in India, caused a media frenzy and brought yogic practice further into Western awareness.

Swami Vishnu's indefatigable teaching and his high-profile peace missions helped popularize yoga and its study method, the retreat. Dubbed "the Flying Swami" by the international press in the '70s, he "bombarded" global trouble spots, tossing marigolds and peace leaflets from a psychedelic Piper Apache, painted with stars and Om symbols by millionaire artist Peter Max. The plane, now suspended in the ashram's museum in Val-Morin, was nearly shot down over the Suez Canal, where Swami Vishnu was chased by Israeli jets and then arrested by the Egyptians. He enjoyed the Cairo prison because it was quiet and he could meditate. When the authorities realized he wasn't a spy, that he was on a peace mission, he went from prisoner to VIP. His captors fed him dates and insisted on taking him out to his first nightclub—which he found so noisy and smoky he asked to be returned to his cell.

Swami Vishnu was 18 in 1945 when he moved in with his teacher, Swami Sivananda, an Indian physician who had given up a lucrative practice to become a wandering monk, and who later founded his first ashram in 1932, the Divine Life Society in 1936 and his teaching organization, the Yoga Vedanta Forest Academy, in 1948. Both still operate in the Himalayan foothills on the bank of the Ganges near Rishikesh, a city of swamis, saints, sadhus and holy people. Swami Vishnu, adept at hatha yoga, was in put charge of that aspect of ashram life—until his master handed him ten rupees and sent him to the West with the encouragement "People are waiting."

Even in cosmopolitan San Francisco in the late '50s, when

Swami Vishnu offered a yoga workshop at Golden Gate Park people thought he was giving away free yogurt. A small brown man in orange robes doing strange acrobatics, he must have seemed extravagantly weird and even dangerous. Like rock and roll before the 1960s, yoga was either unknown or met with bewilderment and hostility. Soon after the penniless young guru's serendipitous arrival in Canada in 1959, he visited members of the Massey family in Ottawa, founded the Montreal Sivananda Yoga Vedanta Centre, still operating today, and established headquarters at the 240-acre Quebec ashram.

Swami Vishnu, who died in 1993, and is yet another guru recently accused of sexual misconduct, modified the ancient gurukula system, in which students would live in a hermitage or monastery in the forest or mountains for education, to better suit his Western students. He geared his residential yoga retreats toward laypeople rather than monastics. And he was among the first—likely the very first—to design retreat programs to train yoga teachers in the West. Intriguingly, counter to the legacy of the first teachers, Swami Vishnu emphasized the physical poses of yoga and then rode the wave of a huge Western cultural shift—the emergence of the mind-body movement. As in India, his yoga students would retreat to ashrams to live, work and study with the senior teachers who resided there, though for shorter periods of time, while maintaining work and family life.

Among the first Westerners to become a Buddhist monk, Namgyal Rinpoche founded our oldest meditation retreat, the Dharma Centre of Canada (DCC) near Kinmount, Ontario, in 1966. The first silent retreat I ever attended, at age 20-something, was at the DCC, a 400-acre sanctuary of forest, meadows, beaver ponds and creeks, the site of a former mink farm. It was a taste of something I hadn't known was missing from my life—solitude, silence, clarity, breathing space. My love for interludes of time apart, and my pattern of retreating and returning to everyday life has become more and more established ever since.

Rinpoche—an honorific given to important teachers that means "precious jewel"—was born Leslie George Dawson, and he bridged traditional methods of Buddhism and modern Western thought. The child of an Irish policeman and a Scottish nurse, he grew up in Toronto's Beaches, attended Jarvis Baptist Seminary and went on to study philosophy and psychology at university in Michigan. He met his teacher while living in London, England, and travelled east, where he was trained and ordained as the Venerable Ananda Bodhi in 1958. During his wandering monk period that followed, he taught in Britain and founded several meditation retreats, including what became the famous Kagyu Samye Ling in Dumfriesshire, still going strong in southern Scotland. As Ananda Bodhi, he travelled the world teaching, often accompanied by his students on ocean-going cargo freighters for months at time. He was provocative, jolting them out of their habits and patterns, and many considered swimming to shore to escape him. He returned to Canada in 1966 with a group of students and founded the DCC.

In 1971 he reordained in the Tibetan Buddhist tradition and was thereafter known as Karma Tenzin Dorje Namgyal Rinpoche. His discourses were captivating and often funny—he was a lively storyteller with a melodious voice—but always he had a serious point, about impermanence, or how to "awaken." He often taught and guided DCC retreats until his death in 2003. Decades ago the DCC was an early manifestation of the kind of multidisciplinary retreats modern people favour today. Rinpoche's interests were vast, incorporating arts and science as ways to enlightenment and paying attention to the planet and its flora and fauna. His was a universalist approach to the dharma: the DCC has always hosted other teachers of various spiritual paths and traditions, along with scientists, artists and healers.

While early yoga and meditation teachers adapted retreats to suit laypeople, today, in a fascinating reversal, the full monastic path is making a comeback in the West—not Christian, but Buddhist, and led by places like Cape Breton's Gampo Abbey. One of the first Tibetan monasteries for Westerners in North America, the abbey is housed in white, red-roofed buildings that perch dramatically on 200-foot-high cliffs above the St. Lawrence. I know this from watching *La Trappe*, a short documentary about the monastics and unlikely allies who also see life as a cycle: the red-robed monks and nuns buy the last catch of lobsters and head out with local fishers to release the creatures back into the sea.

Buddhist nun and bestselling author Pema Chödrön was long the abbey's resident teacher and director—she stepped down in early 2020 after the organization decided that a disgraced teacher, who had left amid allegations of sexual abuse, would be reinstated. Chödrön first took over leadership of the abbey in 1984, three years after she became the first North American woman to be fully ordained as a nun in the Tibetan tradition. She established the monastery for Western monks and nuns on the instruction of her teacher. In one of life's ironies, Chödrön, a celibate nun, has been at once head of Gampo Abbey, which maintains strict, traditional monastic precepts, and the representative of the lineage of the Tibetan meditation master Chögyam Trungpa, as legendary for his wildness—he coined the phrase "crazy wisdom," like divine madness—as for his spiritual realization.

Trungpa was a major figure in the dissemination of the Buddhist retreat in the West from the '60s on and founded about 150 meditation centres worldwide, including Scotland's Kagyu Samye Ling Monastery, where celebrities like David Bowie were among early students. "I was within a month of having my head shaved, taking my vows, and becoming a monk," Bowie said about that period of his life, but the monks advised him to remain a musician because it was how he could most benefit the world.

Trungpa was unorthodox and controversial. After taking up Western habits like drinking he crashed his sports car into a joke shop window and was partially paralyzed. Perhaps he saw it as a karmic sign: when he moved to the United States, he abandoned his robes for Western suits, saying he wanted to get rid of the trappings of spiritual materialism, drank more, married a 16-year-old, and slept with many students. He also taught meditation that was accessible to people of any, or no, religion, and founded the Naropa Institute, "a crossroads where the intellectual-critical mind of the West and the way of experience and meditation of the East could meet head-on." Allen Ginsberg was one illustrious student; Joni Mitchell wrote the 1976 song "Refuge of the Roads" as a tribute to Trungpa, the "friend of spirit" who helped her snap out of a cocaine addiction.

Trungpa first visited Nova Scotia in 1977; in 1983 he established Gampo Abbey in Cape Breton. He shocked his unflappable American followers in 1986 by announcing he had found the earthly location of the mythical, enlightened society of Tibetan legend, Kingdom of Shambhala. "He said, 'We're all moving to Nova Scotia,'" recalls Jeremy Hayward, a senior Buddhist teacher. "We thought it was some kind of joke." Trungpa moved international headquarters from the United States to Halifax and brought many disciples with him, then the next year, died there of alcohol-related causes at age 48. Today the community remains one of Shambhala International's largest.

As a symbol of the dharma's rootedness in Nova Scotia, Trungpa's relics are housed in a stupa at Gampo Abbey. Residents include monks and nuns who have taken life ordination, or temporary ordination, and laypeople. Laypeople can try out abbey life for a week or two on retreat, or do solitary retreats in cabins.

Unlike many places these days, they are specifically *not* intended for creating space for writing, yoga, rest and renewal, but only to study and practise meditation. People can also join practise intensives, or the yearly winter retreat for experienced meditators—the "rainy season" retreat that goes back to time of Buddha, when monks wandered until the weather got wet, then settled together to retreat and meditate. Or, after residing at the Abbey for at least three months, initiates can experience monasticism without a lifetime commitment through temporary ordination, which lasts nine months. The monastics train in disciplines and rituals of a monastic life; after two years, they can ask to become life monastics, which takes another three years.

Increasingly, women are retreating and joining the monastic ranks. Leslie Peters, one of the abbey's newer monastics, took her vows in 2018. Now called Tsöndru Khyung Tso, her head shaven and wearing robes, she follows the strict schedule of her Buddhist practice. From 5:30 a.m. to lights out, the day is scheduled: chanting, work, meditation, silent time, study, meals. This simplicity, she says, brings freedom. "Even if it's temporary," she says, "you go on retreat so that you can have some time to not have to take care of everything. I visited Toronto recently and I was staying with my friends and everyone is so busy. You've got your family, work, you've got to cook, a lot to do just to live in Toronto . . . I feel so much for people, there's no time to ever relax, to really stop."

To retreat, she adds, for any length of time, is a way to actively choose to live differently. As with the lives of Christian hermits and monks who pray for sinners, retreat is not about shutting yourself away from society. The idea is to develop your spiritual path, lead a more useful life, help create a more positive society and help all sentient beings. "We practise every day, not just for ourselves, but for everyone."

That few of us will go on the long-term retreats of advanced meditators or become monastics isn't the point, says Tenzin Palmo, a British Buddhist nun who spent 12 years meditating in a Himalayan cave. "There are many approaches, many ways. What is unrealistic, however, is to become a mother or a businesswoman and at the same time expect to be able to do the same kind of practices designed for hermits . . . Whether one is a monk, a nun, a hermit or a businessman or -woman, at one level it's irrelevant. The practice of being in the moment, of opening one's heart, can be done wherever we are . . . It's just that it's easier to do in a conducive environment away from external and internal distractions," she explains.

Even for short periods, Palmo says, to retreat is valuable: there is more to life than relationships and work. "I think it would be very helpful for many people to have some period of silence and isolation to look within and find out who they really are, when they're not so busy playing roles—being the mother, wife, husband, career person, everybody's best friend, or whatever façade we put up to the world as our identity. It's very good to have an opportunity to be alone with oneself and see who one really is behind all the masks."

Palmo, the daughter of a fishmonger in London, England, became the second Westerner ordained as a Tibetan nun. She was inspired to take to a cave by Milarepa, Tibet's beloved spiritual hero, who disappeared into the Mountain of Solitude and lived for years on nettles, which made his skin turn green. Leaving comfort behind she meditated for years in a cave at 13,000-plus feet. Having prepared for this hard and lonely path for over six years first. She did intensive practices at a remote monastery in the Himalayas—a prerequisite before her teacher agreed she could retreat further up to her mountain cave. With her feat she overturned centuries of tradition.

In her tiny cave Palmo faced blizzards and subzero cold, snowbound for about eight months of the year on the exposed mountain, threatened by wild animals, such as wolves, and the vagaries of her own mind. She sat up in her traditional meditation box, two feet by six inches square, for 12 hours a day meditating. She went in at age 33, seeking the secrets of the inner world and deeper levels of consciousness, and came out at 45.

Asked whether a cave is an anachronism, she says no, not so long as anyone is seeking spiritual understanding. "The advantage of going to a cave is that it gives you time and space to be able to concentrate totally. The practices are complicated [and] require much time and isolation," she says. Using a culinary metaphor, she adds, "Going into retreat gives the opportunity for the food to cook. You have to put all the ingredients into a pot and stew it up. And you have to have constant heat. If you keep turning the heat on and off it is never going to be done. Retreat is like living in a pressure cooker. Everything gets cooked much quicker."

But why do this, live in terrible austerity in a cave, often snowed in, meditating for years alone? "In this age of darkness with its greed, violence and ignorance it's important there are some areas of light in the gloom, something to balance out all the heaviness and darkness. To my mind the contemplatives and the solitary meditators are like lighthouses beaming out love and compassion to the world. Because their beams are focused they are very powerful."

The idea that there's wisdom in the cave that can help others flies in the face of convention, which deems a retreat like this lofty, impractical and useless in times when the world is in crisis. But I like the idea of meditators using their minds as we might a magnifying glass to start a fire—it's not that the sun's rays are stronger than usual, just more focused. Millions attending yoga and meditation retreats are discovering that the cave is not empty, but where an inner flame resides. "The inner—what is it?" writes Rilke, "if not intensified sky, hurled through with birds and deep/ with the winds of homecoming."

In Conclusion

OF HERMITAGES OF THE HEART

White Rooms, Unified Hearts
and Empty Fields

Going nowhere . . . isn't about turning your back on the world; it's about stepping away now and then so that you can see the world more clearly and love it more deeply.

—Leonard Cohen

In the long Western lineage of hermits, monks, naturalists, artists, thinkers, yogis, meditators and assorted rebels, there's a Canadian exemplar who spoke with great eloquence, and often humour, about the role of retreat in a life. Leonard Cohen always kept a space apart for spirit, nature, art and beauty. As both an artist and a former Zen monk—when he says "going nowhere" above, he means a meditation retreat—Cohen was drawn to mountains, both inner and outer. The Edge, guitarist for the band U2, compared Cohen once to Moses, calling him the man "who has come down from the mountaintop with the tablets of stone having been up there and talking to the angels."

I always feel drawn to people like Cohen, who are both spiritual and worldly. His music has a timeless, devotional quality that's not modern, yet he was modern. His intimate, poetic songs draw on ancient wisdom, yet emanate from an international star in an Armani suit, a man who tasted all the world's pleasures yet longed for meaning.

Retreat was vital to Cohen's method. While the geographies changed, his chosen architecture of retreat was constant. "Once his life becomes too cluttered, he moves into an empty room," observed biographer Ira B. Nadel in *Various Positions*. "He removes the debris and starts over again, seeking a clean slate that the bohemian life of Montreal, the remote island of Hydra, and the isolated forest of Mt. Baldy have variously given him." Add to this hotels and rooms in Cohen's own homes, which interviewer after interviewer describe along the same lines: "Leonard's houses in Montreal and L.A. were exquisitely spare: white rooms, with no clutter of books, CDs or magazines, though there was a well-worn edition of Psalms and a rhyming dictionary beside his computer in L.A.," a reporter noted in *Maclean's*.

Cohen was 26 when he found his formative retreat, on the island of Hydra in Greece. With a "huge terrace with a view of a dramatic mountain and shining white houses," as he wrote in a letter to his mother in 1960, its rooms were "cool with deep windows set in thick walls. I suppose it's about 200 years old and many generations of sea-men must have lived here." Cohen bought the rundown three-storey house, which had no plumbing or electricity, with a $1,500 bequest from his grandmother.

Gardenia scent wafted through his room, the green Olivetti Lettera he'd bought in London for £40 sat on the desk and the blue Aegean Sea sparkled just down the hill. In this artistically fruitful space, supported by Marianne Ilhen, Cohen paid deep attention to his work, writing two novels, three books of poetry and starting work on an album—notably titled *Songs from a Room*, with its famous track inspired by a bird on the wire that carried phone service to the island. The wire also brought a realization: "civilization had caught up with me and I wasn't going to be able to escape after all," Cohen told Paul Zollo in the book *Songwriters on Songwriting*. "I wasn't going to be able to live this 11th-century life that I thought I had found for myself." Today, pilgrims go to Cohen's Hydra retreat, lighting candles and leaving flowers on the doorstep of this place of powerful inspiration.

An adept at finding space away from the relentless spotlight, Cohen made retreat a lifelong practice. He was a master of doing so while still keeping his all-consuming "day job," finding interstices to step back. Fascinated by hotel rooms, Cohen withdrew to many, including New York's infamous Chelsea; made a video called *I Am a Hotel*; and was the subject of the 1965 documentary *Ladies and Gentlemen . . . Mr. Leonard Cohen*, filmed in a seedy hotel room in urban Montreal, his hometown. "You always have a feeling in a hotel room that you're on the lam and this is one of the safe moments in the escape," he says as he gets out of bed. "You know that you have found a little place in the grass, and the hounds are going to go by for three more hours. You're going to have a drink, light a cigarette and take a long time shaving." In a later interview Cohen honed his remark, adding, "It's a kind of a refuge, a sanctuary, a sanctuary of a temporary kind and therefore all the more delicious."

Cohen began to retreat in a new way in the 1970s—to the Mount Baldy Zen Center, 6,250 feet above sea level in the high desert of the San Gabriel Mountains near Los Angeles. Initially he went to the zendo fleeing domestic strife and needing "somewhere to cool out"—which is what he found, quite literally. "They had a bunch of these American kids walking around in the snow at 3 a.m. in sandals," Cohen recalls. Snow blew over their food in dining hall. The discipline of the strict form of Rinzai Zen was too severe, and, like many first-time retreaters of all kinds, he ran away. "But there was something about Roshi that I remembered. So several months later I came back again and then I began to study with him and practise with him seriously about 30 years ago," Cohen says in the 2005 documentary *I'm Your Man*. "That is spending several months of the year with him all the time."

It's striking how many people are inspired to retreat after meeting a teacher with admirable qualities they want to emulate. Whenever Cohen spoke of his beloved teacher, his face softened and his eyes shined: their long relationship was one of the most enduring of his life. Kyozan Joshu Sasaki Roshi, the monastery's founder, was a Japanese monk who became one of the most influential Zen Buddhist teachers in the United States, known for his rigorous brand of Zen (and later, after his death in 2014, as a "tainted Zen master," as the *New York Times* wrote, accused of sexual misconduct with students).

"It began," Cohen said of his meditation retreats, "with a need for self-reform." Another time he said of Mount Baldy, "When I go there, it's like scraping off the rust." In the late 1980s Cohen wrote the song "Everybody Knows" about the corrupt, impossible state of the world, signalling his state of mind. By 1993 despair had turned to anguish. On the heels of a difficult tour—Cohen was drinking four bottles of wine to make his knees stop knocking on stage and his personal life was a wreck—he went up the mountain. He said later that he'd felt at an impasse, that a spiritual retreat was the only way forward.

Cohen spent the next six years paying radical attention to his inner life. He became an ascetic Zen monk and Roshi's attendant— his cook, chauffeur and drinking buddy. It was protocol that he be ordained, though he said he wasn't a Buddhist. Becoming a monk was "part of the uniform"—Cohen said that had Roshi, then in his eighties, been a physicist in Heidelberg, he'd have learned German and moved there. "I wasn't looking for a religion," he clarifies. "I already had a perfectly good one [his Jewish faith]. And I certainly wasn't looking for a new series of rituals. But I had a great sense of disorder in my life, of chaos and depression, of distress. And I had no idea where this came from. The prevailing psychoanalytic explanations of the time didn't seem to address the things I felt. Then I bumped into someone who seemed to be at ease with himself and at ease with others," he told the *Independent*.

Like the other monks, Cohen shaved his head, donned black robes, sat at a long wooden table, drank water from small bowl and marched in line. He became Jikhan, which translates as the silence between two thoughts, which tells me his old teacher had a sense of humour. He lived in a small cabin. Aside from his cot, he had his synthesizer and a radio—even on the mountain his worldly ties weren't completely cut—and he worked on music and a collection of poems and sketches. Mostly he devoted himself to the study of Zen Buddhism, which he calls a "study of the self—as it arises and how the self disappears." He joined a sect that, not so humbly for humble monks, consider themselves the Marines of the spiritual world due to their intense physical practices and dislike for conceptual thinking.

Far from offering the seclusion one might imagine, a retreat at the zendo is designed to eliminate the desire for privacy. Cohen quotes a saying: "Like pebbles in a bag, the monks polish one another." Depending on your duties, days on retreat might begin at 2:30 in the morning and go until midnight, most of the time in silence. Cohen was expected to comply with daily routines, but was given dispensation to go down the mountain sometimes to take care of his affairs and see his kids. Though he liked communal life and living simply in a little shack, after six years, in 1999, he left the zendo, calling his time as a monk a "phase of my training." Ever ironic, he once said that perhaps if he'd waited longer he could have spared himself the trouble of all that meditation, because anxiety naturally diminishes with age. Another time, asked by one of his biographers what his retreat with Roshi and Rinzai Zen contributed to his work and life, Cohen was unequivocal: "Survival."

One week after he went down the mountain Cohen got on a plane to Mumbai, where he spent a year with Ramesh Balsekar, a Hindu mentor whose books he'd read, to learn about Advaita Vedanta, or nondualism. There he lived in a small, unadorned hotel room "with a desk and a narrow bed pushed against the wall. A wood-framed air-conditioner and mirror took up much of the opposite wall. On the desk lay a cassette recorder and tapes of Indian music," his friend told BBC.

For reasons Cohen said are "impossible to penetrate," his lifelong depression lifted. His old teacher and his new teacher had similar ideas, Cohen's biographer notes: "There was a great deal of consistency in their doctrines: overcoming the ego, nonattachment, universal consciousness, tendrel, the interrelatedness of all things."

Spiritually transformed by his retreat years, he emerged to confront a new challenge: his material life was in a shambles after his trusted manager embezzled him out of more than $5 million. Broke and in a blaze of creativity, and expressing no bitterness, at age 73 Cohen made his late-career comeback, going on the road for five years starting in 2008. The shows—I attended one in Kingston, as much communion as concert—were routinely deemed the best performances reviewers had ever seen. "Is this cabaret or prayer-hall, you may wonder," wrote Pico Iyer in his astute program notes. I had the exhilarating feeling of witnessing an artist fulfilling himself, hat off, hand over his heart—and of being in a wry, spiritual presence.

Afterwards I kept wondering why Cohen had called his band the Unified Heart Touring Company. So one early summer day I went to investigate, visiting his archive in the University of Toronto's Thomas Fisher Rare Book Library. Inside the 11 boxes I found, among other things, clippings from the *Montreal Gazette* and the *New Yorker*, a note from Nana Mouskouri, the proofs of *Death of a Lady's Man* with an ink sketch and fan event materials with a symbol, like a Star of David but with two interlocking hearts.

Cohen had designed the symbol for an order of spiritual chivalry he'd created, I learned from a *Globe and Mail* clipping. He called it the Order of the Unified Heart. This made me smile—whimsical, unexpected. He gave out rings and pins for this "dream of an order," as he called it when speaking to the reporter. "There is no organization. There's no hierarchy," he'd explained. "There's just a pin for people of a very broadly designated similar intent." Asked about his intent he replied, "To just make things better on a very personal level. You're just not scattered all over the place. There is a tiny moment when you might gather around some decent intention." Asked about his own intentions, he replied slyly that he couldn't think of any, though there must be a couple. The reporter suggested beauty, and he responded, "Beauty, certainly."

I packed up the archive boxes and handed them back to the librarian, disappointed not to have discovered anything conclusive. I had been struck, however, by Cohen's typically postmodern, pragmatic approach to spirituality, of taking whatever interested him from different sources. Religion and spirit had always played a role in Cohen's life: he was Jewish, grew up in Montreal, with its Catholic sensibility, called Jesus "a beautiful guy," dedicated a book to Kahnawà:ke's Indigenous saint, Kateri Tekakwitha—a lover of the divine feminine, he had a shrine to her in his kitchen—and embraced Eastern ideas. "Anything, Roman Catholicism, Buddhism, LSD, I'm for anything that works," Cohen once remarked. Of the word God he said, "People often have difficult reactions, but it's easier to say 'God' than 'Some un-nameable mysterious power that motivates all living things.'" He also believed everyone has a spiritual side, whether they knew or admitted it or not.

Walking down Harbord Street, the trees newly in leaf and birds singing, it was suddenly obvious: Cohen's retreats, practised over a lifetime, had accorded him a unified heart. Hedonist or hermit, poet or musician, worldly lover or ascetic, philosopher or comedian, Jewish rabbi's grandson or Zen monk—he integrated the contradictions.

Once, when told by an interviewer that Dylan had compared his songs to prayers, and that works like "Hallelujah" convey a sense of sanctity and holiness in a world that seems to value neither, Cohen gave a reply that fascinates me—and seems to apply to our retreats. "I understand that they forgot how to build the arch for several hundred years," he told Paul Zollo, as recorded in *Songwriters on Songwriting*. "Masons forgot how to do certain kinds of arches, it was lost. So it is in our time that certain spiritual mechanisms that were very useful have been abandoned and forgot [sic]. Redemption, repentance, resurrection. All those ideas are thrown out with the bathwater. People became suspicious of religion plus all these redemptive mechanisms."

Like building arches after the fall of Rome and other "useful" religious mechanisms, the idea of retreat—of sacred space—was forgotten for a time, and we are reinventing it for our anxious, chaotic world. Over his life Cohen stepped back with increasing regularity into retreats that helped him hold the tension of being a worldly person, an artistic person and a spiritual one, "part wolf and part angel" as his friend Anjelica Huston called him.

"I think there's an appetite for seriousness," Cohen told Huston in an article published in *Interview* magazine in 1995. Though speaking 25 years ago, his words sound more relevant than ever. "Seriousness is voluptuous, and very few people have allowed themselves the luxury of it. Seriousness is not Calvinistic, it's not a renunciation, it's the very opposite of that. Seriousness is the deepest pleasure we have. But now I see people allowing their lives to diminish, to become shallow, so they can't enjoy the deep wells of experience."

Denying ourselves this solemnity, he added in the same interview, has consequences. "Maybe it's always been this way, when the heart tends to shut down. If only the heart shut down and there were no repercussions, it would be OK, but when the heart shuts down, the whole system goes into a kind of despair that is intolerable." Despair, he says, is why he chose the "radical solution" of retreating to the zendo—which he stresses is not for everyone. "You only address the problem of soul if you feel that you're losing it," he told NPR's *Fresh Air* in an interview about *Book of Longing*, the poems he wrote on Mount Baldy.

For Cohen, the opposite of despair was clarity—why he says in our "very shabby moment," making space for what's sacred and spiritual helps. "We're in the midst of a Flood of biblical proportions," he told writer Pico Iyer in 2004 in *Sun After Dark: Flights into the Foreign*, in prophetic mode once again. "It's both exterior and interior. At this point it's more devastating on the interior level, but it's leaking into the real world. I see everybody holding on in their individual way to an orange crate, to a piece of wood, and we're passing each other in this swollen river that has pretty well taken down all the landmarks, and pretty well over-turned everything we've got."

I admire Cohen's heroic devotion to his sacred precinct—even more steadfast in the face of deluge and death. To him, step-ping back to pay attention to spirit, art, truth and beauty was of vital importance, a powerful and positive force against darkness. Cohen's art and spiritual practice came together in what his son, Adam, called "a monastic discipline." In the modest home that he shared with his daughter, Lorca, and her dogs in Los Angeles, not far from Adam, he got up early to work in his "tower of song"—a sparsely furnished white room like the one on Hydra, a simple retreat not unlike a monk's cell. There he'd enter the wise silence and write in complete solitude, his lifelong sacred vocation until the day he died. In his last days he worked to finish his book of poetry, *The Flame*, published posthumously. His work, said his son, "was a mandate from God."

Among the final lines of the final song on Cohen's album that was released weeks before he died, he touches on the ultimate gift of retreat in a life—transformation. In "Treaty," we hear Cohen sing in his dolorous, wry voice of a shift from "broken" to "borderline."

Cohen's retreat experiences, and the others within these pages, are meant to gesture toward the ways time apart can help us gain wisdom, amplify the good and resist the intolerable—"a way to act human in these years the stars / look past," as William Stafford writes.

Paying passionate attention to what is most meaningful to us, to what we have reverence for, is urgent in a desacralized world. Retreat is like the mote of dust the raindrop forms around, or Cohen's "decent intention." In difficult times especially, I believe it's one of the best things we can do. After all, refusing easy despair, and seeking meaning in the face of our certain deaths, is part of what makes humans matter.

Our places of retreat—holy rivers, mountains and deserts, hermitages, monasteries, pilgrim's paths, cabins in the woods, arts temples, ashrams, garden sheds, simple white rooms and empty spaces—mark divine territory, both outer and inner. They stand today as among our least assailable sanctuaries for independent thinking, solitude, silence, spirit, creativity and for connection with self, others and the planet. We step over the threshold and encounter the unmediated and the real. We come to know ourselves, and being fully present, paradoxically, we can return and respond fully to the world in all its beauty and darkness.

A retreat is a place, but it is also an act of independence. A resolute effort of will is required. While it's easier to go with the powerful tide of the mainstream, which requires no thought or cultivation, we can choose to withdraw our attention, step back. Like prayer, piano playing, tennis, yoga and meditation, retreat is a practice—the effort you put in shapes what you get out of it. The practice of retreat attunes you to the extraordinary, to the sacramental world.

When I began writing this book I suspected my retreats made *me* suspect. Now I realize I'm part of a long lineage, a network like mycelium, under the ground, centuries old. Of dissidents, who, over the ages, have accorded with Walt Whitman to "resist much, obey little" when it comes to claiming time apart. I feel confident now that there will always be people who seek a slower, gentler, more contemplative life, and that retreat is more valuable as a method than ever.

Most of us, even in this accelerated age, can devise ways to step away temporarily. Just look to the edges. The margins hold retreat spaces, where we can connect to the total attention of the hermit, to the gentleness and simplicity of the monk, to the pilgrim's sacred ground, to the naturalist's reverence, to the artist's and thinker's passion for truth and beauty, to the embodied inner journey of the yogi and meditator.

Retreat is not a flight, but a way of real engagement. Often it's not a comfortable place to be. When we give serious attention to the fullness and possibility that exists in the inner world, we bump into our own contradictions and chaos, which is reflected in the outer world. Retreat is a gentle call to a certain kind of inaction, one that encourages us to contact our clearest selves and poses the question, What constitutes action anyway?

As for the ancient split—fulfillment in contemplative or active life, the solitary or the social—the lessons of this book confirm for me that these supposed opposites are actually indivisible parts of a whole. There can be no words or music without silence—simply noise. A candle can flicker only within darkness.

To retreat is to unify and transform: we can reconfigure ourselves, and the world, and find within us an enduring kind of liberation. "Freedom is a pretty strange thing," artist Ai Weiwei said. "Once you've experienced it, it remains in your heart and no one can take it away."

An image has stayed with me throughout the writing of this book. It's a fallow field. The brown earth slopes up to nine trees on the horizon and open sky beyond.

Most days during my spring writing retreat in Scotland I walked a narrow footpath that led between the field and its wild margin, where old apple trees with foraging bees in the white blossoms grew amid a tangle of thistles, nettles and wild garlic. It was also the way to the bus stop for the double-decker to Edinburgh, where I often waited, studying the empty field. I made many notes and took photos.

The image of the field has been drifting in and out of my consciousness ever since. With strange frequency, pages of "field notes" resurface in the chaos of my study, like a reminder. Right now the image is in my mind's eye, tugging insistently at my attention as I consider my conclusions.

What is it about this field that feels significant? It's something about the receptive, open space, the blank slate of earth sweeping up to the faraway line of old trees. And how things slowly appeared: the yellow flowers that shot out of the horse dung along the path's edge, the spindly green shoots that pushed up from the soil. The field wasn't fallow. Over the weeks I saw it fill with the unexpected, turn a luxuriant green and begin to ripple in the wind.

I watched with amazement as the invisible transformed the world.

The field, it strikes me now, like retreat, is ground where we can grow invisibly—"like corn in the night," as Thoreau said.

Quantum fields, scientists tell us today, are the stuff everything is made of. To the best of our ability to know, the universe is actually made from nothing but fields, with no smaller parts—which dramatically changes our ideas about empty space. There is no such thing. Emptiness is full, the field of infinite possibility. All retreats are fields, where the extraordinary comes into being.

Epilogue:
June 8, 2020

I'm sitting on the bridge over Beaver Creek, the threshold from here to there. The waters flow swiftly below me as I reread what I'd written about retreat and its role in our modern lives—before the world changed so quickly.

In a strange synchronicity, I submitted the book's first draft on December 31, 2019, the same day reports of a strange illness trickled out of China. Now as I make the finishing touches, in Canada we're in roughly the third month of an unprecedented experiment in collective, involuntary retreat.

When I was writing this book there was no crisis. I was courting possibility, exploring how our retreats—to make space for nature, spirit, imagination and embodiment—give our lives amplitude and meaning.

Our current emergency is not a retreat, because it's unsought. Yet as I revisit this book, I'm struck to find ideas from our chosen retreats apply in times of crisis—including this raw moment, when many have been forced to step back from active and social lives amid fear, instability and tragedy.

"In difficult times you should always carry something beautiful in your mind," wrote Blaise Pascal in the 1600s, touching on a guiding impulse for our retreats. Humans long to connect with beauty, truth, nature and spirit, with larger forces beyond our understanding. Doing so helps us amplify the good—and to endure much.

A retreat is one way to bring the beauty and light inside, like a gem we can pull out anytime, anywhere. A physical retreat, transformed by imagination and memory, becomes a sustaining place, an inner sanctuary. Every retreat is a retreat to the self—not necessarily a place, but a state of mind and heart.

Now the neglected half of reality, the receptive and solitary, has come to the fore. For some, this forced pause may hold space for a choice: to focus inward, develop calm and connect to what we love—which comes before our actions, and is action.

The desert hermits, among the other companions of this book, knew that a retreat is not an escape, but a way to wisdom. We need a rethink, personal and planetary. Our radical attention is needed to protect what has meaning for us, what is sacred and holy—in the sense of hālig, from old English, meaning healthy, whole, uninjured.

Historically, retreat has often been a corrective, and a way to invent brave new ideas—its ancient fruit. The pandemic has underlined that we are all interconnected. We are all vulnerable. May these difficult days hold space to reflect, to connect to our vast inner resources and help create the kind of world we want to live in once the pandemic has passed.

For all its powers, I most value retreat for itself, for the experience of exploring emptiness, which I find stimulating and challenging. I love the heightened receptivity, the not-knowing and the strange alchemy that leads to transformation. How it schools us in the active surrender life often requires.

At its essence, any retreat, whether voluntary or a pause imposed by life, is an encounter with the unknown—which is limitless possibility. What are we on the threshold of?

I watch the quicksilver waters of the creek pour, unpredictable as ever, though flowing within familiar banks. Words surface that seem to speak to our retreats, and our lives. "All is experiment and adventure," Virginia Woolf writes in *The Waves*. "We are for ever mixing ourselves with unknown quantities."

The Lake Isle of Innisfree

I will arise and go now, and go to Innisfree,
And a small cabin build there, of clay and wattles made;
Nine bean-rows will I have there, a hive for the honey-bee,
And live alone in the bee-loud glade.

And I shall have some peace there, for peace comes dropping slow,
Dropping from the veils of the morning to where the cricket sings;
There midnight's all a glimmer, and noon a purple glow,
And evening full of the linnet's wings.

I will arise and go now, for always night and day
I hear lake water lapping with low sounds by the shore;
While I stand on the roadway, or on the pavements grey,
I hear it in the deep heart's core.

WILLIAM BUTLER YEATS

Acknowledgements

For a book about taking a step back and retreating from society, I have a great many people to thank.

My husband, Marco, for love and compassion—as well as trumpet playing, a wayfaring spirit, and many of the photos in this book.

My two beloved Katharine MacLeods, mother and sister, whose ideas enrich everything.

Helen Humphreys and the not-so-shaggy allies, Charlotte and Fig. Solvitur ambulando—"It is solved by walking."

The Villanelles, bright stars: Ashley-Elizabeth Best, Nancy Jo Cullen, Ying Lee, Sadiqa de Meijer, Susan Olding, Sarah Tsiang.

Kindred spirits at ECW: Susan Renouf—for encouragement, warmth and editorial expertise. And for sharing the weirdness of working on a book about retreat as the world took a history-making, collective step back. Jen Knoch—for well-considered and often-hilarious editorial comments.

With gratitude to Sara Maitland, author-hermit and patron saint of this book.

Special thanks also to:

Shannon Parr for expert book-wrangling, and everyone at ECW who fielded my million questions with grace.

Cyndy Baskin, Mi'kmaq and Celtic Nations, Associate Professor of Social Work at Ryerson University in Toronto, for Indigenous cultural expertise in reviewing the pilgrimage chapter.

Coleman Barks, Chen Chen, Daniel Ladinsky and Karen Solie, for great generosity in granting permission to reprint their luminous work.

Jeff Cramer at the Walden Woods Project for astute advice and sharing images.

Swami Lalitananda and the kind people of Yasodhara.

Dr. Valentina Bold, scholar and storyteller, for resources on Scottish pilgrimage and St. Ninian.

Hamish, Ruth and the Hawthornden writers—gratitude for your thoughts, research suggestions and shared meals at the castle after long days spent writing. Thanks also to the Hawthornden International Residency and the late Mrs. Drue Heinz.

The New Quarterly for publishing "The Hermit Diaries," "Green Cathedral" and "The Retreat." In particular, thanks to Pamela Mulloy, and to Susan Scott, who expertly edited my first book, including the two chapters reprinted here.

I gratefully acknowledge financial support from the Access Copyright Foundation and Ontario Arts Council.

Perpetual gratitude goes to:

My steadfast wonders—Mel McCallum and Cary Silverstein.

Maira Reiter for the pilgrimage. Aline, Ingrit, Janete, Karin, Silvana and all the dear Brazilians—Abraços para todos.

Janet Crocker and Eric Tenn—for taking us to the wilds, and for moving to town.

Ed Vreeke and Leslie Shanks—for glorious swims, time and space to write at Weatherhead, and for the motivating "Hazelnoot."

Susan Mockler, for Wednesdays of shared writing and friendship.

Anita Jansman and Sarah Withrow, fine pilgrims, writers and pals.

Katrina and Roddy Beaton—for love, hospitality and for introducing me to *The Living Mountain* by Nan Shepard.

Marilyn Birmingham and Matthew Gventer—for book loans, ideas, leads, research, adventures with chickens and other neighbourly pleasures.

The Le Moine Point and Cataraqui conservation areas.

Jennifer Payne, for greater ease, and my yoga community—in particular Mona Warner and Janati Yoga, and the Drifting Dragons, for sharing their light.

And many thanks to you.

Notes

Epigraph

"I will arise and go now" (page vii): from William Butler Yeats, "The Lake Isle of Innisfree," *The Collected Works of W.B. Yeats Volume I: The Poems*, revised second edition, Simon & Schuster, page 39. First published in the *National Observer* in 1890.

An Introduction

"Lao-Tzu dictated" (page 5): from Stephen Mitchell, trans., *Tao Te Ching*, HarperPerennial, 2000, page vii.

"Wilhelm, who translated" (page 5): from Richard Wilhelm, trans., *The I Ching, or Book of Changes*, Princeton University Press, 1990, page 129–132. (See the Retreat hexagram.)

"To quote the *Tao Te Ching*" (page 6): from Stephen Mitchell, trans., *Tao Te Ching*, HarperPerennial, 2000, page 78.

Green Cathedral

"from *The Lonely Forest Dweller*" (page 11): from Prince Tissa Kumara, see https://www.buddhistinquiry.org/article/the-lonely-forest-dweller/. trans., Andew Olendzki, "The Lonely Forest Dweller," Spring 2003.

"We are driven to distraction by the pursuit of the fragmentary" (page 13): see https://www.tagoreweb.in/Render/ShowContent.aspx?ct=Essays&bi=72EE92F5-BE50-40D7-AE6E-0F7410664DA3&ti=72EE92F5-BE50-4A47-4E6E-0F7410664DA3&ch=c. "The Poet's Religion," retrieved Nov. 8, 2020.

"misery of manilla folders" (page 15): from Theodore Roethke, "Dolor," *The Collected Poems of Theodore Roethke*, Faber & Faber, 1968. See https://www.thetimes.co.uk/article/poets-corner-dolor-by-theodore-roethke-8x592ckc0dg.

"Asked to explain this to my urban friends, I'd quote" (page 17): from Dorothy Parker, "Sanctuary," *Complete Poems*, Penguin Classics, 2010. Appears in essay: https://www.poetryfoundation.org/poetrymagazine/articles/69664/dorothy-parkers-perfect-contempt.

"I like to think of myself as a praise poet" (page 21): see Maria Shriver, "Maria Shriver Interviews the Famously Private Poet Mary Oliver's "Upstream," *Oprah Magazine*,

March 2011. https://www.oprah.com/entertainment/maria-shriver-interviews-poet-mary-oliver/3.

"Attention is the beginning of devotion" (page 22): from Mary Oliver, *Blue Iris: Poems and Essays*, Beacon Press, 2006.

The Art of Retreat

"Now and again" (page 30): from Morihei Ueshiba, *The Art of Peace*, Shambhala Publications, 2007, page 25.

"more devalued than it has been in a long time" (page 32): see Brent Crane, "The Virtues of Isolation," *The Atlantic*, March 30, 2017. https://www.theatlantic.com/health/archive/2017/03/the-virtues-of-isolation/521100/.

"The dream had a wistful feeling" (page 33): from Chen Chen, "I'm not a religious person but," *Poetry*, June 2015, *When I Grow Up I Want to Be a List of Further Possibilities* (BOA Editions, 2017).

"I look to Marie Howe" (page 36): from Marie Howe, reading at Boston University, School of Theology, March 18, 2016. https://www.youtube.com/watch?v=DVYpwxmMl7g.

"like taking behavioural cocaine" (page 36): from Hilary Andersson, "Social Media Apps Are 'Deliberately' Addictive to Users," BBC Panorama, July 3, 2018. https://www.bbc.com/news/technology-44640959.

"Join the Attention Resistance" (page 38): from Cal Newport, *Digital Minimalism: Choosing a Focused Life in a Noisy World*, Portfolio, 2019.

"Neurologist Oliver Sacks wrote in his essay" (page 38): see Oliver Sacks, "The Machine Stops," *The New Yorker*, February 11, 2019.

"Privacy is no longer a 'social norm'" (page 38): see Bobbie Johnson's "Privacy no longer a social norm, says Facebook founder," *The Guardian*, January 11, 2010.

"Your wi-fi router could spy" (page 39): from "June 22 — Is your Wi-Fi watching you? Dog's manipulative eyebrows, Darwin's finches in danger and more . . ." *Quirks & Quarks*, CBC Radio, June 22, 2019. https://www.cbc.ca/radio/quirks/june-22-is-your-wi-fi-watching-you-dog-s-manipulative-eyebrows-darwin-s-finches-in-danger-and-more-1.5182752/your-wi-fi-router-could-be-used-to-watch-you-breathe-and-monitor-your-heartbeat-1.5182770.

"a seventh-century Scottish hermit" (page 40): from Karen Solie, "Origin Story," *The Caiplie Caves*, House of Anansi Press, 2019, pages 69–70.

"'To pay attention'" (page 41): from Mary Oliver, "Yes! No!" *Owls and Other Fantasies: Poems and Essays*, Beacon Press, 2003, page 27.

"Intrigued, I decided to consult" (page 44): see *I Ching* Online, https://www.ichingonline.net/.

"The being one creates of oneself" (page 46): from Alice Koller, *The Stations of Solitude*, William Morrow and Co., Inc., page 23. 1990.

"'Escaping to such a solitary place'" (page 47): from Philip Koch, *Solitude: A Philosophical Encounter*, Carus Publishing, 1999. Page 102.

"In *How to Be Alone*" (page 47): from Sara Maitland, *How to Be Alone*, Macmillan, 2014, page 117.

"'Removing oneself voluntarily from one's habitual environment'" (page 48): from Anthony Storr, *Solitude: A Return to the Self*, The Free Press, 1988. Page 34.

"the terrible epidemic of loneliness in the West" (page 53): see Faye Bound Alberti, "The invention of loneliness: why being 'unhappy alone' is a surprisingly modern idea" [not dated, retrieved Nov 8, 2020]. https://www.historyextra.com/period/victorian/invention-loneliness-mental-health-lonely-history-modern-unhappy-self-isolation-alone/ and *A Biography of Loneliness: The History of an Emotion* by British historian Fay Bound Alberti, who ties modern loneliness to capitalism and secularism. Oxford University Press, 2019.

"'Aloneness implies a conscious choice'" (page 54): see Brent Crane, "The Virtues of Isolation," *The Atlantic*, March 30, 2017. https://www.theatlantic.com/health/archive/2017/03/the-virtues-of-isolation/521100/.

"Similarly, clinical psychologist" (page 56): from Ester Schaler Bucholz, *The Call of Solitude: Alonetime in a World of Attachment*, Simon & Schuster, 1999, page 21.

"the desert to become 'wholly aflame'" (page 57): In a story of the desert fathers a hermit goes to see Abba Joseph and entreats, "I fast a little, I pray and meditate, I live in peace as far as I can, I purify my thoughts. What else can I do?" Abba Joseph lifts his hands up to heaven, and his ten fingers blaze like lamps of fire. "If you will, you can become all aflame," he replies, a man transfigured.

"talk of 'the rise of millennial hermits'" (page 58): see Sarah Todd, "Why Millennials Never Want to Leave Their Apartments Anymore," *Quartz*, November 15, 2019, https://qz.com/quartzy/1748191/how-millennials-became-a-generation-of-homebodies/.

"youthful 'rubber tramps'" (page 58): see Matt Derrick, "The Rise of the Rubber Tramps," *Squat the Planet*, May 27, 2019. https://squattheplanet.com/threads/the-rise-of-the-rubber-tramps.38472/.

"cloud-connected 'hobos'" (page 58): see Drew Magary, "This Hobo Life," *GQ*, March 28, 2016. https://www.gq.com/story/millennial-hobo-life.

"Swedish environmental activist Greta Thunberg" (page 58): see Emily Witt, "Greta Thunberg's Slow Boat to New York," *The New Yorker*, September 9, 2019.

"Temperament is a well-studied aspect of personality" (page 58): see Jonathan Rauch, "Caring for Your Introvert," *The Atlantic*, March 2003.

"it was deemed more desirable to be an introvert" (page 59): from Merve Emre, *The Personality Brokers: The Strange History of Myers-Briggs and the Birth of Personality Testing*, Random

House Canada, 2018. Tim Lewis, "Myers-Briggs personality tests: what kind of person are you?" The Guardian, September 15, 2018. https://www.theguardian.com/science/2018/sep/15/myers-briggs-not-sure-youre-really-our-type-merve-emre-author-origins-validity-personality-tests.

"in Shanghai and Southern Ontario" (page 59): from Susan Cain, *Quiet: The Power of Introverts in a World that Can't Stop Talking*, Broadway Books, 2013, page 187; and Xinyin Chen, Kenneth H. Rubin and Yuerong Sun, "Social Reputation and Peer Relationships in Chinese and Canadian Children: A Cross-Cultural Study," *Child Development* 63(6), December 1992, pages 1336–1343. DOI: 10.1111/j.1467-8624.1992.tb01698.

"no one can say with certainty why we sleep" (page 60): see Jerome Groopman, "The Secrets of Sleep," *The New Yorker*, October 16, 2017.

"writes Czech philosopher Erazim Kohák" (page 60): from Wojciech W. Gasparski, *Environmental Political Philosophy*, Routledge, 2017, page 273.

A Hut of One's Own

"'To live as a hermit'" (page 63): from Meng-hu, "Sayings in the Hermitary Style," Hermitary, https://www.hermitary.com/sayings/ https://www.hermitary.com/sayings/.

"a stylite living atop a pillar" (page 66): see Laura Freeman, "The Art of the Hermit," *The Spectator*, April 4, 2020. St. Simeon Stylites was the first, a fifth-century Syrian monk who genuflected on a ruined pillar for 37 years in the desert sun, trying to get as near to God as possible. His attempt provoked many imitators who tried to surpass his austerities— suspended in cages, walled up in hermitages, buried in cisterns. When pillar hermits reached wintry Europe the tradition mostly died out, deemed impossible because the ascetics would freeze to their pillars. St. Simeon's life involved many extreme retreats: he bricked himself into a hut, chained himself to a rock and lived at the bottom of a well.

"Father Maxime Qavtaradze climbed up the 50-metre Katshki pillar" (page 66): for vivid photos of his eyrie see the works of Amos Chapple, a wandering photojournalist from New Zealand. https://www.rferl.org/a/25102766.html.

"Take Pete, 'one of New Zealand's last hermits'" (page 67): see Tess McClure, "What It's Like to Be a Hermit in New Zealand," *The Wireless*, June 2, 2016.

"'invited her to accompany him to a lecture by Germaine Greer whom he had heard had great legs'" (page 68): see "All Quiet on the Western Front," *The Scotsman*, November 6, 2008.

"'sad, mad or bad'" (page 69): from Sara Maitland, *How to Be Alone*, Macmillan, 2014, page 15.

"a cowled man with a lantern, suggesting Diogenes the Cynic" (page 71): The ideals of Diogenes, the Greek proto-hermit, were radical truth, freedom and simplicity, and he laid down tracks for the first Western hermits, whose influence bridges the ancient and modern worlds. Diogenes thought life had become artificial and called for a return to simplicity, with dogs as role models because they slept anywhere, ate anything and did their natural functions without shame in public—all of which he also did. At a banquet, after guests tossed him bones, the sage lifted his leg and urinated on them. He scandalized people with indecent behaviour in the marketplace, unapologetically remarking that he "wished it were as easy to relieve hunger by rubbing an empty stomach."

His wild transgressions were meant as a shortcut to virtue: he embraced poverty, spurned the material and cultural trappings of Greek life, and asserted that the individual was more important than social rules—a new line of thought that has inspired rebels who have chosen to live outside society ever since. He was the most eminent of the Greek Cynics. Many Cynics joined the early Christian hermits, sharing their hostility for Greco-Roman civilization, and praising self-discipline and the mendicant lifestyle.

"He was the ancient philosopher who demanded the most from himself and his followers in terms of asceticism, cheerful acceptance of hardship, verbal freedom and absolute physical and intellectual self-sufficiency," writes David Mazella in *The Making of Modern Cynicism*. University of Virginia, 2007, page 13.

"Months later I read a dark, often-hilarious article" (page 76): see Sam Knight, "Back to the Garden," *The New Yorker*, September 4, 2017.

"'closyd in an hows of ston'" (page 78): Anchorites were symbolically buried alive, entombed. Last rites were administered in an elaborate ceremony before the cell was bricked up, with only a hard bed, a crucifix and an altar, and their own grave—anchorites were often buried in their cells. "Admiring their own white hands is bad for many anchoresses who keep them too beautiful . . . they should scrape up the earth every day from the grave in which they will rot," advised *Ancrene Wisse*, a guide for enclosed women written by an unknown author. Like other hermits, anchorites were rarely alone. Typically the anchorhold had three windows. A narrow slit called a squint gave a view of the church altar, and many cells were designed so that the anchorite had to kneel in her own grave to see it. There was a food hatch and an assistant: anchorites had to have funding to pay for food and servants before the bishop would agree to enclosure, but this wasn't difficult to arrange. Patrons got divine credits with their support and were repaid through prayer. At a third window, people could come for wisdom, prayer and counsel. Anchorites often worked, doing sedentary tasks like producing books and textiles.

"Ornamental hermits" (page 78): from Gordon Campbell, *The Hermit in the Garden: From Imperial Rome to Ornamental Gnome*, Oxford University Press, 2013, page 2.

This marked the return of the hermit after hundreds of years. In the sixth century, the Protestant Reformation that split the Church ended the extreme religious lifestyle of hermits, monks and anchorites in many countries. In Britain, where traditions had lasted five centuries, anchorites such as a 100-year-old woman were turfed out at the Dissolution of the Monasteries. Traditions languished or disappeared in Protestant countries for centuries. Hermit life continued, but mainly under the auspices of monastic orders in Europe. But when hermits made their comeback in the 1800s, they couldn't have been less like the fiery desert ascetics of St. Anthony's vintage, or the hermits who lived in isolation to pursue higher spiritual enlightenment once so common in Europe's landscape. Now, hermits were the ultimate accessory for busy landowners who hired them to show their meditative sides—by outsourcing them.

"Revelations of Divine Love" (page 79): Julian of Norwich, who was walled up in middle age for her last 26 years, had been twice married before choosing a mystical marriage. Though her real name is unknown, she was born in 1343, the same year as Chaucer, and her cell adjoined the church of St. Julian in Norwich. From there she dispensed comfort and advice to visitors through a grille, and wrote *Revelations of Divine Love*. To my surprise I'm familiar with a passage from her ancient writings, though I'd never known its source: "All shall be well, and all shall be well, and all manner of things shall be well." Curious: I repeat a version of this when I'm truly in a panic, poetic words of comfort that echo down the centuries.

"the first true Western hermits" (page 79): The desert fathers and mothers broke from convention and followed the example of St. Anthony, the Old Testament prophets and Christ, who spent 40 days and nights in the wilderness—by going to fight Satan in desert. This was a practical solution to cleanse sin. Holy hermits, in their ability to endure physical suffering and torture the flesh, "were believed to be able to wear away the curtain that separated the visible world from the divine," writes William Dalrymple in From the *Holy Mountain*, "and by reaching through they gained direct access to God, something that was thought to be impossible for the ordinary believer." Flamingo, 1998, page 162.

"Mortifications. Why?" (page 80): I'm not the only one who finds these ascetic practices repellant. Historian Edward Gibbon, author of *The History of the Decline and Fall of the Roman Empire*, published in 1776, described what he saw as an ascetic epidemic: "A hideous, distorted and emaciated maniac without knowledge, without patriotism, without natural affection, spending his life in a long routine of useless and atrocious self-torture, and quailing before the ghastly phantoms of his delirious brain had become the ideal of nations which had known the writings of Plato and Cicero and the lives of Socrates and Cato."

"intercessors with God" (page 80): "Oh hermit's life, bathtub of souls, annihilation of sins, purgatory of the soiled, you purify secret thoughts, wash away the filth of wicked deeds, and lead souls to the brilliance of angelic cleanness," wrote 11th-century monastic leader and Church reformer Peter Damian, quoted in a wonderful book by Tom Licence, *Hermits and Recluses in English Society*, 950–1200, Oxford University Press, 2011, page 149.

"St. Anthony, the first desert ascetic" (page 80): St. Anthony was born in the Nile to a rich landowning family but left behind what he saw as the corrupt worldly life of 270 AD Egypt in disgust. He retreated alone to an abandoned tomb, where he was locked in, praying to God. Logistics? I'm not sure, but history records that he had friends to feed him. I've seen Anthony's tomb, beautiful and full of birds, on TV. A church has been built over top. Fleeing followers, he later moved to his famous desert cave. Anthony might have lingered at this retreat a few decades longer, but devotees broke into his cell. And when God told him in a vision to go to the desert and he moved into the ruins of an old desert fort in the eastern Sinai, many went along. Bedouins led him through the sands to the mountains near the Red Sea, which are riddled with caves, where he found a life-giving spring. As is often the fate of religious hermits, people—in this case, adoring Greco-Roman intellectuals from Alexandria—kept after Anthony, seeking spiritual advice. Hermits withdrew from society but were asked to give back, to dispense wisdom about how to live. Soon, the inhospitable desert was full of hermits, thousands of them, occupying the mountain caves in the harshest imaginable wilderness, a feared place of privation and death. Anthony did manage to spend the last years of life alone in his cave. The world's first monastery was founded on his burial site in 356 AD. He is often credited with giving birth to two traditions for contemplative life: the eremitic (solitary) and the coenobitic (communal) that gradually become the norm, in which the self is submerged in obedience and collective discipline.

"most repeated subjects in Western literature and art" (page 81): Flaubert wrote *The Temptation of St. Anthony*, in which the saint lusts after the Virgin Mary; Michelangelo's earliest known painting is of Anthony ambushed and beaten in mid-air by devils; and Salvador Dalí depicts a naked Anthony in the desert facing down exotic temptations. Hieronymous Bosch's celebrated triptych that reflects Anthony amid grotesqueries, venalities and ordeals feels contemporary.

"the most wild and deserted places" (page 81): from William Dalrymple, *From the Holy Mountain*, Flamingo, 1998, page 106.

"portals of prayer" (page 82): see William Dalrymple, "Everything is illuminated," *The Guardian*, July 12, 2003. https://www.theguardian.com/artanddesign/2003/jul/12/art.

"The *Scotsman* journalist writes of Maitland" (page 90): see "Five Hermits Who Have Called Scotland home," *The Scotsman*, June 2, 2017.

"asked why he made films" (page 89): Federico Fellini and Charlotte Chandler *I, Fellini*, Cooper Square Press, Lanham, MA, 2001, page 215.

"silence is more like a plan" (page 94): from Adrienne Rich, "Cartographies of Silence," *The Dream of a Common Language*, W.W. Norton & Co., 1978.

Monasticism for Moderns

"There are hundreds of ways" (page 95): from Jalaluddin Rumi, *The Essential Rumi*, trans. by Coleman Barks and John Moyne, HarperOne, 2004, page 36. "the travellers slipped past": see Mathieu Drouin, Canada's History, "Ursulines and Augustinians: Educating and Healing Canada Since 1639," July 23, 2014. https://www.canadashistory.ca/explore/women/ursulines-and-augustinians-educating-and-healing-canada-since-1639.

"Great was their disappointment" (page 97): see Loretta La Palm, "The Hotel Dieu of Quebec," Journal of Canadian Catholic Historical Association, CCHA Study Sessions, 41(1974), pages 53-64. https://www.cchahistory.ca/journal/CCHA1974/LaPalm.pdf.

"With their organic, artisanal products made with care and simplicity" (page 110): from "Monastic Merchandise: Products Made by Monks," *Under the Influence*, CBC Radio, January 31, 2019.

"'stepping outside' the confines of the self" (page 110): from Karen Armstrong, (introduction), *A Time to Keep Silence*, St. Martin's Press, 1997, page x.

"under an abbot's authority" (page 111): Benedict's monks lived apart from society and were self-sufficient, farming and keeping bees and learning the artisanal skills they are still famous for today. Another new idea was that after a long probation in the monastic community, with permission, a monk could become a hermit, which was still considered the peak of monastic life. This meant monks had training first, to avoid the difficulties and spiritual dangers of the Egyptian ascetic way to God.

Pilgrim Ways

"Traveller, there is no path" (page 120): from Antonio Machado, *Campos de Castilla* (*Plains of Castile*), Ediciones Catedra S.A., 2006 (first published in 1912), trans. by Kirsteen MacLeod.

"kinetic ritual" (page 122): from Edith Turner, *Image and Pilgrimage in Christian Culture*, Columbia University Press, 1995, page xiii.

"We depart in search of" (page 122): from Rebecca Solnit, *Wanderlust: A History of Walking*, Penguin Books, 2001, page 45.

"It's heartening that" (page 127): see Christine Luckasavitch, "A Brief History of the Madaoueskarini Algonquin People," MuskokaRegion.com, June 6, 2019.

"Hybla Gospel Tabernacle" (page 132): from Ontario Abandoned Places, https://www.ontarioabandonedplaces.com/Hybla-(semi-ghost-town)_loc732.html.

"Not doing it for religious reasons" (page 146): see Bob Walker, "Walk of faith: 500 km of sugar, storms and blisters," BBC News, July 23, 2015. https://www.bbc.com/news/magazine-33550932.

"Most sought-after pilgrimage goal" (page 149): from Edith Turner, *Image and Pilgrimage in Christian Culture*, Columbia University Press, 1995, page xvii.

"Substitution shrine" (page 151): from Edith Turner, *Image and Pilgrimage in Christian Culture*, Columbia University Press, 1995, page xvi.

"Members of the Driftpile First Nation often arrive" (page 152): see Amber Bracken, "The Healing Waters of Lac Ste. Anne," *The Globe and Mail*, July 30, 2015. Ernie Giroux, president of the Driftpile Cree Nations Pilgrimage Society, each year leads a group of his people from their home in Lesser Slave Lake to Lac Ste Anne. "We're here for our ancestors who had made the journey before and passed on. We do it to honour their memory and follow in their footsteps," he says. See Caitlan Kehoe, "Lac Ste. Anne pilgrims united by tradition and faith," *The Grove Examiner*, July 25, 2014.

"1995's *Healing Waters*" (page 152): from Steve Simon, *Healing Waters: The Pilgrimage to Lac Ste. Anne*, University of Alberta Press, 1995. Another resource about the pilgrimage is the master's thesis, "'Rendezvous' for renewal at 'Lake of the Great Spirit': The French pilgrimage and Indigenous journey to Lac Ste-Anne, Alberta, 1870–1896," by Jessica Anne Buresi (University of Calgary, 2012). "Since its very inception," she writes, "the Lac Ste-Anne Pilgrimage has also been a manifestation of the Aboriginal people's will to both adopt and resist aspects of the colonialist mindset, including new religious ideas and a popular form of Catholic worship, while continuing to also adapt older cultural gathering practices of their own to the new event, based on their relationship to the land."

"In Manitoba there is a spiritual place" (page 154): from Robert Houle, "Where the Gods are Present," in *The Good Lands: Canada Through the Eyes of Artists*, Figure 1 Publishing, 2017, page 261.

"Border Angels, women who walk" (page 155): see Jackie Bryant, "Pilgrimage," *Sierra*, November/December 2019; and see "Life, Death, and the Border Patrol," November 6, 2019, https://www.sierraclub.org/sierra/2019-6-november-december/last-words/life-death-and-border-patrol.

"To wander is the Taoist code word" (page 158): from

Rebecca Solnit, *Wanderlust: A History of Walking*, Penguin Books, 2001, page 144.

"meditation versus action" (page 158): from Youtube, "Glenn Gould reads from The Three Cornered World." https://www.youtube.com/watch?v=jvI5a3kZl0M.

"I read an old copy of" (page 159): Aldo Leopold, *A Sand County Almanac*, Ballatine Books, 1986, pages 294–295 (first published by Oxford University Press, 1949).

"'I fill my glass for you, dear pilgrim'" (page 161): from Hafiz, *The Gift*, trans. by Daniel Ladinsky, Penguin Compass, 1999, page 262.

I Will Go to the Wild Woods

"the genius of Henry David Thoreau" (page 170): Terry Tempest Williams, quoted from radio interview, *To the Best of Our Knowledge*. http://archive.ttbook.org/book/transcript/transcript-terry-tempest-williams-thoreau [no date given].

"of sacred geographies" (page 174): from Courtney Milne, *The Sacred Earth*, (quoting the Dalai Lama), Western Producer Prairie Books, 1991, page 174.

"literate monks and hermits" (page 181): see Kathleen Jamie, "Lone Enraptured Male," *London Review of Books*, March 6, 2008. https://www.lrb.co.uk/the-paper/v30/n05/kathleen-jamie/a-lone-enraptured-male.

"her family and schoolmates publicly professed their belief

in Christ" (page 182): from the Emily Dickinson Museum, see "Emily Dickinson and the church," https://www. emilydickinsonmuseum.org/emily-dickinson/biography/ special-topics/emily-dickinson-and-the-church/. The site observes, "In Dickinson's teen years, a wave of religious revivals moved through New England. Although she agonized over her relationship to God, Dickinson ultimately did not join the church—not out of defiance but in order to remain true to herself: 'I feel that the world holds a predominant place in my affections. I do not feel that I could give up all for Christ, were I called to die,' she said."

"she studied botany" (page 184): from Judith Farr, *The Gardens of Emily Dickinson*, Harvard University Press, 2005, page 3.

"the place of a gaping mouth" (page 189): Ken Burns, *The National Parks* (series), PBS, 2009. http://www.pbs.org/ nationalparks/history/ep1/.

"Colonial crime scenes" (page 189): see Robert Jago, "Canada's National Parks are Colonial Crime Scenes," *The Walrus*, June 30, 2017.

"forced off their lands" (page 189): see Kevin Mcnamee and Maxwell W. Finkelstein, National Parks of Canada, *The Canadian Encyclopedia*, 2012 and updated 2019. http://www. pbs.org/nationalparks/history/ep1/.

"the backwoods of northern Ontario" (page 193): 'She of the Loghouse Nest': from Kirsten Greer and Sonje Bols, "Gendering Historical Ecological Reconstructions in Northern Ontario," *Historical Geography Volume 44* (2016): pages 45-67. https://d2cu82y6eo7f22.cloudfront. net/2020/01/08220733/05HG44-Greer.pdf.

"under the cottage microscope" (page 194): see Jill Lepore, "The Right Way to Remember Rachel Carson," *New Yorker*, March 26, 2018.https://www.newyorker. com/magazine/2018/03/26/the-right-way-to-remember-rachel-carson.

"'Has Rachel Carson's prevision really come true?'" (page 193): see Jim Daley, "Silent Skies," *Scientific American*, September 19, 2019.

"her beloved friend" (page 197): from Rachel Carson, *Always, Rachel: the Letters of Rachel Carson and Dorothy Freeman*, 1952-1964, Beacon Press, 1995, page 394.

"Li's science" (page 205): see Qing Li, "Effect of Forest Bathing Trips on Human Immune Function," Published online 2009 Mar 25. doi: 10.1007/s12199-008-0068-3. https:// www.ncbi.nlm.nih.gov/pmc/articles/PMC2793341/ and Dr. Qing Li, *Forest Bathing: How Trees Can Help You Find Health and Happiness*, Penguin Random House, 2018.

"aerosols emitted by evergreens and many other trees" (page 206): see Florence Williams, "Take Two Hours of Pine Forest and Call Me in the Morning," *Outside*, November 28, 2012.

"The nature cure is an idea" (page 206): see James Hamblin, "The Nature Cure," *The Atlantic*, October 2015.

"'Throughout our evolution'" (page 207): from Florence Williams, *The Nature Fix: Why Nature Makes Us Happier, Healthier, and More Creative*, W.W. Norton & Co., 2017, page 23 (quoting Yoshifumi Miyazaki).

"they're right, says David Strayer" (page 207): ibid., page 187 (quoting David Strayer).

"Li's advice is similar" (page 207): ibid., page 218 (quoting Qing Li).

"because a chronic disconnection" (page 208): ibid., page 3 (quoting Elizabeth Nisbet).

"We evolved in nature" (page 208): ibid., page 13 (quoting Elizabeth Nisbet).

"Researchers say 27 per cent" (page 209): see Alison Flood, "Scientists use Thoreau's journal notes to track climate change," *The Guardian*, March 14, 2012. https://www.theguardian.com/books/2012/mar/14/henry-david-thoreau-climate-change.

"that's killing the planet we depend on for life" (page 210): see Damian Carrington, "Survival of the Natural World Is in the Balance," *The Guardian*, June 24, 2019.

"what are people doing" (page 210): see Curt Stager, "Henry David Thoreau's Walden Pond is Being spoiled by climate change - and urine," As It Happens, CBC Radio, April 5, 2018. https://www.cbc.ca/radio/asithappens/as-it-happens-thursday-full-episode-1.4606389/

henry-david-thoreau-s-walden-pond-is-being-spoiled-by-climate-change-and-urine-1.4606651.

"his temple was made of wood" (page 211): see Laura Dassow Walls, lecture, *The Morgan Library and Museum*, New York, 2017.https://www.themorgan.org/videos/henry-david-thoreau-life.

Artists, Writers, Creative Thinkers, Dreamers

"Best of any song" (page 213): from Wendell Berry, *A Timbered Choir: The Sabbath Poems*, Counterpoint, 1999, page 207.

"Thoreau, who wrote up a storm at Walden" (page 215): see "Thoreau's writing," https://www.walden.org/education/for-students/thoreaus-writing/. He kept field notes, started his lifelong journal there and also wrote *A Week on the Concord and Merrimack Rivers* and the first draft of *Walden*, among other writings.

"servant of the hours" (page 218): from Mary Oliver, "Of Power and Time," *Upstream: Selected Essays*, Penguin Books, 2016.

"Opera now serves as" (page 219): see Vanessa Thorpe, "Opera leaves me transfigured," *The Guardian*, June 23, 2018. https://www.theguardian.com/theobserver/2018/jun/23/rufus-wainwright-opera-transfigured-second-classical-release-change-direction.

"appreciating art can change us" (page 219): see Bill Moyers, *Moyers on Democracy*, "The Wisdom of Faith with Huston

Smith," March 26, 1996. https://billmoyers.com/content/wisdom-faith-hinduism-buddhism/.

"it's my default position" (page 219): see Susan Gonzales, "Writing Is Simply an 'Alibi' for Living Says Poet and Novelist Eileen Myles," *YaleNews*, September 20, 2019.

"much less fully heard" (page 220): see Meena Alexander, "What Use is Poetry?" *World Literature Today*, September 2013. https://www.worldliteraturetoday.org/2013/september/what-use-poetry-meena-alexander.

"Whoever is unwilling" (page 222): see "In Search of Ludwig Wittgenstein's Secluded Hut in Norway, April 25, 2016. http://www.openculture.com/2016/04/in-search-of-ludwig-wittgensteins-secluded-hut-in-norway-a-short-travel-film.html.

"'great veteran pines'" (page 222): from Emily Carr, *Hundreds and Thousands*, Irwin Publishing, 1986, page 103.

"nobody pesters you" (page 223): from Emily Carr, ibid., page 120.

"'we never seem crowded'" (page 223): from Emily Carr, ibid., page 133.

"'my tabernacle, my refuge'" (page 224): from Susan Crean, *The Laughing One*, HarperFlamingo Canada, 2001, page 372.

"Six acres of boreal forest" (page 225): see Portrait of

Marlene Creates, 2019 #GGARTS winner. https://www. youtube.com/watch?v=7apC0qVneE8&feature=youtu.be.

"tiny urban hut" (page 243): see Jessica Stewart, "Designer Suspends Tiny Hidden Art Studio Under a Bridge," *My Modern Met*, August 21, 2017. https://mymodernmet.com/fernando-abellanas-art-studio/.

The Inner Temple

"Consider the experiences of" (page 248): see Jodi Ettenberg, "My exhausting meditation retreat: 10 days of Vipassana, silence and spiders," *The Guardian*, March 31, 2016.

"which share the same ancient source" (page 248): from Philip Goldberg, *American Veda*, Harmony Books, 2010, page 3.

"'the breath within the breath,'" (page 250): from Kabir, *The Enlightened Heart*, ed. Stephen Mitchell, trans. Robert Bly, HarperPerennial, 1993, page 72.

"these traditions filled" (page 250): from Philip Goldberg, *American Veda*, Harmony Books, 2010, pages 14–15.

"The handsome, dignified monk" (page 252): from Rick Fields, *How the Swans Came to the Lake: A Narrative History of Buddhism in America*, Shambhala Publications, 1992, page 121.

"'famously declaring that all traditions can lead to the infinite'" (page 252): from Philip Goldberg, *American Veda*, pages 68–69.

"The first wave of yogis" (page 253): Robert Love, *The Great Oom: The Improbable Birth of Yoga in America*, Viking, New York, 2010, pages 72-73.

"Vivekananda Cottage" (page 253): see the website of the Ramakrishna-Vivekananda Centre of New York, "Vivekananda Cottage Visitors' Information" https:// ramakrishna.org/cottage.html.

"yoga from the head up" (page 253): from Stefanie Syman, *The Subtle Body*, Farrar, Straus and Giroux, 2010.

"Elvis visited often" (page 254): from Louis Sahagun, "Guru's Followers Mark Legacy of a Star's Teachings," *Los Angeles Times*, August 6, 2006.

"I'll share the story of two yoga retreats" (page 262): Both stories appeared originally in my book *The Animal Game*, Tightrope Books, 2016.

"The band was approached" (page 285): from the Beatles, *The Beatles Anthology*, Chronicle Books, 2000, page 167. In *American Veda*, Goldberg writes, "It may have been the most momentous spiritual retreat since Jesus spent those 40 days in the wilderness," page 7.

"Pema Chödrön was long the abbey's resident teacher" (page 289): see Matthew Abrahams, "Pema Chödrön Steps Down as Senior Teacher at Shambhala," *Tricycle*, January 17, 2020.

"the monks advised him" (page 289): see Rod Meade Sperry,

"That Time David Bowie Almost Became a Buddhist Monk," *Lion's Roar*, January 15, 2016.

"'We're all moving to Nova Scotia'" (page 290): see Suzannah Showler, "Kingdom Come," *The Walrus*, December 2010.

"women are retreating" (page 291): see "The freeing power of restricting your freedom," Out in the Open, CBC Radio, February 2, 2018. https://www.cbc.ca/radio/outintheopen/freedom-ltd-1.4505386/the-freeing-power-of-restricting-your-freedom-1.4505921.

"'away from external and internal distractions'" (page 292): from Vicki Mackenzie, *Cave in the Snow: A Western Woman's Quest for Enlightenment*, Bloomsbury Press, 1999, pages 197-8.

"'who one really is behind all the masks'" (page 292): ibid., page 198.

"'Everything gets cooked much quicker'" (page 293): ibid., pages 197–198.

"their beams are focused" (page 293): ibid., page 196.

White Rooms, Unified Hearts and Empty Fields

"calling him the man" (page 298): *I'm Your Man*, DVD release, 2006.

"'Once his life becomes too cluttered'" (page 298): from Ira B. Nadel, *Various Positions*, Random House of Canada, 1996, page 271.

"along the same lines" (page 298): see Brian D. Johnson, "Life of Lady's Man," Maclean's, December 7, 1992.

"snow at 3 am in sandals" (page 300): *Various Positions*, page 190.

"a need for self-reform" (page 300): ibid., page 190.

"'it's like scraping off the rust'" (page 300): ibid., page 202.

"he went up the mountain" (page 301): ibid., page 190.

"wasn't looking for a religion" (page 301): see Simon Worall, "Leonard Cohen: Out of the Monastery and Back on the Road," *The Independent*, June 15, 2008. https://www.independent.co.uk/arts-entertainment/music/features/leonard-cohen-out-of-the-monastery-and-back-on-the-road-845789.html.

"Like pebbles in a bag" (page 302): see "Leonard Cohen on Poetry, Music and Why He Left the Zen Monastery," *Fresh Air*, NPR, March 22, 2006. https://www.npr.org/2016/10/21/498810429/leonard-cohen-on-poetry-music-and-why-he-left-the-zen-monastery.

"'On the desk lay a cassette'" (page 302): from Soutik Biswas, "When the Light Got in for Leonard Cohen," BBC News, November 16, 2016. https://www.bbc.com/news/world-asia-india-37971848.

"'tendrel, the interrelatedness of all things'" (page 302): from Sylvie Simmons, *I'm Your Man*, McClelland & Stewart, 2012, page 425.

"'Beauty, certainly'" (page 304): see Sarah Hampson, "Hampson on Leonard Cohen," *The Globe and Mail*, May 29, 2007.

"Anything, Roman Catholicism" (page 304): see David Remnick, "Leonard Cohen makes it Darker," *New Yorker*, October 17, 2016. https://www.newyorker.com/magazine/2016/10/17/leonard-cohen-makes-it-darker.

"Of the word God" (page 304): see Douglas Todd, "Leonard Cohen: Jewish, Buddhist and Christian too," *Vancouver Sun*, November 25, 2016.

"'they forgot how to build the arch'" (page 304): from Paul Zollo, *Songwriters on Songwriting*, Da Capo Press, 2003, page 344.

"not for everyone" (page 305): see "Leonard Cohen's 'Book of Longing,'" Fresh Air, NPR, January 1, 2007. https://www.npr.org/templates/story/story.php?storyId=6696573.

"there's an appetite" (page 305): see Angelica Huston, "Leonard Cohen," Interview, November 1995. Posted as "Remembering Leonard Cohen," November 11, 2016. https://www.interviewmagazine.com/music/leonard-cohen.

"a monastic discipline" (page 306): see Scott Timberg, "Romance, Regrets and Notebooks in the Freezer: Leonard Cohen's Son on his father's final poems," *The Guardian*, September 28, 2018. https://www.theguardian.com/books/2018/sep/28/leonard-cohen-poetry-the-flame-adam-cohen-interview.

"we hear Cohen sing" (page 306): from Mikal Gilmore, quoted in "Leonard Cohen, Remembering the Life and Legacy of Brokenness," *Rolling Stone*, November 30, 2016 (quoting Leonard Cohen).

"'the stars look past'" (page 307): from William Young, "William Stafford, The Art of Poetry No. 67," *The Paris Review*, Winter 1993.

Selected Bibliography

Ansell, Neil. *Deep Country*. London: Hamish Hamilton, 2012.

Ansell, Neil. *The Last Wilderness: A Journey into Silence*. London: Tinder Press, Headline Publishing Group, 2018.

Armstrong, Karen. *A Short History of Myth*. Toronto: Vintage Canada, 2006.

Badé, William Frederic. *The Life and Letters of John Muir*. New York: Houghton Mifflin Company, 1924.

Bakewell, Sara. *How to Live: A Life of Montaigne in One Question and Twenty Attempts at an Answer*. London: Vintage Books, 2011.

Berger, John. *Confabulations*. London: Penguin Books, 2016.

Buchholz, Esther. *The Call of Solitude: Alonetime in a World of Attachment*. New York: Simon & Schuster, 1999.

Carr, Emily. *Hundreds and Thousands: The Journals of an Artist*. Toronto: Irwin Publishing, 1986.

Carson, Rachel. *Always, Rachel: the Letters of Rachel Carson and Dorothy Freeman, 1952-1964*. Boston: Beacon Press, 1995.

Carson, Rachel. *Silent Spring*. New York: Houghton Mifflin Company, 1962.

Clifford, Amos. *Your Guide to Forest Bathing*. Newburyport, MA: Conari Press, 2018.

Colegate, Isabel. *A Pelican in the Wilderness: Hermits, Solitaries and Recluses*. London: HarperCollins, 2002.

Crean, Susan. *The Laughing One: A Journey to Emily Carr*. Toronto: HarperFlamingo Canada, 2001.

Dalrymple, William. *From the Holy Mountain*. London: Flamingo, 1998.

Dassow-Walls, Laura. *Henry David Thoreau: A Life*. Chicago: University of Chicago Press, 2017.

David-Neel, Alexandra. *My Journey to Lhasa*. New York: Harper Perennial, 2005.

Dickinson, Emily. *The Complete Poems of Emily Dickinson*. Edited by Thomas H. Johnson. New York: A Back Bay Book, Little, Brown and Co., 1961.

Dillard, Annie. *Pilgrim at Tinker Creek*. New York: Harper Perennial Modern Classics, 2013.

Emre, Merv. *The Personality Brokers: The Strange History of Myers-Briggs and the Birth of Personality Testing*. Toronto: Random House Canada, 2018.

Fermor, Patrick Leigh. *A Time to Keep Silence*. New York: New York Review of Book Classics, 2007.

Fields, Rick. *When the Swans Came to the Lake: A Narrative History of Buddhism in America*. Boston: Shambhala Publications, 1992.

France, Peter. *Hermits: The Insights of Solitude*. New York: St. Martin's Press, 1997.

Goldberg, Philip. *American Veda*. New York: Harmony Books, 2010.

Hass, Robert. *The Essential Haiku*. New York: Ecco, 1994.

Hirshfield, Jane. *Nine Gates: Entering the Mind of Poetry*. New York: HarperCollins, 1998.

Isherwood, Christopher. *My Guru and His Disciple*. New York: Penguin Books, 1981.

Iyengar, B.K.S., *Light on Life*. Vancouver: Raincoast Books, 2005.

Iyer, Pico. *Sun After Dark: Flights into the Foreign*. New York: Vintage Departures, 2004.

James, William. *The Varieties of Religious Experience*. New York: Penguin Classics, 1985.

Koch, Philip. *Solitude: A Philosophical Encounter*. Peru, IL: Open Court Publishing Inc., 1994.

Koller, Alice. *The Stations of Solitude*. New York: Bantam, 1991.

Koller, Alice. *An Unknown Woman*. New York: Bantam, 1991.

LaBastille, Anne. *Woodswoman*. New York: Penguin Books, 1992.

Ladinsky, Daniel, translator. *The Gift, Poems by Hafiz*. New York: Penguin Compass, 1999.

Lawrence, Louise de Kiriline. *The Loghouse Nest*. Toronto: Natural Heritage/History Inc., 1988.

Leopold, Aldo. *A Sand County Almanac and Sketches Here and There*. New York: Oxford University Press, 1949.

Li, Quing. *Forest Bathing: How Trees Can Help You Find Health and Happiness*. New York: Penguin Random House, 2018.

Licence, Tom. *Hermits and Recluses in English Society, 950–1200*. London: Oxford University Press, 2011.

Lindbergh, Anne Morrow. *Gift from the Sea*. New York: Pantheon Books, 2005.

Mabey, Richard. *Nature Cure*. London: Chatto & Windus, 2005.

MacAvoy, Liz Herbert and Mari Hughes-Edward, eds. *Anchorites, Wombs and Tombs: Intersections of Gender and Enclosure in the Middle Ages*. Cardiff: University of Wales Press, 2010.

Macfarlane, Robert. *The Old Ways*. London: Hamish Hamilton, 2012.

Macfarlane, Robert. *The Wild Places*. London: Granta Books, 2008.

Mackenzie, Vicki. *Cave in the Snow*. London: Bloomsbury, 1998.

Maitland, Sara. *A Book of Silence*. London: Granta Books, 2009.

Maitland, Sara. *How to Be Alone*. London: Pan Macmillan, 2014.

Merton, Thomas. *Thoughts in Solitude*. New York: Farrar, Straus and Giroux, 1999.

Mitchell, Stephen, ed. *The Enlightened Heart*. New York: Harper Perennial, 1993.

Mitchell, Stephen, trans. *Tao Te Ching*. New York: Perennial, 2000.

Nadel, Ira B. *Various Positions*. Toronto: Random House of Canada, 1996.

Norris, Kathleen. *Cloister Walk*. New York: Riverhead Books, 1996.

Norris, Kathleen. *Dakota: A Spiritual Geography*. New York: First Mariner Books, 2001.

Oliver, Mary. *Blue Iris: Poems and Essays*. Boston: Beacon Press, 2006.

Oliver, Mary. *Upstream: Selected Essays*. New York: Penguin Books, 2016.

Radha, Swami Sivananda. *Radha: Diary of a Woman's Search*. Palo Alto, CA: Timeless Books, 1990.

Rich, Adrienne. *The Dream of a Common Language*. New York: W.W. Norton & Co., 1978.

Ritter, Christiane. *A Woman in the Polar Night*. New York: E.P. Dutton and Co., 1954.

Sarton, May. *Journal of a Solitude*. New York: W.W. Norton & Co., 1992.

Scott, Susan, ed. *Body & Soul: Stories for Skeptics and Seekers*. Halfmoon Bay, BC: Caitlan Press, 2019.

Sebald, W.G. *The Rings of Saturn*. Translated by Michael Hulse. London: The Harvill Press, 1998.

Simmons, Sylvie. *I'm Your Man*. Toronto: McClelland & Stewart, 2012.

Simon, Steve. *Healing Waters: The Pilgrimage to Lac Ste. Anne*. Edmonton: University of Alberta Press, 1995.

Solie, Karen. *The Caiplie Caves*. Toronto: House of Anansi Press, 2019.

Solnit, Rebecca. *Wanderlust: A History of Walking*. New York: Penguin Books, 2001.

Stark, Freya. *Bagdad Sketches*. New York: E.P. Dutton and Co., 1938.

Storr, Anthony. *Solitude: A Return to the Self*. New York: The Free Press, a Division of Macmillan, 1988.

Strayed, Cheryl. *Wild: From Lost to Found on the Pacific Coast Trail*. New York: Vintage Books, 2003.

Symons, Stefanie. *The Subtle Body: The Story of Yoga in America*. New York: Farrar, Straus and Giroux, 2010.

Tagore, Rabindranath. *Creative Unity*. Portland, OR: The Floating Press, 2009.

Thoreau, Henry David. *Walden: Or Life in the Woods*. New York: Penguin Classic, 2016.

Thorson, Robert M. *The Guide to Walden Pond*. Boston: Houghton Mifflin Harcourt, 2018.

Turner, Victor, and Edith Turner. *Image and Pilgrimage in Christian Culture*. New York: Columbia University Press, 2011.

Ueshiba, Morihei. *The Art of Peace*. Boston: Shambhala Publications, 2007.

Wilhelm, Richard. *The I Ching, Or Book of Changes*. Princeton, NJ: Translated by Cary F. Baynes. Princeton University Press, 1990.

Williams, Florence. *The Nature Fix*. New York: W.W. Norton & Co., 2017.

Williams, Terry Tempest. *The Hour of the Land*. New York: Sara Crichton Books, 2016.

Woolf, Virginia. *A Room of One's Own and Three Guineas*. New York: Penguin Modern Classics, 2000.

Woolf, Virginia. *A Writer's Diary*. Edited by Leonard Woolf. London: The Hogarth Press, 1953.

Worster, Donald. *A Passion for Nature: The Life of John Muir*. New York: Oxford University Press, 2018.

Yogananda, Paramahansa. *Autobiography of a Yogi*. Los Angeles: Self-Realization Fellowship, 1971.

Zollo, Paul. *Songwriters on Songwriting*. Boston: Da Capo Press, 2016.

Image Credits

Section 1: Mapping the Ground—Of Sacred Groves, Inner Mountains and the Art of Retreat, p. 1
Poet on a Mountaintop, Shen Zhou, late 15th century, China. (Wikimedia Commons)

An Introduction, p. 3
The bridge at Beaver Creek. (Kirsteen MacLeod)

Green Cathedral, p. 8
The cabin at Beaver Creek. (Marco Reiter)

The Art of Retreat, p. 30
Travelers in Autumn Mountains, Sheng Mou, 1271–1368, China. (Creative Commons, Gift of Mr. and Mrs. Severance A. Millikin 1963.589, courtesy of Cleveland Museum of Art)

Section 2: The Old Ways—Of Hermit Caves, Monasteries and Pilgrim Paths, p. 61

IN PRAISE OF RETREAT

St. Paul and St. Anthony and the raven that brought them bread. Every effort has been made to contact copyright holders; in the event of an inadvertent omission or error, please notify the publisher so full acknowledgement can be given in future editions. (Icon with St. Anthony visiting St. Paul of Thebes Inv. No. 3418 Painted wood H: 55 cm, W: 56 cm Old Cairo, Monastery of Mercurius (Abu Sayfayn), 1777 Coptic Museum, Cairo)

A Hut of One's Own, p. 63
The hermitage in northwestern Scotland. (Marco Reiter)

Monasticism for Moderns, p. 95
Nuns in the garden at Le Monastère, Quebec 1937. With permission from the archives of Le Monastère des Augustines (HG-A-26.22.11.1.6)

Pilgrim Ways, p. 120
The Hastings Heritage Trail north of Bancroft, Ontario. (Marco Reiter)

Section 3: The New Deities: Nature and Culture—Of Forest Cabins, National Parks and Creative Sanctuaries, p. 165
Original title page of *Walden* drawn by Sophia Thoreau. (Courtesy of Walden Woods Project)

I Will Go to the Wild Woods, p. 167
A drawing of Walden Woods. (Wikimedia Commons)

Artists, Writers, Creative Thinkers, Dreamers, p. 213
Emily Carr and company at her caravan, "the Elephant," at the southwest end of Esquimalt Lagoon in 1934.
Image F-07885 courtesy of the Royal BC Museum and Archives

Section 4: Light of the East, p. 245
Drawing of a sacred grove in India, 1782. (Wikipedia)

The Inner Temple, p. 247
At the Hermitage, folio from the Ramayana, 1780. (Creative Commons 1.0 universal public domain dedication)

Section 5: In Conclusion—Of Hermitages of the Heart, p. 295
Hawthornden Castle near Edinburgh, Scotland. (Kirsteen MacLeod)

White Rooms, Unified Hearts and Empty Fields, p. 297
Meditation cabin in the mountains of British Columbia. (Marco Reiter)

Permissions

Grateful acknowledgement is made to the following for permission to reprint previously published material:

COLEMAN BARKS, MAYPOP BOOKS: One line from Jalal ad-Din Rumi, *The Essential Rumi*, translated by Coleman Barks and John Moyne, HarperOne, 2004. Reprinted by permission of Coleman Barks. Page 95.

WENDELL BERRY: one line from A *Timbered Choir: The Sabbath Poems*, Copyright 1998 by Wendell Berry. Reprinted by permission of Counterpoint Press. Page 213.

CHEN CHEN: two lines from "I'm not a religious person but," from *When I Grow Up I Want to Be a List of Further Possibilities*, BOA Editions, 2017. Reprinted by permission of Fred Courtright, The Permissions Company, LLC Rights Agency for BOA Editions, Ltd. Page 33.

Purchase the print edition and receive the eBook free!
Just send an email to ebook@ecwpress.com and include:

• the book title
• the name of the store where you purchased it
• your receipt number
• your preference of file type: PDF or ePub

A real person will respond to your email with your eBook attached.
And thanks for supporting an independently owned Canadian publisher
with your purchase!